PRAISE FOR *HOW TO BE LESS ST*
BY CRYSTAL M. FLE

"Fleming upbraids us all (herself included) for our ignorance about race, but her breathtaking (and wig-snatching) lessons assure that racial illiteracy has a cure. By page 15 of this book you are already supremely smarter, having learned all the terms you need to sound knowledgeable, and by page 20, you won't be as susceptible to making common mistakes in racial thought. Along the way you will surely laugh, and by the end you may even find yourself listening to black women! Don't be stupid about race. Buy this book."

—Vilna Bashi Treitler, author of *The Ethnic Project: Transforming Racial Fiction into Ethnic Factions*

"Crystal Marie Fleming is one of the most forceful sociological voices of this new generation. *How to Be Less Stupid About Race* is a brilliant contribution to the long African American tradition of bridging dark humor with social critique. Fleming has written a timely analysis of systemic racism and white supremacy that is both deadly serious and seriously funny. With its deft mix of satire, memoir, and empirical evidence, her book is a groundbreaking model of public scholarship and sure to be an instant classic. Everyone needs to read this book, and I for one will assign it in my classes!"

—Eduardo Bonilla-Silva, former president of the American Sociological Association and author of *Racism Without Racists: Colorblind Racism and the Persistence of Racial Inequality in America*

"*How to Be Less Stupid About Race* is the perfect combination of Racism 101, critical race theory, and powerful analysis, woven with Dr. Crystal Fleming's personal journey from racial naiveté to one of the most incisive critics of white supremacy. Anyone who wants a straightforward education on race, racism, and white supremacy should buy this book immediately. Dr. Fleming minces no words in her exposition of racism in both the Obama and Trump eras. This bold and brave book is a must-read for anyone who wants to understand white supremacy in the United States."

—Tanya Golash-Boza, author of *Race and Racisms: A Critical Approach*

"Bold . . . and irreverent . . . *How to Be Less Stupid About Race* is an explosive book revealing the roots and nature of racism in our psyche, our interactions with each other, our institutions, our politics, our media, our gender relations, and even our love lives. . . . While racism is based on power and economic inequalities, it is also anchored in ignorance and stupidity. If Americans are willing to initiate the long journey of eradicating racism, they must wipe away the ignorance that sustains it."

—Aldon Morris, author of *The Scholar Denied: W. E. B. Du Bois and the Birth of American Sociology*

"Well, damn! I wrongly assumed *How to Be Less Stupid About Race* would be a how-to guide for naive Kumbaya-singing and 'colorblind' folks. My bad. This is a bold, carefully researched, and intimate take on the race conversation that points the finger at all of us: Yes, even those of us who know what intersectional means. Yes, even those of us who voted for Obama. Yes, even us Obama voters who know what intersectional means and have all Black friends. Beyond finger-pointing, it also offers solutions so we can hopefully—finally—throw off our racial dunce caps. For those looking for a distinctly smart, humorous, and intellectually challenging read on a much-needed complex racial conversation, *How to Be Less Stupid About Race* is essential reading."

—Angela Nissel, author of *The Broke Diaries* and *Mixed*

"Dr. Fleming offers a straight-no-chaser critique of our collective complicit ignorance regarding the state of race in the United States. In particular, she calls out the lack of resolve, especially among the political class, to admit and address the generational damage caused by institutional racism. This book will leave you thinking, offended, and transformed."

—Nina Turner, former Ohio state senator

"Fleming's strength is her expertise as a sociologist. . . . She wields her data like a sword, shredding racist nonsense."

—Christina G. Kukuk, *The Christian Century*

HOW TO BE LESS STUPID ABOUT RACE

HOW TO BE LESS STUPID ABOUT RACE

ON RACISM, WHITE SUPREMACY, AND THE RACIAL DIVIDE

CRYSTAL M. FLEMING

BEACON PRESS, BOSTON

BEACON PRESS
Boston, Massachusetts
www.beacon.org

Beacon Press books
are published under the auspices of
the Unitarian Universalist Association of Congregations.

Printed in the United States of America

22 21 20 8 7 6 5 4 (pbk.)
21 20 8 7 6 5 (hc.)

This book is printed on acid-free paper that meets the uncoated paper
ANSI/NISO specifications for permanence as revised in 1992.

Text design and composition by Kim Arney

Library of Congress Cataloging-in-Publication Data

Fleming, Crystal Marie, author.
Title: How to be less stupid about race : on racism, white supremacy,
and the racial divide / Crystal M. Fleming.
Description: Boston, Massachusetts : Beacon Press, [2018] |
Includes bibliographical references.
Identifiers: LCCN 2018009257 (print) | LCCN 2018028000 (ebook) |
ISBN 9780807050781 (ebook) | ISBN 9780807039847 (pbk. : alk.
paper) | ISBN 9780807050774 (hc. : alk. paper)
Subjects: LCSH: United States—Race relations. | Race awareness—
United States. | Racism—United States.
Classification: LCC E184.A1 (ebook) | LCC E184.A1 F576 2018 (print) |
DDC 305.800973—dc23
LC record available at https://lccn.loc.gov/2018009257

This book is dedicated to my students,
for helping me become less stupid
about a whole lotta things.

Contents

Introduction

THE ORIGINS OF RACIAL STUPIDITY

It is an aspect of their sense of superiority that the white people of America believe they have so little to learn.

—MARTIN LUTHER KING JR.[1]

Hundreds of years after establishing a nation on colonial genocide and chattel slavery, people are kinda-sorta-maybe-possibly waking up to the sad reality that our racial politics are (still) garbage. But as our society increasingly confronts the social realities of race, we are faced with a barrage of confusing developments. How could the same country that twice voted for an Ivy League–educated black president end up electing an overt racist who can barely string together two coherent sentences? Why do white liberals who can't even confront their Trump-supporting friends and family members think they can lead the "Resistance"? Democrats who didn't care about mass deportations or the treatment of Muslims under Obama suddenly care now that a Republican is in charge. While black and brown people are being crushed by systemic white supremacy, the rapper Common thinks we can all "get over race" by extending a "hand in love."[2] Don Lemon still has a job. Rachel Dolezal exists. Everyone has an opinion about race, but

99 percent of the population has never studied it. And even many textbooks that "talk about race" are filled with lies, inaccuracies, and alternative facts.[3] With so much racial ignorance in the world, how will we ever find our way to that glorious mountaintop Martin Luther King Jr. glimpsed right before a white racist killed him?

Although race is an inherently divisive topic—the cause of continual controversy, Facebook feuds, and endless debate—there is exactly one thing and one thing only that we can probably all touch and agree on regardless of our racial or ethnic identity, gender, age, political beliefs, or shoe size:

We are surrounded by racial stupidity.

From the White House to Waffle House, from the classroom to the internet comments section, from the television to the tiki-torch aisle of your local Pier One—we are surrounded and, at times, astounded by the ignorant and dangerous ideas people express about this thing called "race."

Why are so many people so incredibly confused and misinformed about race? It's the white supremacy, stupid! As I'll demonstrate throughout this book, one of the main consequences of centuries of racism is that we are all systematically exposed to racial stupidity and racist beliefs that warp our understandings of society, history, and ourselves. In other words, living in a racist society socializes us to be stupid about race. Of course, as you well know, some people are more afflicted by racial stupidity than others. We'll get into the nature of these variations a bit later. For now, I want to emphasize just how widespread and ubiquitous racial ignorance truly is. Politicians routinely spout racist distortions of reality and lie about the existence and nature of racial oppression. Absurd racial stereotypes pervade our various forms of media. And as noted, textbooks systematically misrepresent racial history in ways that minimize or erase racism altogether, and, all too often, teachers themselves are undereducated or miseducated about the history and ongoing realities of racial oppression.

How to Be Less Stupid About Race explores precisely how and why racial stupidity has become so terribly pervasive and examines the cesspool of silly ideas, half-truths, and ridiculous misconceptions that have thoroughly corrupted the way race and racism are represented in the classroom, pop culture, media, and politics. The key idea that I'll come back to again and again is that living in a racist society exposes us all to absurd and harmful ideas that, in turn, help maintain the racial status quo. Drawing from my own experience as an educator—and as someone who continually confronts my own racial ignorance—I'll also share some concrete steps that you (as well as your racist friends, ignorant family members, and clueless coworkers) can take to become *less* stupid about race and better equipped to detect and dismantle racial oppression. While I don't personally believe in postracial utopias, and I don't put a lot of faith in reaching glorious mountaintops, I know for sure that the very first step in challenging racism is having a clear understanding of what it actually is.

Not only are we surrounded by stupid ideas *about* race; we are even surrounded by stupid ideas about how to talk about race. In May 2015, Starbucks launched a doomed campaign called #RaceTogether to encourage baristas and coffee drinkers around the country to "have a conversation" about race. Although many might have mistaken the campaign for a satirical entry on *The Onion*, Starbucks announced that its employees had the option of arbitrarily writing the hashtag "#RaceTogether" on a random customer's cup. Aspiring coffee drinkers minding their own damned business would then be obliged to say something to the barista about race. After a steady stream of criticism and mockery on social media by antiracists across the color spectrum (yours truly included), the company eventually backpedaled and canceled the initiative.

To some, encouraging random people to talk about race sounds like a step in the right direction. Don't we need more profit-driven corporations to take a stand and say that "race" is a legitimate and important topic of conversation? Well, no, we don't. Rather than thinking through the best practices that might foster a *productive* discussion about racism, the company executives thought best to just sort of tell everyone else to figure it out without providing any educational resources, training, or guidelines whatsoever. In a letter to employees, Starbucks chairman Howard Schultz stated that he conceived of the idea "not to point fingers and not because we have answers, but because staying silent is not who we are."[4] When asked whether Starbucks employees received diversity training before being instructed to initiate conversations about race, the company replied: "We don't presume to educate communities on race, only to encourage an open dialogue."[5] In other words, though Schultz thought race was a really important topic, he had nothing in particular to say about it except that there is no one to blame for racism.

But a clueless dialogue "about race" that doesn't center on racism is not particularly helpful and can even be destructive. When I heard about this silly campaign, several questions immediately sprang to my mind. I mean, first and foremost: *How you gon' talmabout race . . . if you've never studied race?* Who signed off on this foolishness? What civil rights groups, antiracist organizations, scholars, or diversity experts did Starbucks consult in crafting "Race Together"? One can easily imagine that both white and nonwhite people might feel racially profiled when receiving a cup with the hashtag. Did the company provide employees with guidelines for how to select customers to "join" in the conversation? There is also the issue of consent. What about those of us who have no desire to be asked about a potentially painful topic by a perfect stranger? Would people of color have to wear T-shirts to Starbucks saying: "*Please don't ask me about race and don't touch my hair*"? What happens when conflict arises, as it inevitably will in any public discussion of race? Would Starbucks provide conflict resolution, mediation, or therapy for employees and customers who feel troubled or traumatized by the racist ideas they are sure to hear in their stores? On social media, the #RaceTogether hashtag was quickly hijacked by racists. But, of course, there was no one to blame.

Ill-conceived campaigns like "Race Together" contribute to the misconception that "race" is a topic that requires no education whatsoever to discuss. As I'll argue throughout this book, conversations "about race" based entirely on racial ignorance are actually quite harmful. As an antiracist educator, an occasional coffee drinker, and a black woman, I for one do *not* want to hear random members of the public who have not studied race share their uninformed opinions with or around me in the early morning hours. The unfortunate truth is that the vast majority of US citizens have never taken a class on the subject, attended an antiracist workshop, or seriously studied the history, politics, psychology, and sociology of race relations. Classes dedicated to the topics of racism and ethnic studies are not required for most students in public or private institutions. And, as you know from your own experience, many organizations and businesses do not mandate diversity training with specific attention to racial and ethnic bias and discrimination. As a result, most of us make it through the entirety of our lives without structured opportunities to learn about racism from experts on the subject. Is it any wonder that so many people are so damned racially ignorant?

The costs of taking a superficial approach to addressing racism are quite high—and fall squarely on the shoulders of people of color. Nearly three years after its "Race Together" nonsense, Starbucks made headlines once again, in April 2018, when the manager of a store in Philadelphia called police to arrest two men who were simply waiting for a friend to arrive.[6] When one of them asked to use the bathroom, an employee refused, indicating that the great privilege of using their toilet was limited to paying customers. The employee then demanded that the two men leave. When they declined, the employee called the cops, who accused the men of trespassing and loitering. It didn't matter that the men were realtors who were having a business meeting. It didn't matter that their friend—a white man—arrived and insisted that they were allowed to be there. It didn't matter that multiple witnesses, including white folks, were saying "*They didn't do anything!*" The heavily armed cops surrounded the men, bullied them, and took them away in handcuffs anyway. Video of the arrest went viral almost immediately, juxtaposing the chill jazz vibes of the music playing in the café with the harsh, everyday reality of white supremacist racism. Watching the film was harrowing, as I worried that one wrong move could've resulted in these two brothers being shot to death because of a racist Starbucks employee and the bias that pervades policing. As backlash against the company mounted, yet another Starbucks CEO (this time, Kevin Johnson) was forced to issue a mea culpa and denounce the discriminatory behavior that led to these two black men being racially profiled and criminalized. Shortly thereafter, the company announced that eight thousand stores would be forced to close for an afternoon of racial bias training.[7] Gee, maybe, just maybe, they should have done this years ago instead of trying to force people to "race together?"

I've been rude. I should've introduced myself. My name is Crystal—or Dr. Fleming, if you're nasty. Tens of thousands of people know me by my Twitter handle @alwaystheself. I'm a queer, bisexual black woman. I grew up watching *Columbo*, *Moesha*, and *Star Trek: The Next Generation*. I enjoy Pinot Noir, exotic travels, and the pleasures of hot-stone massage. I may be bougie now, but I'm just one generation removed from poverty. I'm a tenured professor, a long-term student of racial domination, and the author of a book about racism and the legacies of slavery in France. And, although this may be surprising, I had no fucking idea that we in the United States live in a racist (and sexist and classist) society until I was a full-grown adult. More on this later.

Nobody clued me in about the whole racism thing when I was growing up. My mom, a single parent, gave birth to me in our hometown of Chattanooga, Tennessee, when she was nineteen years old. Despite being a child of the 1960s and '70s, and living through the civil rights and Black Power eras, Mom never spoke to me about discrimination or desegregation or anything related to oppression, really—at least, not until I began formally studying these matters in graduate school. When I belatedly found out about racism, I was like *Damn! Why ain't nobody tell me?* In talking about all this with Mom, I learned that she was trying to shield me from harmful beliefs about black people—and for good reason. Research by social psychologist Claude Steele has famously demonstrated the deleterious effects of stereotypes on student performance—a phenomenon he refers to as "stereotype threat." Steele's experiments have shown that when students are primed to be aware of negative expectations about members of their group, they perform poorly.[8] My mom didn't know about Steele's work, but she wanted to create an empowering environment in our home so that I could grow up believing I could do anything.

At school, I was one of those black kids who didn't know they were black. It's not that I denied my racial identity or viewed myself as "white." I just don't remember thinking about myself in racial terms. As a child, I experienced a great deal of bullying—not because I was black or bisexual (I kept that secret to myself until my twenties) but because I came to school dressed in the long skirt, stockings, and hats required of the Pentecostal church my family attended back in the day. What happened to me was not unlike the religious bullying suffered by Muslim girls wearing headscarves.[9] Because I felt excluded due to my ridiculous church outfits, it didn't occur to me to feel marginalized because of my skin color.

Another source of my racial ignorance was the fact that I was labeled as uniquely intelligent early in life. At some point in the first or second grade, a white teacher singled me out and suggested I take an IQ test. Shortly thereafter, I was placed in the "talented and gifted" track. Minorities like me who "make it" in predominately white settings are viewed and treated like unicorns—aberrations from the white (male) supremacist rule. Part of my experience was being made to understand that I was "special" and also relatively rare—not only as a "gifted" person but also specifically as a black gifted person. The exclusivity of the gifted program made it sufficiently clear that we were considered different and, well, more gifted than the vast majority of other students.

Inside the classroom, I was told that I could do anything—that I was special, creative, and valued. But outside the protective bubble of the classroom—in the hallways, on the playground—I felt shunned. After a certain age, kids didn't want to sit with the hat-wearing weirdo at the lunch table. Even the few friends I made were also subject to bullying. One day, walking home from school, my white friend David and I were pelted with rocks. Years later, when I won a scholarship to attend a private school, a white jock attacked me for wearing my hat to school, saying, "*I should shoot you in the head.*" When my mom and I complained to school officials, they did nothing. I dropped out shortly thereafter and found another private school to attend.

Psychologically, I coped with all of this by alternating between pride in my religious piety ("*Don't conform to the ways of this world,*" our erudite pastor intoned on Sundays) and pride in my intellectual "gifts." My self-worth was unhealthily based on my ability to bring home straight As and shine in class. I still remember, as a child, occasionally pulling out the transcript of my IQ test scores, smiling to myself as I noted that my verbal ability tested in the "top 2 percent" of the population. These numbers made me breathe a little easier and feel less worthless. And although as a young girl I didn't have the language to conceptualize or understand social dynamics in terms of race, I do remember noticing that there was only ever one other student who looked like me in the "gifted" program. The vast majority of black kids at the diverse public schools I attended were relegated to the standard academic curriculum.

As an adult, I would come to understand that my reliance on academic achievement to boost my ego no longer served me and that, to the contrary, it represented a kind of internalized oppression. Defining my self-worth in relation to my intellectual accomplishments and external validation wasn't healthy, not only because our worth is inherent but also, as I would later discover, because dominant definitions of "intellect" and "achievement" were intentionally crafted to exclude and oppress women, nonwhites, and economically disenfranchised people—that is to say, *my people.* The more I learned about the history of scientific racism, as well as about the Eurocentric and patriarchal biases of knowledge production more broadly, the more critical I became of the same metrics that were used to define me (a supposedly rare black girl "genius") as a mere exception to the rule of white male superiority.

My experience bears some odd similarities to being socialized as "white" in a white supremacist society: being advantaged by a hierarchical distribution of rewards, not because of any particular merit or achievement of my own but because of how I was labeled (as "gifted"), and then given resources (material, psychological, social, and cultural) because of that hierarchical label. But what no one told me as a child in the "gifted" program is that the criteria that define intellectual "giftedness" are socially constructed—shaped and molded by power relations, including racism and sexism, and largely determined by wealthy white men who, you guessed it, just so happen to situate themselves as intellectually superior to other groups.

I first discovered critiques of standardized tests and IQ scores in graduate school—and I admit that it was hard for me to let go of my attachment to the idea that these scores were as meaningful as I'd been socialized to believe. Although it took years of introspection and brutal honesty to get to the root of my own resistance, I eventually realized that I wanted to believe in the validity of standardized tests because I wanted to hang on to the story I'd held onto since childhood: I was "special," exceptional, and worthy because of my intellectual gifts, as defined by white educators. When you've been told all of your life that you're special—and, implicitly, superior—it can be hard to give that up.

I first learned about racism (and class oppression) from a self-proclaimed "white Jewish guy"—my college professor Ira Silver. His Introduction to Sociology course, which I took in my first year at Wellesley College, got me to switch from my work in biochemistry and molecular pharmacology to sociology. In his class, we read a book that changed my life: Jay MacLeod's *Ain't No Makin' It: Aspirations and Achievement in a Low-Income Neighborhood.* The study, which chronicles the experiences of working-class boys in the Boston area, unveils the dynamics of racism and class oppression, showing that even when young men "play by the rules" and pursue educational success, they often fall prey to structural dynamics that reproduce the poverty and class disadvantage into which they were born. For the first time, I began to see the unjust ways in which resources were concentrated among the wealthy—and the racially privileged. I was also deeply influenced by MacLeod's core argument in the book, that structural changes and social justice require collective action and consciousness-raising. That class was also my first exposure to the work of the French sociologist Pierre Bourdieu and his theories of social reproduction.

Before Dr. Silver's class, I was so deep down the rabbit hole of exceptionalism that I had no knowledge whatsoever about how power relations work. If I had known about racism (and class oppression and sexism) as a teen, I might have been able to understand why I was so unhappy at private school or why I felt oppressed by religious rules that forced women and girls to dress in ways that marked us as targets for bullying—but allowed men to blend into society. Growing up, I lacked the tools required understand racism, classism, and (hetero)sexism, much less their intersections, which is precisely why I decided to write this book. Like, I was *this* close to becoming some version of Ben Carson, Kanye West, or Omarosa. I still shudder thinking about it. I be looking at these fools like "*That could've been me . . .*"

Before we get too lost in the sauce, let me share some basic definitions and concepts. In this book, the term "racial stupidity" refers to

- nonsensical, illogical, ahistorical, or socially inaccurate claims about race and racism
- the denial of racial oppression
- racist beliefs such as the inherent and natural superiority of one race over others
- superficial descriptions of the racial order

Typically, racial stupidity involves the misrepresentation, minimization, denial, and justification of racial domination. Paradoxically, "racists" (that is, people who overtly or covertly support racial oppression) often alternate between denying that racism exists and justifying it.

Let me be clear: I am not suggesting that racial oppression merely derives from "ignorance." Rather, racial stupidity has become routinized and is the result of intentional actions of European colonists and enslavers who sought to justify their capitalist exploitation of non-Europeans through the myth of white superiority.

"Race" is a fundamentally stupid idea that refers to the belief in visible, permanent, hierarchical differences between human groups defined in terms of biology, physical appearance, or ancestry. Race is inherently ridiculous for many reasons, not the least of which is the fact that we now know there is *no biological basis* to dividing humans into "racial" categories. The modern concept of biological race was invented in the mid-nineteenth century by Europeans for the purpose of justifying their exploitation and domination of people they conveniently depicted as inferior. Absurd racial ideas like the one-drop rule, also known as the rule of hypodescent, demonized African ancestry and bolstered white privilege. Like other dominator groups throughout history, Europeans used religious ideology (especially Christian beliefs) to justify stealing land and resources that didn't belong to them. But European colonizers also introduced something new in their efforts to enrich themselves through mass murder, theft, and forced labor: the use of pseudo-science (also known as "scientific racism") to create an ideology of biological racial belonging that positioned their own group as inherently superior and the groups they dominated as inherently inferior. Ultimately, the function of "racist ideology"—the belief in racial inferiority and superiority—was to allow Europeans to exercise power over racial "others" with a clean conscience and to create permanent categories of "sub-humans" who could be exploited, harmed, and even murdered for generations. Obviously, it's much easier to sleep at night when you can rationalize genocide, slavery, and centuries of discrimination by believing that "your people" deserve resources and inferior "racial others" deserve domination—or death.

Sociologists often say that race is "socially constructed," which simply means that human beings create ideas about what race means and these ideas gradually emerged at a specific point in history. The fact that human beings construct the meaning of race means that we produce what Ann Morning calls "racial conceptualizations"—ideas about race that vary across time, space, and cultural contexts.[10] The cultural meanings of racial categories shift and change throughout history. White identity, for example, is not monolithic and involves its own absurd hierarchy of "superior" Europeans (e.g., white Anglo-Saxon Protestants) and "inferior" Europeans (e.g., Italians, Jews, and the Irish).[11]

"Systemic racism" (sometimes referred to as "structural racism") is another key concept, and by wrapping your head around the term, you'll automatically distinguish yourself from billions of people who have no idea what it means. When social scientists describe racism as "systemic," we're referring to collective practices and representations that disadvantage categories of human beings on the basis of their perceived "race." The key word here is "collective." Much of the racial stupidity we encounter in everyday life derives from the fact that people think of racism as individual prejudice rather than a broader system and structure of power.

Speaking of prejudice, it's important to understand that individual biases and negative stereotypes (which we all hold) are not the same as systemic racism (a system of power). Though everyone internalizes stereotypes about social groups, we do not all occupy the same position in the racial order. When members of a so-called "racial" group are able to impose their prejudices in ways that reliably benefit them and disadvantage others, they have managed to successfully *institutionalize* their racist beliefs and protect their racial privileges. "Institutional racism" consists of racist ideas and practices embedded within social organizations and institutions (e.g., policies, laws, families, education). The major insight about systemic and institutional racism is that there is no such thing as "a little bit of racism" or "pockets of racism" or "random incidents of racism" isolated from the rest of society. Whether you realize it or not, racism is systemic, pervasive, and embedded within the core of all of our major institutions. The consequences of systemic racism are vast—from the burgeoning racial wealth gap, political disenfranchisement, mass incarceration and racist immigration policies to micro-aggressions, racial profiling, racist media imagery, and disparities in health, education, employment, and housing.

It's important to be clear about the meaning of racism, particularly systemic racism, because so many people have made up their own definition of what the word means. A common misconception among racists and racial idiots alike is the idea that racism means "making generalizations" or, more specifically, "making generalizations about white people." In fact, some fools think even mentioning the phrase "white people" is inherently racist. It's fascinating watching racists argue *against* basic logic and inference to defend their racism and/or racism denial. The faulty argument often goes like this:

ANTIRACISTS: "White racism is pervasive, and whites control the vast majority of resources."

RACISTS: "Generalizations are wrong!"

ALSO RACISTS: "Whites are the superior race because . . ."

The sad reality is that the very same people who view themselves as the "master race" can't even master basic logic. Racists want to maintain a monopoly on racial generalizations: they'd love to have their racist cake (by making racist comments and generalizations about racial groups) and eat it too (by insisting that the racial generalizations they dislike, especially critiques of white racism, are "racist"). Making generalizations is not inherently "racist" for the simple fact that generalizing is a basic cognitive activity required for existing in and navigating society. We all make generalizations and refer to in-groups and out-groups. And since racism and racialization are core features of our society, we simply have to use language that acknowledges the social, political, and economic realities of racial domination. Being honest about these social realities requires explicitly naming the racial majority and minority groups and acknowledging racial disparities.

Throughout the book, I refer to "antiracists." To be clear, "antiracists" are not "nonracist" people. Rather, antiracists are people of any racial or ethnic background who take a personal, active role in challenging systemic racism. It is debatable whether it is possible for someone socialized in a racist society to rid themselves of "racist" thinking—or even to divest themselves of systemic racial privileges—even if they wanted to. One of the goals of *How to Be Less Stupid About Race* is to help folks of all walks of life recognize and critique the racial order in which we live. That racial order has a name: "white supremacy." White supremacy is the social, political, and economic dominance of people socially defined as "white."[12] Although white supremacy might seem ancient or timeless, it's important to understand that white identity and white supremacist racism are relatively new phenomena. To be clear, the roots of modern racism extend far back in time and encompass religiously justified ethnocentrism and oppression across the globe, as seen in the violent history of anti-Semitism. However, Theodore W. Allen, an influential independent scholar of racism and class relations, convincingly argues that white identity did not yet exist when Europeans first colonized the land that would become the United States. Instead, Allen's study of colonial America shows that belief in a superior "white" race was invented as a form of social control designed to empower and enrich elites by fomenting hatred and conflict between working-class whites and oppressed racial minorities.[13] In a similar vein, historian George Fredrickson points out that "the notion that there was a single pan-European 'white' race was slow to develop and did not crystallize until the 18th century." From that point forward, the intertwined forces of capitalist oppression, European imperialism, and slavery gave rise to a systemic way of structuring society across the globe, as European elites and pseudo-scientists spread the pernicious idea that human groups can be ranked according to made-up "racial" categories, with Northern Europeans on the top, sub-Saharan Africans on the bottom, and everyone else—including some white ethnic groups—in between.[14] It's a mistake to think that people of color are the only ones harmed by white supremacy. Members of stigmatized European groups, like Jews, Italians, and Polish people, have been the targets of white supremacist violence and stigmatization.[15] The stupidity that undergirds white supremacy is now perpetuated from one generation to the next through "socialization," the process through which our families, peer groups, and social environments shape our behavior, beliefs, and identities. As a result, racism is not "in your heart" but rather is "in your head"—and racism is in your head because we live in a racist society.

White supremacy is about power. It's about the intersections of racial domination, class domination, gender domination, and other forms of oppression. It's about capitalism. It's about colonialism. The bottom line is that white supremacy is about resources: who gets (and retains) access to them, who gets excluded, whose lives are made to matter, and whose lives are rendered disposable.

There are a number of fallacious ideas about white supremacy that I'd like to address up front. These include the KKK Fallacy, the Gaslighting Fallacy, the Class Fallacy, the Whites-Only White

Supremacy Fallacy, the Political Fallacy, and, my personal favorite, the Black Supremacy Unicorn Fallacy.

THE KKK FALLACY

Let me keep it all the way real: even as a college professor with two degrees from Harvard, I didn't personally understand white supremacy as an institutionalized system of power until my early thirties. In fact, many of us tend to think of white supremacy as represented by extremists such as the Ku Klux Klan or the Nazi regime. But the truth is that white supremacy is not something you can isolate among far-right radicals or overt racists. Instead, white supremacy—the dominance of people socially defined as white—is systematically maintained by hundreds of millions of ordinary people, as well as by everyday institutional practices that protect the racial order. The KKK Fallacy is the idea that white supremacy is a cancerous tumor you can remove, when the truth is that white dominance is pervasive. The sad reality is that the social cancer of white supremacy began to metastasize and infiltrate our institutions, laws, and cultural representations centuries ago.

THE GASLIGHTING FALLACY

Have you ever heard racial idiots say that racism doesn't exist simply because they haven't experienced it—or because they don't want to believe those who have been targeted by racial exploitation and terror? This is an example of racial gaslighting: denying the existence of racial oppression. "Gaslighting" is a term for psychological manipulation in which an abuser denies that any harm is taking place, prompting the target of abuse to question reality.[16] People who experience racism, sexism, and any other form of oppression are familiar with what it feels like for others to deny that their experience of abuse was real. Racial gaslighting happens at both the interpersonal level and the structural level.

Given the prevalence of racism denial, the bar for intelligent racial discourse is so low that merely saying "systemic racism exists" is often viewed as a genius-level intervention. And, given how hegemonic racism denial is, I can see how and why that happens. People still get cookies for merely saying "people of color should not be killed" or "white supremacy is wrong." It's a lamentable situation. One might even say deplorable.

The denial of systemic white supremacy and structural racism is so widespread that even the ice cream company Ben & Jerry's found it necessary to create a webpage entitled "7 Ways We Know Systemic Racism Is Real," complete with educational resources and empirical data about the racial wealth gap (whites hoard 90 percent of the nation's wealth!) and discrimination in housing, employment, education, criminal justice, surveillance, and health care.[17] I mean, you know things are really bad when a gotdamn *ice-cream company* has to debunk the pervasive belief that racial oppression is a thing of the past because schools, academics, politicians, and journalists are failing to do so.

THE CLASS FALLACY

Though wealthy whites benefit the most from white supremacy, somehow the myth that poor whites or "rednecks" are the Real Racists™ persists. This fallacious and empirically discredited idea reemerged with fierceness in the wake of the 2016 presidential election as well-to-do white liberals attempted to portray Trump's electoral college victory as the result of white working class "resentment." The Class Fallacy is the wrong-headed notion that wealthy and "educated" whites are somehow immune to racism and absolved from complicity with racial domination. But sociologists such as Joe Feagin and Eduardo Bonilla-Silva point out that racist views and discriminatory behavior are widespread among whites regardless of their class status.[18] Moreover, it is well established that the richest whites exercise the most economic and political control over our society. According to an analysis of data published by the Federal Reserve in 2013, the top 10 percent of the wealthiest white families "own almost everything."[19]

In his magisterial work *Black Reconstruction in America*, W. E. B. Du Bois cogently demonstrates that poor and working-class whites were distracted from their own alienation and class exploitation by the psychological "wages" of whiteness.[20] More recently, critical race philosopher Shannon Sullivan has argued that middle-class whites bolster their sense of moral goodness by defining themselves as "good white people"—in contrast to "racist" rednecks, whom they regard as "poor white trash." Meanwhile, these same middle-class (and even wealthy) whites typically have no idea just how much more wealth they hold compared to people of color.[21] Although white households typically hold ten to thirteen times more wealth than black and Hispanic families, almost everyone assumes that the wealth gap isn't as wide as it really is. A 2017 study by psychologists at Yale University shows that both whites and blacks tend to severely underestimate the extent of the racial wealth gap by about 25 percent, expressing what the authors call "unfounded optimism" about the extent of progress made in addressing racial economic inequality.[22] What all this means is that hundreds of millions of US citizens are both racially and economically ignorant in ways that minimize systemic racism and class oppression.

THE WHITES-ONLY WHITE SUPREMACY FALLACY

Because many people walk around with a sociologically superficial, ahistorical, and vague understanding of racism, the notion that people of color can and do contribute to white supremacy is often dismissed. A simple-minded view of racism holds that white supremacy only exists if and when all resources and all power are held by "whites only." If any person of color holds a position of authority or experiences any degree of success, their mere existence is taken to be evidence that systemic racism and white privilege do not exist. This is what I call the Whites-Only White-Supremacy Fallacy, the foolish idea that proof of white supremacy requires every single person of color to be deprived of all rights and resources. People who believe this fallacy are also likely to point to the existence of a few wealthy women and women professionals as "proof" that sexism doesn't exist, disregarding both the fact that women are systematically disadvantaged in every sphere of power and the fact that women certainly absorb misogynist beliefs that harm themselves and other women. Just as patriarchy makes room for women—especially when they remain subordinate to men—white supremacy has historically made room for people of color who were willing to accommodate white dominance. And, to some extent, almost all people of color are forced to make certain accommodations to white supremacy while surviving within a violent, unjust system. Anyone who has ever studied racism knows that though people of color tend to be more knowledgeable about racism (due to direct experience) and more opposed to racial oppression than whites, they can also actively participate in maintaining white supremacy—and be rewarded for doing so through their individual advancement (while members of their racial group remain collectively oppressed). Prominent examples include Booker T. Washington, Clarence Thomas, Dinesh D'Souza, and Barack Obama. Yeah, I said it: your man Barack. We'll come back to Obama's role in whitewashing white supremacy in chapter 3.

THE POLITICAL FALLACY

On the topic of politics: Can we please, pretty please, finally dispense with the bald-faced lie that only people of a certain political persuasion can be "racist"? I am so gotdamn tired of hearing liberals depict racism as a thing that only conservatives do—and bored to tears with conservatives who concern-troll liberal racism while turning a blind eye to their own embrace of white supremacy. As historian Ibram X. Kendi shows in his incisive 2016 book *Stamped from the Beginning: The Definitive History of Racist Ideas in America*, systemic white supremacy pervades politics on the left and the right. The complicity of liberals and conservatives in maintaining white supremacy is a running theme of this book—one that we'll explore in depth in chapter 4.

THE BLACK SUPREMACY UNICORN FALLACY

As someone with an active social media platform, I'm occasionally asked by an internet troll to comment on this mythical thing called "black supremacy." One hundred percent of the time, references to black supremacy are designed to deflect critiques of white supremacy. But since the term comes up so often in white supremacist circles, let's go ahead and address the black supremacy unicorn in the room. If, for example, black people in these United States set up a system of racial oppression that involved an ideology of racial superiority and the centuries-long enslavement, torture, and systemic rape of white people; or if black people invented pseudo-sciences to justify their racial domination of whites and others; or if blacks built their wealth through settler-colonial genocide against indigenous people and forced white slaves to work for free for generations upon generations upon generations; or if blacks set up a system of antiwhite discrimination resulting in the widespread demonization of whites throughout society; or if black people developed and institutionalized a belief system that portrayed whites as subhuman animals, and if they collectively succeeded in integrating the dehumanization of whiteness into the educational system; or if blacks held a quasi-monopoly on all major political parties and branches of the government; or if black people monopolized economic resources; or if nearly all the private schools and well-funded educational institutions and well-resourced neighborhoods in this country were dominated by black people and whites were relegated to shitty schools and toxic living environments—that is to say, if black people did to white people what white people have done to us, then yes, we could talk about "black supremacy" in the United States. And if that racial world existed, it would be as contemptible as this one.

But you know, just as well as I do, that there is no such thing as black supremacy in the US, just as there is no such thing as unicorns (sorry to break the news). And though racial biases and denigrating stereotypes are widespread among all of us regardless of our racial or ethnic background, the fact remains that there is only one racist system in the United States, and that system is called white supremacy.

There are a certain number of prerequisites for the course that you will find between these pages. These include critical thinking, reflexivity, compassion, and a willingness to experience and sit with discomfort. By "critical thinking," I mean the ability to challenge what you may think of as common sense—to ask questions and subject your own beliefs to empirical validation. Reflexivity is an important part of any antiracist's toolkit, because it involves being able to take a look at your own experiences, beliefs, and behavior. For me, mindfulness and meditation (practices designed to bring attention to the present moment) help foster an awareness of my own feelings and thoughts, including my racial socialization. This awareness, in turn, is useful for coming to terms with our racialized beliefs, biases, and behavior. I also think that compassion—for others and for ourselves—is key to doing this kind of critical work. Oppression of any kind is a difficult subject to address and being able to empathize with other people's experiences—and to generate compassion for our own suffering and shortcomings—keeps us connected to the higher, life-sustaining energies of love and community. Compassionate mindfulness can also help us as we learn to sit with and tolerate the uncomfortable feelings that will inevitably come up when we confront power relations, injustice, and domination.

But let's get one thing clear: as much as I value compassion, I also believe in telling the hard, painful truths. This book is not going to be everyone's cup of tea. I am not going to coddle you. I am not going to hold your hand. What I am going to do is wig-snatch the hell outta white supremacy. And I am going to explain how the racial stupidity that developed as a consequence of white dominance screws up our understanding of the past, impoverishes our understanding of the present, and endangers the future of life on this planet. If a vulgar word here or there makes you clutch your pearls, then you best get to clutchin'. In case there was any ambiguity, let the record reflect that I have no fucks to give about respectability politics. I am tired of pretending that we should be polite about calling out a violent, oppressive system that is responsible for the mass killing, enslavement, exploitation, and methodical disadvantaging of millions of people.

To begin the ongoing process of challenging racial domination—and exploring our implication with it—we need to get really clear about the nature of systemic racism. We also need to confront how racial stupidity functions to keep large majorities of the population ignorant about the social, political, historical, and economic realities of racial oppression. Racial stupidity serves to justify and reinforce racism. And if we're ever going to build a better world, we will need to fearlessly identify and dismantle the many forms of ignorance that keep so many of us in bondage.

Chapter 1

THE IDIOT'S GUIDE TO CRITICAL RACE THEORY

The legal legacy of slavery and of the seizure of land from Native American peoples is not merely a regime of property law that is (mis)informed by racist and ethnocentric themes. Rather, the law has established and protected an actual property interest in whiteness itself.

—CHERYL HARRIS[1]

Some of the best and most insightful scholarship on racism is sequestered in a lively academic field known as critical race theory, or CRT. Predictably, this revelatory work has been maligned by tin-foil-hat-wearing white supremacists who believe that the only kind of racism that exists is "antiwhite racism." But critical race theory is something everyone needs to know about, not only because scholars working in this area were on the vanguard of debunking the myth of color blindness but also because they helped develop powerful theories of white supremacy as a pervasive system of racial oppression, rather than the narrow idea that white supremacy can only be found in the beliefs and practices of white nationalists.

Using the insights of critical race theory, I'm going to break down the "what," "when," "where," "why," and "how" of white supremacy, after which you'll be well ahead of the vast majority of the population, who have no idea what white supremacist racism really is, where it came from, or what could possibly be done about it. I'm going to review and simplify a lot of complex history, but here are several important things to bear in mind. First: white supremacy is, most fundamentally, a system of power designed to channel material resources to people socially defined as white. Second: white supremacy is *not* just neo-Nazis and white nationalism. It's also the way our society has come to be structured, such that political, economic, and other forms of capital are predominately maintained by elite whites. Long before op-ed columnists and contemporary activists began using the term "white supremacy," critical race scholars and radical progressives such as Derrick Bell, Kimberlé Crenshaw, and Cornel West were leading the way with strident critiques of structural racism (and its interconnections with sexism, class oppression, and other forms of domination). Finally: white supremacy is inextricably linked to other systems of domination. This is the major insight of intersectionality, a concept I will come back to later. For now, simply remember that racism goes hand in hand with class oppression, patriarchy, and other forms of domination.

This chapter will also introduce you to the brilliant work of critical race philosopher Charles Mills, who has been consistently, eloquently snatching white supremacist wigs for decades. I'll spend some time explaining his best-known concept: the *epistemology of ignorance.* If many of these terms are new to you, get ready to have some of your most basic assumptions about race challenged. *Buckle up your seatbelt, baby: this is gonna be a bumpy ride.*

If you grew up like most people in the United States (including me), you probably learned very little about the history and current realities of racism in school. If anything, you were likely taught that racism, while unfortunate, is mainly a thing of the past, something to view through the rearview mirror. In his excellent books

Lies My Teacher Told Me and *Lies Across America*, sociologist James Loewen clearly demonstrates that racial history is routinely minimized and distorted within our (mis)educational system. Not only is it highly unlikely that you learned much of substance about race or racism at school; it is also highly likely that you absorbed racist propaganda. To the extent that our schools typically fail to teach students how to intelligently connect the racial past to the present, many of us end up with *preracial* or color-blind understandings of history and society. In the introduction, I mentioned that I didn't grow up consciously thinking about race or racism. In fact, I was so lost in the sauce in middle school that when our class read those precious few lines about slavery and the Civil War in our history book, I thought, "Gee, how sad for those people." *Those people.* As in, the enslaved Africans and their descendants—some of whom are *my* ancestors!

Prior to going to college, I don't recall having *any* teacher, from elementary on through high school, draw clear connections between past and present racism, or even acknowledge that systemic racism was a serious, ongoing problem in the United States (not to mention the rest of the globe!). In schools across the country, young people are indoctrinated with a rosy origin myth of the United States, a lie that frames indigenous people as noble savages who happily sat down with the Pilgrims to "celebrate" Thanksgiving over turkey and squash as their people were being systematically slaughtered through genocide.[2] To the extent that racial oppression is referenced at all, it is generally framed as a bad thing that happened a long time ago. One of the sad ironies of oppression is that it's completely possible to grow up in a society ravaged by multiple forms of domination and *not know* that your society is ravaged by multiple forms of domination, especially when our educational system manufactures feel-good histories and progress narratives. I concur with Ibram X. Kendi, who argues that our nation's emphasis on racial progress has obscured "racist progress"—the evolution of racist ideas and practices alongside antiracist transformations. The end result is a society where racism is routinely misrepresented, denied, and difficult to detect—unless, of course, you experience it directly *and* have the political and historical lens needed to *know* you're experiencing it.

This is precisely why civil rights lawyers and experts developed critical race theory: to address and redress widespread racial misinformation and to promote racial justice. Between the intentional efforts of bigots to whitewash racism and massive historical ignorance pervading our social institutions, it's no wonder that millions of people struggle with racial denial—including the denial of racism itself. Depending on which racial idiot you ask, the United States hasn't been racist since Obama's election, the civil rights movement, the dawn of the twentieth century, or ever. In 2017, former NFL player and coach Mike Ditka proclaimed that there has been "no oppression" of any kind in the last "one hundred years."[3] And for some misguided minorities, the gains of the civil rights movement and certainly the election of the nation's first biracial president were interpreted as signs that significant racial barriers are no longer with us. In the wake of Obama's 2008 election, the conservative African American linguist John McWhorter went so far as to pen an op-ed in *Forbes* entitled "Racism in America Is Over." In keeping with his long career of minimizing racism, McWhorter enthusiastically declared the end of "serious" racial oppression: "Of course, nothing magically changed when Obama was declared president-elect. However, our proper concern is not whether racism still exists, but whether it remains a serious problem. The election of Obama proved, as nothing else could have, that it no longer does."[4]

I'm sitting here scratching my head over an author saying that his concern is not "whether racism still exists" in an article entitled "Racism in America Is Over." Now, to be fair, it's possible that McWhorter did not choose the title of his essay, as editors often provide the headlines, but let's be clear: there is a logical contradiction between declaring the end of racism and then backpedaling to the more restricted (but still delusional) claim that "serious" racism no longer exists.

McWhorter's position is not *postracial*, strictly speaking. He predicted that during the Obama era "a noose or three will be hung somewhere, some employer will be revealed to have used the N-word on tapes of a meeting," but racial oppression, he maintained, was now definitively a thing of the past. McWhorter gave lip service to acknowledging trivial remnants of racism—an apparently harmless act of racial terrorism or awkward racial epithet here or there. But, from his perspective, these acts of bigotry were minor, individual human failings in contrast to systemic oppression, which he depicted as the relic of a bygone era. We can think of this line of argumentation as *post-really-bad racism*. Thus, McWhorter writes:

> It's not an accident . . . that increasingly . . . alleged cases of racism are tough calls, reflecting the complexity of human affairs rather than the stark injustice of Jim Crow or even redlining. A young black man is shot dead by three police officers and only one of them is white. A white radio host uses a jocular slur against black women—used for decades in the exact same way by black rappers celebrated as bards. . . . But anyone who wants to take this line from now on will have to grapple with the elephant in the middle of the room: the president of AmeriKKKa is black. If the racism that America is "all about" is the kind that allows a black man to become president, then I'm afraid the nature of this "all about" is too abstract for me to follow, and most Americans will feel similarly. It's time to change the discussion.

It's safe to say that McWhorter didn't see the Black Lives Matter movement or the election of a KKK-endorsed president coming (to be fair, very few of us did). But what I want to point out here is that the denial that our society is always already racialized can take many forms, from individual proclamations of color blindness (*"I don't see color!"*) and disavowals of *significant, systemic* racial oppression to the complete denial of all forms of racism. And nonwhites are, unfortunately, not immune to absorbing and disseminating distortions of racial reality.

In many respects, my own discipline of sociology bears some responsibility for obscuring the maintenance of systemic racism and white supremacy.[5] Although sociologists are often framed as "liberal," the truth is that sociology in the United States was founded on overtly white supremacist ideas. And, as Eduardo Bonilla-Silva and Gianpolo Baiocci argue in their 2007 article "Anything but Racism," sociologists from the twentieth century to the present day have often downplayed the existence of structural racism in their analyses.[6] This is perhaps especially true of scholars who emphasize the role of culture or class in explaining the persistence of group-based inequalities. It's probably no coincidence that some of the most revered and highly cited sociologists responsible for pushing the *post-really-bad-racism* trope have been devastatingly brilliant black sociologists employed by Harvard University, my alma mater. These include Orlando Patterson (one of my doctoral advisors) and William Julius Wilson, author of a classic 1978 text, *The Declining Significance of Race*, which was met with wide-eyed enthusiasm and nearly orgasmic praise by white elites.[7]

While the post-really-bad-racism trope has been long dominant in and outside sociology, there is a vibrant counter-discourse emerging from scholars working in the intellectual and political tradition of W. E. B. Du Bois and Ida B. Wells-Barnett. From Joyce Ladner in 1973 to Aldon Morris, Vilna Bashi-Treitler, and Noel Cazenave more recently, critical sociologists have argued that sociological analyses purporting to be racially progressive often minimized or masked structural racism and white dominance. Many sociologists who emphasize the complicity of sociological research in masking racial oppression and white domination throughout US history have been heavily influenced by the insights of critical race theory.

As stated previously, we live in a society where the phrase "white supremacy" has been traditionally used to refer to neo-Nazis and extremists rather than to the dominance of people socially defined as white. But legal scholars, social scientists, and political philosophers working in the robust field of critical race theory have developed conceptual tools for recognizing and responding to systemic racism and white supremacy. Critical race theory is an interdisciplinary body of scholarship that emerged in the aftermath of the civil rights movement as legal theorists grappled with naming and challenging the persistence of racism after the fall of de jure segregation. Born in the mid-1970s, CRT boldly embraced an overtly activist agenda: the promotion of racial justice and the eradication of racial oppression. Bridging legal analysis with storytelling and narratives centering the experiences of people of color, critical race theorists set about to unveil and address the persistence of racism and white dominance. And, importantly, scholars in this tradition also acknowledge the intersections of racism with sexism, class oppression, and other systems of inequality. One of the most important and helpful features of critical race theory is its clear analysis of white supremacy in the so-called post–civil rights era, a period in US history when politicians and the majority population increasingly portrayed themselves as "beyond race" or "nonracist."

Critical race theory is kryptonite for the myth of color-blindness and helps cut through the bullshit of postracial propaganda by specifying the role of social institutions (especially laws and legal practices) in reproducing racism. From a critical race perspective, the United States is not (and never was) a benevolent "nation of immigrants." Rather, it is a nation of settler-colonialism, genocide, white nationalism, racial slavery, legal torture, and institutionalized rape. Since the inception of this country, laws and legal practices systematically favored whites economically, politically, and socially. In fact, critical race scholar Cheryl Harris, in 1993, described whiteness as a form of protected "property" within the US racial hierarchy, a category of privilege tied to the accumulation of economic resources and the subjugation of racialized "others." From this perspective, laws and legal institutions within this country have continually converted white identity into a valuable, exclusive mechanism for maintaining power.

Few people realize that the nation's very first immigration law, the Naturalization Act of 1790, was explicitly white supremacist, restricting naturalization to "free White persons," though white women were left out of this exclusionary understanding of "freedom." Granting citizenship to free white men was quite literally a government handout—for whites only. As you might have noticed, history keeps coming up here, quite simply because critical race theorists encourage historical consciousness. In order to understand present-day racial realities, we will have to look to the past. This might seem simple or obvious on its face, but the sad truth is that most US citizens have never seriously studied history of any kind, much less racial history. If the vast majority of the population is ignorant of the racist past, how can they understand the impact of that past on the present?

Critical race theorists also challenge the liberal logics that have been used to portray the United States as "beyond race," for example, by analyzing the jurisprudence surrounding the country's affirmative action policies. Scholars such as Richard Delgado, Kimberlé Crenshaw, and Derrick Bell (the last of whom was a professor of Barack Obama's at Harvard Law School) have shown that legal assumptions about meritocracy and fairness that are used by conservatives to undermine affirmative action programs are logically inconsistent with the existence of institutional racism.[8] Other scholars who take a critical or "systemic" approach to the study of racism have shown that the nation's first affirmative action programs and government handouts were conceived *by* white Americans *for* white Americans.[9] From using racially justified mass murder, land theft, and labor exploitation to enacting racist citizenship laws, people socially defined as "white" have built generations of wealth and political power by playing the race card and founding an entire nation on white identity politics. To take just one example, the 1862 Homestead Act gleefully gave away *millions* of acres of stolen land almost exclusively to whites.[10] And, quiet as it's kept, white people continue to be the number-one beneficiaries of affirmative action today. Race scholars are aware that white women are the top recipients of affirmative action, but few have considered that white women's primary access to affirmative action helps maintain the racial wealth gap.[11] Because these white women typically marry white men, their affirmative action benefits are channeled toward their white families. And their access to affirmative action benefits (preferential hiring and federal diversity initiatives) not only helps them but also bolsters the socioeconomic status of white families broadly.

My first serious encounter with critical race theory occurred after I'd already finished my PhD. Although I didn't realize it then, I had chosen to undertake my graduate work in a sociology department that was relatively conservative in terms of its racial politics—there was little in the way of overlap or exchange with more radical or progressive elements at the university. Certainly, none of my professors were intensely collaborating with critical race theorists. Nonetheless, for most of my seven years of doctoral work, I felt confident that I was being educated by some of the world's most insightful experts on race. As well-meaning as the Harvard sociologists might have been, the truth is that their work typically downplayed racial oppression or focused on conceptually vague "cultural elements" of race rather than systemic racism. This was even demonstrated in how specialty areas were named for our general exams, a sink-or-swim, high-stakes assessment at the end of our first year of graduate school in which each student had to absorb information from nearly ten thousand pages of scholarly articles and books. One of the optional specialties offered to students was called "Race and Ethnicity"—not "Racism." And though we studied racism, the term "white supremacy" was not part of our sociological lexicon. If I had done my due diligence, I would have known that Harvard has a long history of producing dubious scholarship on race—and by "dubious," I mean "racist." Consider the fact that Charles William Eliot, university president from the mid-1800s to the early twentieth century, played a major role in legitimating eugenics, an ideology first developed by white male scientists for the purpose of promoting the genetic erasure of groups deemed to be inferior. Harvard has, in fact, been described as the "brain trust" of the eugenics movement.[12]

The idea that certain human groups are undesirable and should be removed from the face of the planet would later find favor with Adolf Hitler, who drew on eugenics to justify the extermination of millions of Jews and other stigmatized people. To this day, there is still a student dorm named for Charles Eliot. Worse, he is not the only white supremacist currently honored and commemorated at Harvard.[13] Unfortunately, the same could be said for many campuses across the country.

As a graduate student, I was predominately trained to examine racism as a "cultural" phenomenon happening "out there" in the social world, not a structural feature of oppression that shaped what we were taught—and by whom. And so it was that I spent seven whole years of my life thinking I knew a lot about race when in fact I lacked any understanding of the racial politics shaping my own education.

By the time I arrived at Stony Brook as an assistant professor, I had published an award-winning dissertation on racism and collective memory in France, as well as numerous scholarly articles on the dynamics of racism in the United States. But, as painful as this is to admit, I still didn't have a clear understanding of systemic racism in the US until I began to break away from the influence of my old mentors and teach undergraduate and graduate students myself. I also began belatedly talking with other academics who were more politically conscious and radical than I was, the kind of people who proudly and unapologetically framed their scholarship in terms of activism (and, incidentally, the kind of people I did not often encounter in my Harvard bubble). Slowly—with a mix of excitement, shame, and relief—I began to realize that there were entire fields of racial scholarship I'd ignored and brushed aside. As I engaged with intellectually and politically incisive work that had been pushed to the margins at Harvard, I finally understood why so much of what I'd been taught to believe was "important scholarship" actually made me sick. I mean this quite literally. After I finished my PhD and began to establish myself as a scholar, I also increasingly noticed how much I disliked (let me keep it real: *despised*) research that minimized structural racism, ignored white supremacy, or marginalized the critical work of people of color and white antiracists. As a longtime practitioner of mindfulness and meditation, I found that the more I brought my attention to the present moment, the more clearly I could identify the tightness in my chest or revulsion in my stomach when reading racist scholarship. Conversely, I also noticed how invigorated and inspired I felt reading authors who frankly acknowledged the structural, political, and spiritual realities of domination.

And then, one fine day, I had the luck of encountering Dr. Charles Mills—an eminent critical race theorist and political philosopher. Dr. Mills had been invited to Stony Brook to give a provostial lecture on his famous book *The Racial Contract*. Sitting in the amphitheater, I listened intently as the professor threw around terms like "white supremacy" and "epistemology of ignorance," but I confess that I had no friggin' clue what the hell he was talking about. Back then, "white supremacy" still seemed, to my ear, like an odd phrase to describe racism in the United States. How could there be "white supremacy" when the president was black? And how could racial oppression be so persistent if I, an African American woman, held multiple degrees from a prestigious university and had garnered a highly sought-after tenure-track job?

The more I read of Mills's work—and the work of other critical race theorists—the more I began to understand the importance of looking beyond my own individual circumstances. As I would come to see clearly, dominant discourses of individualism, exceptionalism, and meritocracy work to sustain collective denial about racism and other forms of injustice. Paying attention to the conditions of my own students at Stony Brook, a state university, also sensitized me to systemic inequalities. The gap between the limited socioeconomic resources available at a public institution versus the elite private schools I'd grown accustomed to could not be more stark and morally abhorrent. During my office hours,

I met talented, brilliant students who lacked access to basic resources, worked multiple jobs, commuted obscene hours, and even struggled with homelessness. The unfairness of their predicament shocked my conscience. It's also clear, looking back, that the death of Trayvon Martin—and the subsequent emergence of the Movement for Black Lives—opened my eyes to all that had not changed about race in the United States. I understood, then, that "white supremacy" was not merely about a few racist extremists but rather about a system of domination that stretched into the present day and affected every sphere of society.

But if white supremacy is so widespread, why has it been so difficult for some to detect? And how could I, as a black woman, have obtained multiple degrees from elite institutions and studied "race" for nearly a decade without clearly recognizing the fact that we live in a white supremacist society? In Mills's view, white supremacy is a system of power and domination, one founded on racial oppression and which provides material benefits to people socially defined as "white." More broadly, critical race theorists such as Mills emphasize the role of European colonialism, genocide, and chattel slavery in producing intertwined ideologies of white superiority and scientific racism in order to retroactively justify the (continued) exploitation of people socially defined as "nonwhite." And here's the kicker: Mills has convincingly argued that the maintenance of white supremacy involves and requires "cognitive dysfunctions" and warped representations of the social world that conveniently serve the interests of the majority population.[14] These distortions and cognitive errors produce "the ironic outcome that whites [are] in general . . . unable to understand the world they themselves have made."

This brings us back to Mills's rather esoteric phrase: *the epistemology of ignorance*. The word "epistemology" refers to the study of knowledge and its formation, so an epistemology of ignorance would involve creating "knowledge" based on . . . a profound *lack of knowledge* or stupidity. Using fancy academic language, Mills is basically saying that whites' ideas "about race" are fundamentally based on misrepresentations and distortions of social reality, but their "not knowing," their ignorance, gets routinely repackaged as credible, authoritative "knowledge," even as "science."[15] But racial ignorance is not restricted to white folks, unfortunately. My sociological interpretation of Mills's argument is that racist societies socialize *all of us* to be racial idiots, insofar as we are exposed to forms of racial ignorance. Moreover, this widespread ignorance sustains the racial power structure, and the racial order, in turn, helps maintain the economic power of capitalist elites. The powerful always thrive on the miseducation of groups they seek to exploit and control. As long as everyday citizens are fed a daily mental diet of white supremacist ideology, historical ignorance, and disinformation, the overall power structure remains difficult to detect—and oppose. Thus, becoming less stupid about race involves discovering how we've all been socialized in ways that obscure the realities of racial domination for the benefit of white male property owners. I would eventually come to see that even something as simple as referring to "race" or "racism" without describing the overall racial order (the approach I absorbed in graduate school) could have the unintended effect of reproducing that very same racial order.

The concepts and words we use to represent (or misrepresent) racism have a lot to do with how the system perpetuates itself. Imagine if you went to the doctor for an annual checkup and your physician sat across from you, looking very somber. Peering over her glasses, she says, "*I'm very sorry to break this news to you, but . . . you have an illness.*"

Alarmed and anxious you ask, "*What kind of illness?*"

But instead of answering your question, the doctor flatly repeats, "*You have an illness.*"

Wouldn't it be helpful to know what the hell kind of illness you have? You see, a general diagnosis is not especially helpful. You don't know what exactly is wrong or what to do. Similarly, using bland, vague words like "race" or "racial" can often disguise what racism is and how it actually works. In fact, scholars Karen E. Fields and Barbara J. Fields make this point in their book *Racecraft*, which argues that racial domination is reinforced by mysterious references to "race" that ignore systemic racism.[16] Describing the collective, systemic nature of racism clearly is an oft-overlooked, prerequisite for taking effective action to challenge racial injustice.

Now that we have defined white supremacy, we turn to the question of *when* it emerged. This bit is super important: white supremacy, as an ideology, would have you believe that white people have been timelessly dominant. This simply isn't true. Remember how long our species (Homo sapiens) has been on the earth: about two hundred thousand years. White supremacy and European global domination have existed for about four hundred years. This means that the entire period of Western colonial power represents an infinitesimal fraction of time—0.2 percent of our history! Of course, this tiny fraction of time encapsulates our entire life and the lifetimes of many ancestral generations.

With all of this said, it is important to understand European domination and modern racism as nestled in a more complex, and longer, history of oppressions. It's also important to bear in mind that ethnicity and ethnic boundaries pre-date the more recent emergence of race. In their 2012 book *Race in North America*, Audrey and Brian Smedley demonstrate that modern ideas about racial (biological) difference were articulated gradually, between the sixteenth and the nineteenth centuries, in the aftermath of European colonial expansion and the onset of the transatlantic slave trade.[17] Thus, the modern race concept served to justify the classification (and exploitation) of racialized others. An intersectional approach to understanding racism specifically, and oppressions more broadly, makes it clear that racial oppression is one of multiple, interlocking systems of domination. And—crucially—it's not the oldest form of oppression.

Certainly the histories of slavery, patriarchy, and class oppression demonstrate that violence and dominance are human problems, not merely "white problems." But in the same way that men invented patriarchy, critical race theorists argue that we must be clear that Europeans invented (and continue to benefit from) modern racism in order to combat misrecognition and misrepresentation. But part of this clear understanding, from my perspective, is seeing white supremacist racism in its proper context: as a relatively new system of oppression that was built on (and integrates) prior (and much longer) systems of oppression including but not limited to class oppression, patriarchy, and gender oppression. And white supremacist racism can poison the mind of everyone socialized within its reach, including minorities, who have the most to lose from internalizing and perpetuating racist ideas.

Let me be clear on this point: I am not drawing a false equivalence between the racial ignorance of people of color and the racial ignorance of the white majority. The "ignorance" of a majority group and that of minority groups are not the same, especially not the same in their effect. In other words, though racial stupidity is ubiquitous, it is ubiquitous due to the violence and dominant discourses of the majority population. It so happens that this majority population is white but, of course, from an intersectional perspective, almost everyone belongs to both "majority" and "minority" groups. And though people of color are subject to being socialized in a racist society and absorbing the biases and stereotypes inherent within such a society, they are typically not as racially stupid as their majority counterparts. That's not because they are fundamentally better than white people or inherently more insightful, but for the simple reason that they are more likely to encounter racism and therefore are able to identify it and oppose it. Of course, to borrow from the language of sociology, these dynamics are *probabilistic* rather than *deterministic*: we can't know for sure, based on someone's racial identity, how she sees the world or how racially obtuse she is. But it's indisputable that on average, white people know a lot less about race and racism than people of color.

Now that we've covered the "what" and the "when," we have to know the "where" of white supremacy. Well, the first important step is to acknowledge that white supremacy exists right now within the United States. However, critical race theory scholars have also argued that global white supremacy has come to be consolidated and maintained by other Western nations. My own work examines the politics of white supremacy in France, while scholars such as Melissa Weiner and Gloria Wekker have unveiled dynamics of white domination in Scandinavian countries, and France Winddance Twine has analyzed the maintenance of white supremacy in Brazil.

As for the "why" of white supremacy, that's easy: Europeans wanted to exploit other human beings for material profit, take shit that didn't belong to them, and feel good about it in the process. The mythology of white superiority and scientific racism developed over time in the aftermath of colonial conquest and slavery to justify socioeconomic exploitation and theft. As long as the endemic, systemic nature of white supremacy is successfully minimized or denied, as long as "conversations about race" are mainly about individual attitudes, prejudice, or the actions of a few extremists, then attention is drawn away from the structures and pattern of racial inequality hiding in plain sight. Nationwide, white families hold thirteen times the wealth of black families. In Washington, DC, alone, white households (a numerical minority in this "chocolate city") are *eighty-one times more wealthy than black households.*[18] And, so, we come back to class relations—and why Bernie Bros get it wrong every time they insist that we should talk about class instead of race. The truth is that these two concepts are intimately intertwined. In fact, modern race and white supremacy can both be understood as capitalist inventions. There is nothing really very original, of course, about creating a system of domination to monopolize resources. A quick review of history evinces widespread use of religious ideology to oppress, murder, exploit, and enslave.

Wondering *how* white supremacy endures? Good news: political scientist Charles Hamilton and activist Stokely Carmichael (later known as Kwame Ture) answered this question fifty years ago in their book *Black Power.* As Hamilton and Carmichael noted: "Racism is both overt and covert. It takes two, closely related forms: individual whites acting against individual blacks, and acts by the total white community against the black community. We call these individual racism and institutional racism. The first consists of overt acts by individuals, which cause death, injury or the violent destruction of property. This type can be recorded by television cameras; it can frequently be observed in the process of commission."[19]

One of the outcomes of the Black Power and civil rights movements was a major advance in our understanding of racial oppression. The key, as Hamilton and Carmichael point out, is that racism comprises both individual *and* institutional components, though most people only think about racism as an individual, personal trait. But if you're going to wrap your head around how racial oppression actually operates, you have to move beyond simplistic individual notions and grasp how racism becomes *institutionalized* in the ideas and routine practices of our social organizations: our families, our laws and policies, our educational system and decisions and structures shaping the representation of race we absorb from the media. From mass incarceration to sentencing laws to racial discrimination in housing and home loans, the invisibility of institutional racism is maintained by the fact that it is literally hard to *see.* Hamilton and Carmichael describe institutional racism as "less overt, far more subtle, less identifiable in terms of specific individuals committing the acts."[20] For example, most of us are not present when racist decisions are made in the courtroom or when laws and policies with racist consequences are being drafted. And the self-imposed racial isolation and social apartheid preferred by many whites means that most members of the majority population have *no* meaningful relationships with people of color and, consequently, no significant exposure to the realities of systemic, institutionalized racial oppression. Unless you directly experience the injustice of living in a polluted neighborhood decimated by environmental racism, unless you've been racially profiled or abused by police, how could you know it's happening—especially if such matters aren't addressed in school? And even if you personally experience the consequences of institutionalized racism, how could you know it's occurring on a wider scale? Even the language of "structures" and "institutions" can be a barrier for understanding and visualizing social relations; the terms are, admittedly, abstract. Most of us are not used to thinking about society in terms of historical patterns and distributions of power and resources. Hamilton and Carmichael are careful to point out that for institutional racism (and, therefore, white supremacy) to exist does not mean that every white citizen must hold racist beliefs or engage in individual acts of racism. Because institutional racism is a systemic power structure, it functions through collective action and systemic practices. As such, it is "deliberately maintained . . . by the power structure and through [whites'] indifference, inertia and lack of courage."[21]

We can draw an important connection between the invisibility of institutional racism and Mills's conceptualization of the epistemology of ignorance. Both of these ideas point to aspects of systemic racism that are difficult to detect, despite (and perhaps even because of) their durability and ubiquity. White supremacy endures, ironically—and chronically—through the widespread erasure of its systemic and chronic nature. These erasures include covert forms of institutional racism as well as denial, misrepresentation, and disinformation by those who intentionally seek to secure resources for "whites," as well as the "unintentional" and institutionalized distortions of racial reality that result from vague and imprecise descriptions of ongoing racialized social and historical realities. In this way, systemic racism is reproduced and extended through everyday practices that allow people to live in a racist society but fail to make meaningful connections between their own observations, their nation's history, and broader patterns of domination.

Once established as an ideological and political system, white supremacy reproduces itself through repertoires of silence, denial, misrepresentation, disinformation, deflection, willful ignorance, justification, and—when all else fails—brute violence and force. This is the case no matter how or when white supremacy is established in a nation's history. As the racial order takes hold, the population that benefits from its maintenance is generally socialized in ways that ensure the system remains in place. Within white supremacist societies, members of the majority population are socialized to draw upon every discursive and coercive tool at their disposal to maintain dominance without regard to logical coherence, empirical evidence, reason, or morality. Ordinary racists *and* their extremist counterparts employ liberal, inclusive, and even, at times, "antiracist" ideas in order to obscure the racist intentions and effects of their actions and institutional arrangements. The combination of racist and antiracist ideas is, in fact, one of the most prominent and pernicious methods used to mask or justify continual white dominance and to uphold the "non-racist" pose that has become politically expedient in the wake of World War II and the US civil rights movement.

Let me give you a really concrete example of the epistemology of ignorance and racial denial. After the white supremacist rally and domestic terrorist attack in Charlottesville, Virginia, in August 2017, I penned an op-ed for *The Root* about the origins of white supremacy in the United States.[22] The next day, I started getting emails telling me to turn on CNN, which is normally against my religion because, my God, CNN is hot trash fire. But it turned out that Ohio state senator Nina Turner had referenced my work twice on the network's Sunday morning politics show *State of the Union*, hosted by Jake Tapper. The response of her panelist, noted homophobe Rick Santorum, was white supremacist deflection 101:

NINA TURNER: I want to read a brief quote from Dr. Crystal Fleming. . . . "It is clear that our nation is in the midst of a very public—and painful—reckoning with the memory (and ongoing realities) of white supremacy." And that's it. That, in other words, what transpired in Virginia was just a tipping point, but this has been happening in this country all along. And until we go deeper, showing disgust for and standing up very clearly and unified against racism and bigotry like the neo-Nazis and KKK inspired, but we've got to go deeper to deal with mass incarceration in this country that locks up more black and brown folks and poor folks. We got to deal with income and wealth inequality—inequality in our school system. So dealing with neo-Nazis is one thing, but dealing with systemic racism is another. And this is a day of reckoning for our country.

JAKE TAPPER: Senator?

RICK SANTORUM: Yes. That kind of talk that really, I think, causes problems for a lot of America that says somehow or another that if you're white, you're somehow racist. And—I mean—

NINA TURNER: Nobody ever said that.

RICK SANTORUM: You talked about—you talked about systemic racism and as opposed to neo-Nazis, I agree. I mean, I think everybody has stood up and said, you know, that we're obviously against white supremacy. I don't know of anybody who has spoken in favor of . . . Certainly nobody that I'm aware of, but the idea of then saying, well, this is a, you know, a larger problem that is that— I just would say that, you know, we have problems of racism in this country. But that's not— Tying that to white supremacists, I think, is a —

NINA TURNER: Two hundred and fifty years' worth of slavery—250 years' worth of slavery. Almost a hundred years' worth of Jim Crow in this country, the fact that the systems in this country still treat black folks, in particular, African-American folks as second-class citizens. And part of what the senator doesn't want to face is also part of the problem. No one has said . . . that all white people are racists. But we do, in this country, have racist institutions. Look there were white folks out there, marching against the neo-Nazis and the KKK. But the fact that we can't deal with systemic racism in this country, something is wrong with that.[23]

There's so much racial stupidity here on Santorum's part that one scarcely knows where to begin. But let's just start with the simple fact that rather than acknowledge centuries of systemic racism, he immediately denied that white supremacy exists as a system of racial domination. The man literally said that he refused to "tie" (connect) "problems of racism" to white supremacy. Somehow, racism, in his mind, apparently exists independent of white supremacy. Instead of admitting that larger, institutional dynamics exist, Santorum tried to impose an individualist framing of racism. White supremacists are just a faction of extremists, floating in the ether, disconnected from structural forces. Senator Turner successfully pushed back, cogently acknowledging the systemic nature of racism and the historical legacies of racial oppression.

Just as Charles Hamilton and Stokely Carmichael, referenced earlier, made it clear that systemic racism doesn't need every white citizen to be personally racist in order to exist, so Senator Nina Turner emphasized the institutional, collective forces that create institutional racism. But to make what should be very basic points, she was forced to address and counter the pathological denial, historical ignorance, racial stupidity, and general dumbassery of Rick Santorum.

And the inconvenient truth is that there are millions of Rick Santorums in our midst.

Repertoires of denial, erasure, and distancing are widespread in white supremacist Western societies, but the specific discourses and strategies of deflection (and especially their degree of "success" and hegemony) differ across national contexts. For example, the fact that whites practiced slavery and genocide within the geographic confines of the United States means that US citizens cannot easily pretend that chattel slavery and "race" are irrelevant issues here without completely disregarding basic history and ongoing social issues. This does not mean, however, that US citizens (especially whites) do not try to disregard racial history and present-day racial issues—color-blind discourses certainly exist here, for sure. But color-blind ideology in the US is frequently contested and perhaps more easily detected as erroneous given the plethora of empirical evidence of past and present racism and the long-term, significant presence of immigrants and racial minorities.

But color-blind racism, though widespread among the US white majority, is even more hegemonic in European countries, which also practiced racial violence and developed a white supremacist ideology.[24] Because European nations can more convincingly frame "race" as a distant issue (both geographically and politically), they have more success imposing racial denial than their US counterparts. The fact that continental Europeans (1) existed prior to the elaboration of modern white supremacy; (2) largely practiced racialized violence overseas through colonial domination of non-Europeans; and (3) managed to prevent the mass immigration of non-Europeans until relatively recently makes it easier for their majority population to deny the social existence and salience of race. A fourth geopolitical issue also fosters the erasure of past and present racism in European societies: the ever-present boogeyman of the overtly racist United States. As Northern liberals frequently point to Southern (and/or conservative) racists in order to deny their own racism, so, too, do Europeans frequently point to the overt evidence of racism in the United States to portray their own societies as nonracist, racially benign, or "less racist." Whites in the United States cannot easily employ this tool of comparative denial, not only because the global media ecosystem routinely portrays the US as "more racist" than other nations but also because many whites in the United States do not know much about racism in other societies.

Becoming antiracist involves developing the historical and sociological literacy needed to decode the ongoing impact of the racial past on the present. It means becoming familiar with the typical tropes of minimization, deflection, and denial that allow racism to persist unrecognized and/or justified on a daily basis. And it means going far beyond "calling out" your racist friend or family members for their racist comments and behavior (something the vast majority of whites do not do). If we are ever to move beyond this racial order, then we will also have to dismantle the system of unearned privilege attached to being socially defined as "white." If being racist is about supporting a system of racist domination, then becoming antiracist is about recognizing and opposing this system. This recognition is the very first step to becoming less stupid about race and developing strategies capable of challenging racism in the present and building a more just future. Critical race theory and systemic approaches to studying racism are incredibly helpful for developing this literacy, as these perspectives provide not only an explanation of the origins and functioning of racism, but also a theory about how this system of domination is ideologically sustained through commonplace modes of misrepresentation and denial.

As a system, white supremacy needs people to believe that it (1) doesn't exist, (2) has been overcome, or (3) only exists among extremists. White supremacy can't tolerate millions of people finally realizing that it is pervasive and systemic. It needs us ignorant and hopeful. And it needs us to cling to a particular kind of hope—a hope that reinforces racial ignorance and denial of white supremacy. A hope that sells you neoliberal inclusion and "feel-good" tokenism—the kind of hope that cannot threaten the racial status quo.

Antiracists have to learn how to recognize racism in its subtle political, psychological, and sociological forms: the workings of institutions, publications, laws, families. Adopting a systemic view of racism requires noticing the cooperation of both major parties (and corporate media) with the economic and political forces of white supremacy. And you must see how your own socialization, behavior, and choices are complicit with multiple systems of oppression, racism included. The fact that racism (and patriarchy, class domination, and so on) are systemic means that none of us are exempt from these dynamics. White supremacy continues to persist, in part, due to the widespread temptation to only see and condemn *other people's racism*—racism is always someone else's crime.

If it's not already clear to you, there is also a moral dimension to critical race theory, for it involves challenging the values and principles that justify (implicitly or explicitly) racial domination. From a critical race perspective—one that centers the views and voices of the marginalized—we can (and must) do better than what the "Founding Fathers" did. We don't need to mythologize their moral integrity.

The only way a nation founded on white supremacy, colonial violence, and hypercapitalism can be framed as a moral entity is to continually devalue the lives of those it has repeatedly diminished, in our case women, indigenous populations, and black, brown, working-class, and poor people.

In order to envision and build a more just society, we will have to collectively recognize the foundational immorality of the Founding Fathers and commit to creating a world better than the one they conceived. People of conscience must eventually admit that we do not need to keep making excuses for white supremacists and enslavers—even those who putatively embraced ideas of "freedom"—because the freedom they had in mind was not honorable.

As this chapter has explained, the freedom conceived by white supremacists was specifically crafted by and for white male property owners. It was always morally abhorrent. For white male supremacists, "liberty" was conceived as consistent with oppressing marginalized others: women, indigenous people, Africans, the poor. This should go without saying, but people who base their concept and practice of freedom on genocide, slavery, and rape aren't moral models. A true moral revolution requires letting go of the need to elevate those who justified exploitation, murder, and oppression.

Some will contend that the founders' redemptive values of freedom outweighed their actual practice of oppression. (*"Gotta see both sides . . ."*) But the opposite is true: the founders' actual practice of oppression reveals that they used the language of freedom to justify domination. Others will object and say that condemning the founders for their moral crimes against humanity is unfair, because it means using our current values to judge historical figures. But this narrative—long dominant (and typically invoked by white men)—deliberately ignores the fact that people spoke out against and opposed white supremacist genocide and chattel slavery *while these things were happening*. Unsurprisingly, the people calling out these moral wrongs were often those being targeted. The histories of indigenous resistance against European aggression, slave rebellions, and abolitionism clearly demonstrate that there were people who knew it was wrong to treat other human beings as if they were disposable. But there were also European "whites" who spoke against these moral wrongs at every stage of our history, a very small but important minority among the majority population who rejected theses of racial inequality and justifications of oppression.

Wouldn't a more perfect union be a society in which white supremacists, enslavers, and rapists are no longer honored? A society in which indigenous people, black people, people of color, and white antiracists who fought against oppression are held in higher esteem than those who defended the indefensible? What kind of transformations—social, political, economic, and moral—would need to happen to build a more perfect union?

There have always been voices challenging racial oppression, pointing out its horror and moral wrong. But throughout our history, these voices have been opposed and drowned out. We must not allow these voices to be marginalized any longer. We must be clear: racism is morally wrong and racists do not deserve to be honored, whether they were members of the Confederacy or the signatories of the Declaration of Independence. But we can certainly learn from the past. And maybe—just maybe—the way to correct the moral errors of those who came before us is to decide, with conviction, not to repeat them.

If there is anything to learn from the Founding Fathers, it's that we have the right to call out tyranny by its name and transform our society. But we don't have to remain enslaved to the limited moral imaginations of those who rationalized slavery and genocide. We can dream better, more inclusive dreams and create a more just society. And even if we aren't able to bring about all the positive change we would like to see in our lifetime, at the very least, we can begin to imagine it.

Chapter 2

LISTEN TO BLACK WOMEN

The history of white women who are unable to hear black women's words or to maintain dialogue with us is long and discouraging.

—AUDRE LORDE[1]

White (male) supremacy socializes us to devalue the critical insights of black women and girls. And we're all the more stupid as a society because of this collective refusal to take black women's knowledge seriously. Black women such as Sojourner Truth, Anna Julia Cooper, Ida B. Wells, the Nardal sisters, and Fannie Lou Hamer have been on the forefront of theorizing and challenging multiple forms of domination for generations, but our perspectives are routinely brushed aside.[2] Dismissing black women and girls is embedded in the DNA of our nation. And worse, when this erasure is called out and critiqued by black women, we are almost always met with efforts that trivialize the harm we routinely experience.

Imagine publicly silencing a black woman for speaking about the racial and sexist violence she's experienced—and then writing an op-ed about the sexual violence you experienced. Well, that's exactly what Salma Hayek, the famous Mexican American actress, did when she penned an essay for the *New York Times* in December of 2017 about her traumatic encounters with movie producer Harvey Weinstein—only months after shaming a black actress for speaking up about racism.[3] In the midst of the #MeToo movement (itself a product of a black woman's labor), Hayek decided to break her own silence and acknowledge that she had been victimized by Weinstein's relentless harassment and predation. But back in January of that year, Hayek earned black folks' collective scorn for her racially stupid remarks to Jessica Williams, a young black comedian, at a swanky luncheon for women filmmakers.[4] The star-studded event, which included well-known luminaries such as Shirley MacLaine and Alfre Woodard, as well as younger artists and actresses including Williams, took place in the wake of the historic Women's March, the largest protest in US history. Issues of identity, difference, and solidarity were discussed over gourmet food as the women debated the meaning of solidarity and intersectionality. (We'll come back to that buzzword later.)

As the women discussed the implications of Trump's election, Shirley MacLaine mentioned a connection between "democracy" and identity. Soon thereafter, Salma Hayek criticized what she referred to as "victimization." "I don't want to be hired because I'm a girl," she said. "I want them to see I'm fabulous. Don't give me a job because I'm a girl. It's condescending." At this point, Williams, best known for her appearances on *The Daily Show*, intervened to ask MacLaine: "I have a question for you. . . . What if you are a person of color or a transgendered [*sic*] person who—just from how you look—you already are in a conflict?" MacLaine shot her down. "Right, but change your point of view. Change your point of view of being victimized. I'm saying, 'Find the democracy inside.'" Then Salma Hayek decided to gang up on Jessica too. "I'm sorry," she said to Williams. "Can I ask you a question? Who are you when you're not black and you're not a woman? Who are you and what have you got to give?"

I'll let Amy Kaufman of the *Los Angeles Times* report what happened next:

> Williams took a deep breath. "A lot. But some days, I'm just black, and I'm just a woman," she said. "Like, it's not my choice. I know who I am. I know I'm Jessica, and I'm the hottest bitch on the planet I know."
>
> "No, no, no," Hayek said. "Take the time to investigate. That's the trap! . . . There is so much more."
>
> "Right," agreed MacLaine. "The more is inside."

The more is inside. What the hell does this patronizing phrase even mean? Evidently, acknowledging the "more" that MacLaine and Hayek believe is "inside" does not include speaking up about the racism and sexism that black women experience. And so Jessica Williams tried, once again, to explain the futility and stupidity of what she was being told—essentially to ignore the discrimination she encountered as a result of how her black womanhood is viewed and framed in a racist and sexist society. Williams said:

> "I think what you're saying is valid, but I also think that what you're saying doesn't apply to all women. I think that's impossible."
>
> "What part of it is impossible?" Hayek responded. "You're giving attention to how the other one feels."
>
> "Because I have to," Williams said.
>
> "If you have to do that, then do that," Hayek said. "Then that's your journey. But I want to inspire other people to know it's a choice."

As some of the women in attendance vaguely spoke to the need for women to "support each other" regardless of their background, Williams went on to try to articulate the importance of recognizing black women's specific oppression:

> When I talk about feminism, sometimes I feel like being a black woman is cast aside. I always feel like I'm warring with my womanhood and wanting the world to be better, and with my

> blackness—which is the opposite of whiteness . . . I think there is a fear that if we present an idea that, "Hey, maybe [black women] have it a little bit harder in this country"—because we do; black women and trans women do—if we're having it a little bit harder, it doesn't invalidate your experience. I really am begging you to not take it personally.

Hayek's response, below, was appalling:

> Can I interrupt, because I feel misunderstood. . . . It's not shutting you up. I feel misunderstood on one point: We should be also curious about our brain. By being the best that you can be. That's what I was trying to say to you. Let's not just spend all the time in the anger, but in the investigation. Baby, I'm Mexican and Arab. . . . I'm from another generation, baby, when this was not even a possibility. My generation, they said, "Go back to Mexico. You'll never be anything other than a maid in this country." By the heads of studios! There was no movement. Latino women were not even anywhere near where you guys are. I was the first one. I'm 50 years old. So I understand."
>
> "You don't understand," Williams managed to reply.

What's so interesting—and infuriating—about this exchange is that Jessica Williams clearly said that the specific concerns and vulnerabilities faced by black women and trans women are often cast aside in discussions about feminism, and yet Salma Hayek decided to go right ahead and cast aside those concerns anyway. Hayek, a woman of color, interrupted and imposed her views, dismissed Williams's cogent and well-argued points, deployed the "angry black woman" stereotype, and implied that Williams didn't understand the importance of "the brain"—all while framing herself as being "misunderstood." Apparently, addressing the discrimination and mistreatment that black women and transgender women experience was a choice Salma Hayek found uninspiring and brainless. But of course, only months later, she was inspired to speak up about her own experience of harassment and abuse.

Imagine if someone turned to Hayek and asked, "*Who are you when you're not a woman?*" in response to her disclosure of experiencing harassment and sexist violence. Wouldn't that be ridiculous and downright cruel? And yet, so many people feel justified in shutting down black women when we talk about the manifold ways in which we experience systemic discrimination and harm. *Can't we all just get along?* No, we can't all just get along, precisely because so many people—including white women and nonblack women of color—refuse to listen to black women.

The difficult dialogue between Williams, MacLaine, and Hayek reminds me of an observation made by Audre Lorde, the well-known black lesbian feminist, in her brilliant 1984 essay "The Uses of Anger": "I have seen situations where white women hear a racist remark, resent what has been said, become filled with fury, and remain silent because they are afraid. That unexpressed anger lies within them like an undetonated device, usually to be hurled at the first woman of color who talks about racism."[5]

In other words, white women's (and nonblack women of color's) hostility toward black women is related to their unwillingness to openly challenge the dynamics of oppression in their own lives. Given Hayek's subsequent revelations about her difficulty speaking up about sexual harassment, there's a lot to be said about the role of internalized oppression in her attempt to bully Williams into silence. Even so, it's hard to imagine Shirley MacLaine—or anyone else, really—instructing Salma Hayek to "find the democracy inside." Could it be that her pain is taken seriously, while black women's pain is dismissed, even and especially by other women who claim to "understand"?

When I read about this conversation, I felt a familiar confluence of fury and fatigue. Fury, because there is nothing quite as demoralizing as the wall of apathy that meets black women when we speak to the unique intersections of racism, sexism, and other forms of oppression that we confront—and fatigue for the very same reason. Black women are well acquainted with being framed as inappropriately "angry" or "playing the victim" when we simply acknowledge the conditions of our lives. I suspect that when she had her "Me Too" moment, Hayek was not only inspired by the women who spoke up about Weinstein and other sexual predators but also, ironically, by the very same black woman she scolded for speaking up about racism and intolerance among women. There are all these ways in which black women's courage and outspokenness are shamed and denigrated by the very same people we "inspire." It's part of the invisible labor of being a black woman. We are told to keep quiet by the same people who, in the next breath, the next hour, week, or year work up the courage to speak out about their pain.

It's now widely known that the Me Too movement didn't start in 2017. It originated in 2006 with a black woman, civil rights activist Tarana Burke, more than a decade before actress Alyssa Milano used the phrase on Twitter. But the fact that a black woman created Me Too specifically to support girls of color in healing from sexual trauma and violence would have gone unnoticed if black women hadn't organized online to prevent her erasure. What kind of sick irony is it that black women have been collectively screaming "Me too!," only for our pain to be trampled again and again by other people's suffering?[6] And don't get me started about Tarana Burke being left off the cover of *Time* magazine when the movement she formed was recognized as "Person of the Year."

There's an energetic parasitism about all of this. Black women's labor (emotional, intellectual, political, and otherwise) gets routinely shamed and silenced even as it is appropriated and exploited by those who feel threatened by our legitimate critiques—and, yes, by our reasonable anger.

I know what you're thinking. It's mighty convenient for me, a black woman, to write a chapter with this title. But the importance of listening to black women was not always obvious to me. (Just ask my mom.) Sometimes people assume that outspoken black women—perhaps especially outspoken black women professors—came out of the womb wearing a "Black Girl Magic" T-shirt and quoting Angela Davis. But the truth is that like most people in this country, I was not socialized to take black women's knowledge seriously—which of course means that I was not socialized to take my *own* knowledge seriously. Many black women have had to struggle against the intertwined forces of patriarchy, racism, and class oppression that keep us silenced, ignored, and marginalized. So, yes, even as a black woman, it took me several decades to begin to understand that black women and girls have been uniquely and violently oppressed in our white male supremacist society—and that listening to black women is key to challenging multiple forms of oppression.

There are, of course, lots of really good reasons to listen to black women. Your food will almost certainly taste better. You could summon otherworldly powers of resilience and begin living your best life. You'd become familiar with the art of throwing shade and cussin' a mofo out in multiple languages without saying a word. Listening to and learning from black women mathematicians and engineers such as Mary Jackson and Christine Darden could teach us all how to pioneer mathematics, revolutionize engineering, and author dozens of papers on the subtleties of the supersonic boom all while making sure our edges are laid. And if millions of US citizens had listened to black women and girls several centuries ago, we wouldn't have had to wait until 2017 to begin collectively acknowledging the centrality of sexual harassment and assault in our society.

As far as I'm concerned, one of the very best reasons to listen to black women is because doing so will better equip you to understand the complexity of oppression and what we can do to challenge it. Listening to black women (and girls) is vitally important, because those of us who pay attention to the condition of our lives are aware that we're marginalized by multiple forces of discrimination. The hard-won knowledge we gain from reflecting on our experiences of oppression holds valuable insights for anyone interested in building a more just society. Now, let me be clear. There's nothing inherent about being a black woman that guarantees some kind of existential insight into the dynamics of racism, sexism, or both. Obviously, racially ignorant black women exist—I used to be one of them—and some black women, like Stacey Dash, are still *clueless*. But on the whole, our vulnerability to multiple forms of oppression render black women more sensitized to and knowledgeable about the complexities of racism, sexism, classism, and so on.

In many ways, growing up in the 1980s and '90s meant, for me, being surrounded by facile notions of (black) girl power. I heard Whitney sing "I'm Every Woman," bowed down to Oprah Winfrey every day after school, saw Janet Jackson leading troops to the beat of *Rhythm Nation*, watched Clair Huxtable run a law practice and her household on *The Cosby Show*. And like most of the rest of the world, I had no idea that Bill was drugging and raping women when he wasn't on stage. If black women and girls were oppressed, it wasn't especially apparent to me. My mother created an environment that insulated me from the realities of racism and, to some degree, sexism as well. While I may not have always listened to every single thing she said, Mom has always been my shero. It didn't occur to me growing up that she had to battle the systemic and intertwined challenges of racism, sexism, and poverty. *You can do anything you set your mind to. We can make a way out of no way.* These were the mantras that filled our home. At church, we were taught to believe in the power of supernatural forces to vanquish our enemies and remove any obstacle. *If God is for us, who can be against us?* While prioritizing her own professional goals, she also poured her energies into supporting my education, nurturing my spirit, and ensuring that I would have a chance to lead a life of unimaginable possibilities. I saw my mom pursue continuing education in her nonexistent spare time, despite having had to drop out of college to work full time and raise me. I saw her leave an abusive relationship, take on multiple jobs, overcome poverty, enter the middle class, and make a way out of no way. She worked for an insurance company and for university hospitals, took temp jobs (including a stint at a movie theatre, which meant free movies for me—yay!), and eventually established a successful career in corporate America. And after working long hours, she'd come home and help me with my homework. I sometimes chuckle when I hear stereotypical talk about the "immigrant work ethic"—as opposed to the rest of us? No one in my immediate family is an immigrant, but they have all worked their asses off. In my mind, there was nothing Mom couldn't do. And I wanted to be just like her: professional, poised, and powerful.

It wasn't until many years later that Mom began to share with me the contours of her own struggles as a single black mother in a racist, sexist society. I would come to understand that sheltering me from the harsh realities of her own experience was her way of trying to create some space for me, for us, to exist in this world with less harm, violence, and injury. As a kid, I had no idea what my mother had to go through to provide for us and beat the considerable odds stacked against us. She went far beyond merely putting food on the table. Her hourly goal and determination was to give me a platform on which to grow, expand, and learn, and to have a life with many more academic, financial, and social options than those afforded to poor and working-class black women like her. In all honesty, she made raising me look easy. Meanwhile, the imagery of black female empowerment that permeated my childhood—and hers—was devoid of structural analysis. Although the modern black feminist movement began to germinate just a few years before my birth, it might as well have happened on another planet. My mother was herself a teenager when important volumes like *This Bridge Called My Back: Writings by Radical Women of Color* (1981) and *All the Women Are White, All the Blacks Are Men, but Some of Us Are Brave* (1982) were published. I wouldn't read these texts or even come to know of their existence until my thirties. Clearly, one of the reasons black feminism didn't make its way into our household is because many of these initiatives were led by black lesbian feminists. Everyone in my immediate family attended our insular, patriarchal, homophobic Pentecostal church, where black lesbians weren't exactly guests of honor. Even as a young bisexual black girl, I had no idea other bisexual, queer, and lesbian black girls existed until I arrived at Wellesley College. And I certainly didn't know that they were among the architects of black liberation movements and social justice organizing.

When I finally had a chance to read about Angela Davis in college—and met the Black Power feminist icon herself—I didn't really understand the significance of explicitly asserting the value of black women's knowledge. It wasn't clear to me that black women and girls were still a collectively—and uniquely—marginalized group. The concerns that animated the women's movements of the 1970s seemed far removed from me. No one was burning bras in the streets when I was coming of age.

And there's another uncomfortable truth: as I began to interrogate why it took me so long to begin seriously reading black women's work, I realized how challenging it is to confront and sit with the unique forms of violence to which black women are routinely exposed. Even for black women, it is often easier to "talk about race" without talking about the specific experiences of black women. I've sometimes wondered if black women center black men and boys in narratives about racism because it's too painful and frightening for us to confront just how vulnerable we also are. Focusing on the suffering of black men and boys reinforces patriarchy, to be sure. But it also keeps us from coming to terms with our own pain—and directly facing the unthinkable violence to which black women and girls are routinely subjected.

Though most people understand racism in terms of black men's vulnerability, black women's oppression has been hiding in plain sight, from the intimate space of the family to education, health, employment, popular culture, legal institutions, and policing. Black women are 35 percent more likely to be victimized by domestic abuse than white women and 2.5 times more likely to experience intimate-partner violence than nonblack women of color.[7] Analysts often point out that black women "entered the labor market" earlier than white women, but what this means concretely is that, for generations, black women and girls were forced into slavery and worked to death performing unpaid labor in concentration camps, more commonly referred to as "plantations." Even today, black women still work outside the home at a higher rate than their white counterparts, but "have the lowest pay and occupational status jobs of any race/gender groups."[8]

Historically, black women's bodies were subject not only to enslavement and brutal whippings but also to legally sanctioned assault made all the more grotesque by the fact that their wombs were systematically transformed into incubators for future slaves. For centuries, white slave owners routinely raped black women and young girls and increased their profit margin by enslaving their own children. Scholars such as Adrienne Davis and Angela Davis teach us that chattel slavery was a cauldron of sexual violence and a modern birthplace of what we now call "sexual harassment."[9] Angela Davis in particular describes sexual violence as a technique of terror that white slave owners employed to maintain control over their property and thwart resistance. The routine sexual abuse and exploitation of black women and girls was not some well-kept secret. It happened openly, without punishment, for centuries.

Childbirth has always been a precarious affair for black women. In her groundbreaking book *Killing the Black Body: Race, Reproduction, and the Meaning of Liberty*, sociologist and legal scholar Dorothy Roberts describes how black motherhood has been traditionally stigmatized and exploited in our patriarchal, white supremacist society: "Black motherhood has borne the weight of centuries of disgrace manufactured in both popular culture and academic circles. A lurid mythology of black mothers' unfitness, along with a science devoted to proving black biological inferiority, cast black childbearing as a dangerous activity . . . [and] justified the regulation of every aspect of black women's fertility."[10]

After being "liberated" from centuries of sexualized slavery, black women were then almost immediately targeted by eugenicist campaigns designed to keep us from having any children at all. Today, health disparities continue to suffocate the lives of black women and girls. Black mothers are up to four times more likely than white mothers to die in the midst of pregnancy, and reproductive technologies continue to valorize white women's children while black women's childbearing is policed.[11] As Roberts points out, "We live in a country in which white women disproportionately undergo expensive technologies to enable them to bear children, while black women disproportionately undergo surgery that prevents them from being able to bear any."[12]

Despite the ubiquity and prevalence of violence against black women, portrayals of racial injustice typically center black men. As author and activist Andrea Ritchie reminds us, the prevailing image of police brutality is usually "a white cop beating a Black man (almost always imagined as heterosexual and cisgender) with a baton."[13] In New York City, where I live, black women are just as likely as black men to be arbitrarily harassed, profiled, and arrested by police, but you wouldn't know that from the public debate on "stop and frisk," which focuses on black male victims.[14] Police officers have murdered black women when responding to calls about domestic abuse—sometimes in front of their children. They shot forty-seven-year-old Yvette Smith on sight when she opened her door, then lied and said she had a gun. They killed Aiyana Stanley-Jones, a seven-year-old child, in her sleep. Officers electrocuted thirty-seven-year-old Natasha McKenna to death while she was handcuffed and shackled. *Pearlie Golden. Tarika Wilson. Tanisha Anderson. Miriam Carey. Mya Hall. Renisha McBride. Sandra Bland. Shelly Frey. Malissa Williams. Michelle Cusseaux. Shereese Francis. Kyam Livingston. Meagan Hockaday.* These are just a few of the names of black women who were either directly murdered by officers or died in police custody. If you've never heard of them or don't know their stories, you should put this book down right now and get to work.[15]

Black women and girls are also subject to sexual violence and abuse from predatory policing. Many black women, especially trans black women, know that police are often an aggravating source of systemic violence, not protection from it. To take just one example, Daniel Holtzclaw, in 2013 and 2014, used his position as an armed police officer to sexually assault and rape at least thirteen black women in Oklahoma City. In 2011, CeCe McDonald, a black trans woman and activist, was attacked by a group of violent men, including a white neo-Nazi who physically assaulted her while hurling homophobic and racist slurs. McDonald defended herself and managed to survive the incident, killing one of the attackers in the process. Despite clearly acting in self-defense to ensure her own survival, she was convicted and sent to prison. Speaking at a conference at Barnard College after her release, McDonald recounted how officers arrived on the scene of the attack she survived, only to immediately frame her as the perpetrator. Ignoring the blood pouring down her face, they showed no regard whatsoever for her well-being. Regarding the police, McDonald observed: "A lot of times they're so quick to criminalize and dehumanize you that they can't even, you know, begin to process on how to help you. . . . How can you help someone when you have your cisnormativity and your prejudice blocking your view?"[16]

I could go on and on, citing statistics and stories about the structures of violence that black women and girls encounter in our everyday lives. But what I want you to understand is that these patterns and problems are not side issues for those of us interested in challenging and dismantling white supremacy—they're *central.* Listening to black women makes it crystal clear that we all need to get a lot less stupid about a lot of things—racism, class domination, patriarchy, heterosexism, and cissexism, to name just a few—because these deadly forces are intertwined, and our collective survival demands that we get up off our asses and do the work to connect the dots.

The Combahee River is a forty-mile-long waterway in the South Carolina low country, about fifty miles outside of Charleston.

During the Civil War, the Combahee became the site of a stunning victory for the Union army when Harriet Tubman, the abolitionist and freedom fighter, led troops in a successful effort to free over seven hundred enslaved people trapped in Confederate territory. The Combahee battle was the only wartime effort designed specifically to liberate slaves, and in the process, Tubman became the "first woman in U.S. history to plan and lead a military raid."[17] Over a century later, her remarkable feat would inspire a group of black lesbian socialists to brand themselves the Combahee River Collective and publish a revolutionary black feminist manifesto. Barbara Smith, one of the main authors of the Combahee River Collective Statement, put it this way: "My perspective, and I think it was shared, was let's not name ourselves after a person. Let's name ourselves after an action. A political action. And that's what we did. And not only a political action but a political action for liberation."[18]

What I love about the Combahee statement is that the writers were unapologetic about centering black women's liberation. "Above all else," they wrote, "our politics initially sprang from the shared belief that Black women are inherently valuable, that our liberation is a necessity not as an adjunct to somebody else's but because of our need as human persons for autonomy."[19] The collective's manifesto laid the groundwork for what would later be called "intersectionality," forging connections between racism, sexism, imperialism, and class oppression and grounding their analysis in Marxism. And though they certainly centered black women's suffering, the Combahee women also spoke to the need to practice solidarity with women of color and oppressed people outside the United States.

Though black feminism has a contemporary genealogy within academia, it has a tradition that stretches beyond the ivory tower. For centuries, black women have resisted the intertwined forces of white supremacy and patriarchy to speak to the specific forms of oppression we face. In 1851, Sojourner Truth stood up in the midst of a women's rights convention in Akron, Ohio, and delivered her famous address, "Ain't I a Woman?" Bringing together the concerns of civil rights with the women's movement, Truth raised the question of what was (and was not) being talked about in these mobilizations—namely, black women's experiences:

> Look at me! Look at my arm! I have ploughed and planted, and gathered into barns, and no man could head me! And ain't I a woman? I could work as much and eat as much as a man—when I could get it—and bear the lash as well! And ain't I a woman? I have borne thirteen children, and seen most all sold off to slavery, and when I cried out with my mother's grief, none but Jesus heard me! And ain't I a woman?

Let's just take a step back here to recognize the fact that Sojourner Truth had to get up in the middle of a meeting on women's rights and demand to be seen because the white women leading this movement weren't looking out for women like her. The white abolitionists and black men fighting slavery weren't always looking out for her either.

Okay, now let's take a whole 'nother step back. The account I just shared with you about Sojourner's Truth's speech? Turns out there's a little more to this story. Nell Painter, the esteemed African American historian, convincingly argues that while Truth certainly stood up in Akron and addressed women's rights, the phrase so often attributed to her—*Ain't I a woman?*—was actually the fanciful invention of a white feminist named Frances Dana Gage. Describing the speech twelve long years after it occurred, Gage's version of events has come to define the master narrative. And this is precisely how white supremacy works. Even a black woman's speech about black women's oppression can be appropriated by a white woman.

In the wake of the civil rights movement, black women intellectuals, organizers, and activists began speaking up about the sexism with the black nationalist movement, as well as the racism they encountered in white feminist movements. Black feminists began organizing amongst themselves to give voice to the complex dynamics of oppression and betrayal they bumped up against within political communities that were supposed to be filled with allies. Black women objected to being sidelined in conversations about racial empowerment and told by black nationalists that they must take a back seat to (and literally walk behind) black men. In the words of Michele Wallace, a black feminist writer, "Black men . . . seemed totally confounded when it came to treating Black women like people."[21] As black men dominated many visible movement organizations, black women's humanity and particular vulnerabilities were (and still are) often brushed aside in the name of racial solidarity. Even today, black men like Ta-Nehisi Coates and Cornel West seem to be competing for the mantle of "white liberal whisperer," taking up valuable space and drowning out black women's voices.

In recent years, the terms "intersectionality" and "intersectional feminism" have increasingly emerged as social justice mantras in the public sphere, but many people still have no clue what these words mean—and even fewer recognize their significance to black feminist thought. So let's take a step back and define a few key concepts. To begin with, "black feminism" centers the experiences, knowledge, perspectives, well-being, and empowerment of black women. If you're not a black woman, it may be news to you that black women's experiences, knowledge, and perspectives are routinely ignored, erased, and denigrated in our society. Black feminism, therefore, exists to bring attention to black women's erasure and oppression. "Intersectionality" is a black feminist approach to the study of power and inequality that understands systems of oppression as inextricably linked. Intersectional theory asserts that our social identities can overlap in ways that make us vulnerable to more than one type of discrimination, rather than imagining (as many people do) that sexism, class exploitation, and other axes of inequality are divorced from each other. The concept itself was devised by Kimberlé Crenshaw, a black legal theorist who helped pioneer both critical race studies and black feminism in the academy. In a 1989 article, Crenshaw used the metaphor of a traffic "intersection" to imagine how black women experience discrimination as a result of their specific position within multiple systems of domination: "Discrimination, like traffic through an intersection, may flow in one direction, and it may flow in another. If an accident happens in an intersection, it can be caused by cars traveling from any number of directions, and sometimes, from all of them. Similarly, if a black woman is harmed because she is in the intersection, her injury could result from sex discrimination or race discrimination."[22]

The imagery of intersecting traffic was useful for illustrating how black women's social identities make us vulnerable to more than one type of oppression. Crenshaw was concerned with illuminating the ways in which antidiscrimination laws framed around racism *or* sexism failed to account for the *convergence* of these factors in the marginalization of black women. In other words, black women were (and still are) systemically disadvantaged by multiple axes of oppression—but existing legal frameworks overlooked the ways in which racial and gender bias delimited their lives.

Around the same time that Crenshaw began writing about intersectionality, Patricia Hill Collins revolutionized the field of sociology with her groundbreaking 1990 book *Black Feminist Thought*. Her work challenged the centrality of white male perspectives in social science and, crucially, framed black women as important sources of knowledge. Focusing mainly on the United States, Collins described the social world (and the distribution of resources) as structured by a "matrix of domination" consisting of multiple oppressions. Her work also shows how black women and girls are subject to denigrating stereotypes or controlling images (like the "Mammy" figure or the over-sexed "Jezebel"), while white women are culturally valorized. Building on feminist critiques of knowledge production, Collins insisted on the importance of knowledge produced from black women's standpoint—the social locations black women occupy in a racist, heterosexist, capitalist society. It's difficult to overstate the revolutionary nature of Collins's assertion that black women are valuable producers of knowledge in a society that has traditionally silenced, erased, shamed, and exploited us. As such, Collins urges black women to use our own experiences to learn about the complex dynamics of power that shape our lives.

More recently, Moya Bailey, a queer black feminist scholar, introduced the term "misogynoir" to describe the specific, noxious flavor of sexism and racism that black women experience. Combining the word "misogyny" with the French word for black, "noir," "misogynoir" highlights the intersections of gendered and racialized violence that shape the lives of black women and girls. Describing the origins of the term, Bailey wrote: "[It] is important to me . . . that the term is used to describe the unique ways in which Black women are pathologized in popular culture. What happens to Black women in public space isn't about them being *any* woman of color. It is particular and has to do with the ways that anti-Blackness and misogyny combine to malign black women in our world."[23]As Bailey explains, the concept of misogynoir forges connections between the shaming and stigmatization of black women and girls in various forms of media and our vulnerability to structural disadvantage and violence.

The Combahee River Collective Statement, mentioned earlier, crystallized these concerns. Writing in 1977, the authors affirmed: "We struggle together with Black men against racism, while we also struggle with Black men about sexism."[24] Regarding white women's complicity with racism, they continued: "As Black feminists we are made constantly and painfully aware of how little effort white women have made to understand and combat their racism, which requires among other things, that they have a more than superficial comprehension of race, color and black history and culture."[25]

A similar theme runs through the feminist writings of other black women and women of color, many of them lesbian or queer, who experienced exclusion and marginalization within movements that centered the worldviews and concerns of white women.

A frank appraisal of black feminists' critique of white women's racism reminds us that listening to black women means coming to terms with white women's racism. At no time in the history of this country have white women collectively stood up to condemn white supremacy or to actively oppose the racism from which they benefit on a daily basis. Not once. There has never been a movement to unite tens of thousands of white women (let alone millions) in the sustained work of confronting and dismantling racism. Never. Of course, there are individual antiracist white women. Some of them have suffered dearly for opposing white supremacy, losing family members or even their lives. Yes, white women were involved in the civil rights movement. If you're not familiar with the murder of Viola Liuzzo, a white antiracist activist killed by Ku Klux Klan terrorists in 1965, you should look her up right now. Undoubtedly, you'll see parallels between her death and the killing of Heather Heyer, the white antiracist who was run over by a white supremacist in Charlottesville.

Unfortunately, white women who actively oppose white supremacy are overwhelmingly outnumbered by white women who don't, those who are unwilling to do anything more than give lip service to equality while reaping the benefits of systemic racism, as well as overtly racist white women who are happily invested in white supremacy. Whatever the white women's movement of the 1960s and '70s was, it was not a movement to confront or dismantle racism. And today, white women still fail, on a regular basis, to rigorously acknowledge their racism. This failure was quite obviously on display when, in 2016, 53 percent of white women voted in the presidential election for a white racist endorsed by the KKK.[26]

It's tiresome having to point out again and again how black women are stigmatized and silenced in everyday life. But if we don't do this work, who will? The constant need to contest our erasure—while also supporting adjacent liberation movements—has mobilized black women into action for centuries. It's why Barbara Smith, Audre Lorde, and other black feminists who formed the Combahee River Collective also started Kitchen Table: Women of Color Press in 1980, to amplify the voices of women living at the intersections of racism, sexism, and colonialism. It's why Kimberlé Crenshaw and colleagues at the African American Policy Forum launched the #SayHerName campaign and report in 2015, to highlight black women and girls who have been harassed, abused, and slaughtered by police violence.[27] And it's also why Guilaine Kinouani, a French psychologist, writer, and activist, teamed up with Samantha Asumadu, a filmmaker and founder of Media Diversified, to create the #PredatoryPeaceKeepers campaign to raise awareness about the role of French soldiers and UN troops in sexually abusing and assaulting at least ninety-eight girls in the Central African Republic, Haiti, and elsewhere.[28] The work of the Predatory Peacekeepers campaign chronicles a shocking range of sexual abuse and torture, from French soldiers tying up African girls, urinating on them, raping them, and forcing them to have sex with animals. Bringing together a critique of white supremacy with colonialism and patriarchy, Kinouani notes, "Under colonialism African childhood and womanhood were aggressively denied as part of a conscious effort to dehumanise."[29] Today, the systematic violation of black women and girls continues to be a humanitarian crisis around the globe.

Not long after I began my job at Stony Brook University, a white male colleague pulled me aside and asked what I thought of intersectionality. I remember responding dismissively. Black feminist thought wasn't exactly the mainstay of Harvard's Department of Sociology. My doctoral program, overwhelmingly designed by and for white people, largely disregarded the work of black women. Black feminist scholarship was mentioned in passing—included in a syllabus here or there, usually at the end of the semester, as I recall—but the majority of professors in the department studied racism without centering black women's perspectives in or outside of the academy. I remember one black woman in our graduate program who regularly urged other students (and our professors) to read black feminist work. I also remember that year after year she was rigorously ignored.

The marginalization of black women's perspectives extended far beyond my department. It's the modus operandi of the entire discipline of sociology and academia more broadly. Indeed, when black women's work isn't being ignored by academics, it's often being scoffed at and brushed aside. I received this lesson early on, loud and clear, in graduate school during the review process for one of my first academic publications. In the first draft of the paper, I made sure to cite the work of a brilliant black woman scholar whose work I admired, only to receive anonymous peer review comments (almost certainly from a white scholar) urging me to center the theoretical work of white men and avoid referencing the black woman's scholarship altogether. I pushed back, refusing to remove the citation, but I did acquiesce by including unnecessary caveats about her work. I still regret making this concession, but my younger, less confident, and decidedly un-woke self was also desperate to get another line on my CV. Looking back, I wish I'd been stronger.

The turning point for me in my journey toward embracing black feminism was coming to terms with just how disgusted I was with mainstream academia. After my first year on the tenure track, I realized I was no longer interested in following the path of the scholars who "trained" me. I made a commitment to get clear about—and then prioritize—my own values. For me, that meant coming out about my bisexuality and claiming my identity as a queer black woman. But it also meant coming out about my spirituality and my interest in mindfulness. The (white male supremacist) intellectual environments to which I'd grown accustomed were not spaces where academics interacted with each other as full human beings. I didn't know any academics in my circle who talked openly about their religious or spiritual beliefs, even informally. But as I began deepening my own meditation practice, I began seeking out other people in and outside the academy who shared my interests in meditation, Buddhism, mysticism, and holistic wellness.

The more I set aside time for quiet contemplation and sitting with my emotions, the more clarity I felt about how to navigate my career. Although I didn't know it at the time, integrating these previously disparate aspects of my life and honoring my own intuition were already significant steps toward practicing black feminism. By listening to my inner guidance and honoring my desire to move away from intellectual frameworks and professional relationships that no longer served me, I was already working toward my personal and political liberation.

I also began heeding the advice of folks who were more "woke" about gender than I was. An astute white graduate student in one of my seminars pushed me to complicate my theorization of race by thinking more deeply about patriarchy. On Twitter, I encountered words I'd never seen before, such as "heteropatriarchy" and "misogynoir," and I realized that I had a lot of work to do. I came to understand that my failure to seriously engage the work of black women and women of color also meant that I was alienating myself as a source of knowledge too. When I won a fellowship from the Woodrow Wilson Foundation, I decided to use the year away from teaching to make headway on my first book and read up on black feminist scholarship to bring into my syllabi. That was almost five years ago—and I'm still learning.

Growing beyond our racial ignorance—and getting serious about disrupting white supremacy—requires developing an intersectional sensibility: awareness of interlocking systems of oppression and concern for a wide variety of marginalized groups. To put it bluntly: if you're not thinking about race intersectionally, then you're not thinking about race intelligently. Black feminism teaches us that intersections of power determine whose suffering matters and whose suffering is ignored or justified—even and especially in the context of understanding racism. Black feminists rightly argue against the idea that we can pursue the politics of liberation by focusing on "single issues." This means "class-not-race" Bernie Bros and "race-not-gender" activism both get the black feminist side-eye. Instead, black feminists insist that our intersectional differences should not be ignored or sublimated but, rather, must inform our efforts to challenge multiple forms of injustice.

We see this intersectional sensibility on prominent display in the leadership of the #BlackLivesMatter movement. Founded in 2013 by three black women, BLM activists refuse to frame racism as a single issue. In describing the agenda of the Black Lives Matter network, founders Patrisse Cullors, Alicia Garza, and Opal Tometi assert "the need to center the leadership of women and queer and trans people" and to highlight the specific oppression of black trans women.[30] In this way, movement leaders explicitly bring the problems of antiblackness and state violence into dialogue with the marginalization of queer lives and trans lives. This sophistication and complexity is what black feminism brings to the table: an invitation to move beyond superficial ideas and simplistic politics in favor of radical coalitions that can disrupt the status quo.

Of course, black feminists are far from perfect and must also be pushed to put their intersectional principles into action. Black trans women are undeniably the most vulnerable black women, and cisgender black women have to be challenged to divest from transphobia and cissexism. One of the major insights of intersectionality is that understanding one axis of oppression does not necessarily mean you'll have revolutionary insight into or sympathy for other struggles. Black men's failure to address their sexism and white women's failure to address their racism has made this obvious. Black feminism teaches us that we all need to cultivate reflexivity to examine our own complicity with systems of oppression and compassion for forms of oppression we will never experience. It should come as no surprise, therefore, that transgender black women have had to struggle to be seen and heard in feminist movements. Reflecting on her own experience, Barbara Smith of the Combahee River Collective admitted that it took her circle of cisgender black lesbians about ten years before they were able to undertake the work of making their movement trans inclusive.[31] And in recent years, Chimamanda Adichie, the Nigerian writer whose paean to feminism was sampled in Beyonce's "Flawless," drew widespread criticism for distinguishing between "trans women" and "women." My own journey to confronting my cisgender privilege and transphobia was embarrassingly belated. But learning from brilliant black transgender women such as Janet Mock, Cece McDonald, and Laverne Cox forced me to deepen my intersectional sensibility and better understand trans identities, as well as the centrality of black trans lives to the fight against patriarchy and racism. Complicating our understanding of black womanhood means realizing that if our trans sisters aren't free from violence and terror, then *none* of us are free.

I started this chapter by saying that no one wants to listen to black women. Well, that's not exactly right. You see, there *are* people who do want to listen to black women—people who are *so* interested in what we have to say. The problem is that some of these people don't want to actually recognize and pay black women for our time, labor, and expertise. Every woman has had the experience of saying something in a group setting, being ignored, then having a man say the same thing a few minutes later and be met with a chorus of agreement. Imagine what it's like for black women. Our words get parroted by—and credited to—black men, white men, white women, nonblack people of color.

This is why black women are constantly required to claim credit where credit is due, advocate for ourselves, and, yes, as Auntie Maxine says, *reclaim our time*, because if we don't, the social expectation is that we're just sitting around waiting to be exploited. And not only are we expected to provide our labor for free or pennies on the dollar but we're expected to be grateful for the "opportunity" to do so! I'm at a stage in my career where I'm regularly invited to speak, but I could write entire novels about the so-called invitations I've received to give free talks about racism and slavery at well-funded universities that built their wealth on racism and slavery. There's the "antiracist" white academic who evidently thought she was doing me a favor by asking me to travel across the country and give an unpaid talk for her highly ranked department. Gee, as tempting as it would be for me to enrich your life with my unpaid labor while you rollick in your white privilege, I'm going to have to pass. Then there's the senior critical race scholar—an expert on the reproduction of racism—who asked me to speak at an Ivy League institution. I'm still not sure if she's a white woman or a nonblack woman of color. Regardless, when I asked about the honorarium and funds for travel (which were never mentioned in the "invitation"), I was met first with deflection and then with the frank admission that not only was I being asked to speak at this resource-rich university for nada, I was also expected to cover my own travel. The excuse? "It's a student-organized conference. There's no money!" I nearly fell out laughing. Now why the hell would I want to pay my own way to speak at an Ivy League university for free *when I have two Ivy League degrees?* My response:

> Thanks for clarifying. Of course, I know of student organized events and conferences at [your campus] that pay thousands of dollars for speaker fees. An institution with tens of billions in the coffers can certainly afford it. In any case, thanks for thinking of me but I will have to decline. I do hope the faculty involved in advising the students will teach them about the importance of applying the principles of critical race theory to the practical matter of paying black scholars for our time and labor.
>
> My Best,
> Crystal

Of course by "My Best," I meant "*You tried it!*" Girl, please. I did the electric slide after I sent that email. Incidentally, the very same day I received this ridiculous request, I also received the contract for my largest speaking fee yet—one considerably greater than zero. In fact, it had several zeroes.

But it's not just white folks and nonblack people of color who have a hard time paying black women appropriately for our work.

I was once approached by a black women's organization to give a talk about "self-care" at a rich private school. The catch? They just *couldn't* find the funds to pay me. When I inquired into their budget, it turned out that there was money for hors d'oeuvres, money for entertainment—even money for cocktails!—but no money to actually pay me. I informed the students that I would be declining their "invitation" as an act of self-care.

If you can pay for hard liquor, you can pay for my expertise.

Intersectionality isn't just a theory. It's an invitation to actually change the way we live our lives. At some point in the writing of this chapter, I looked up at the clock and saw that it was already three o'clock in the morning. My eyes were straining, my shoulders were tight, and my neck was aching. I had a choice. I could do what I'd normally do—continue writing and power through the night to try to make a deadline—or I could listen to my body and get some rest.

Unsure of what to do, I picked up my copy of bell hooks's *Sisters of the Yam: Black Women and Self-Recovery*. It was sitting in a stack of black feminist classics piling up in my home office. The pages fell open to the following passage:

> [black] women . . . are so well socialized to push ourselves past healthy limits that we often do not know how to set protective boundaries that would eliminate certain forms of stress in our lives. This problem cuts across class. What's going on when professional black women who "slave" all day on the job, come home and work some more, then provide care and counseling for folks who call late into the night? Is it guilt about material privilege that makes us feel we remain "just plain folks" if we too are working ourselves into the ground even if we don't have to? Rarely are the statistics on heart disease, depression, ulcers, hypertension, and addiction broken down by class so that we might see that black women who "have" are nearly as afflicted

> by these stress-related illnesses as those who "have not." In a society that socializes everyone to believe that black women were put here on this earth to be little worker bees who never stop, it is not surprising that we too have trouble calling a halt.[32]

Knowing that I'd just received a live and direct sermon from the Universe, I closed the book in astonishment and took my ass to sleep.

I sometimes lament the fact that it took me so long to begin engaging black women's work in earnest. Yes, I know that learning is a lifelong affair, but I can't help but imagine what my life would be like if a woke black feminist fairy godmother had intervened just a *little* earlier. Maybe if I'd read and listened to black feminists in my twenties, it wouldn't have taken me so long to leave so many bad relationships. And perhaps I could have been more politically astute, less confused and naive. I would've known that black women should not look to any politician in this racist, sexist society as a knight in shining armor. If only I'd encountered the insights of Audre Lorde earlier in life, I would have known that radical black lesbians and socialists, queer folk, and freedom-fighting dreamers want to develop alternative tools to dismantle the master's house, while people like Barack Obama want to use the master's tools to enter the master's house, wear the master's clothes, get the master's money, and carry out the master's agenda.

Which is to say, if I'd listened to black feminists, I could've saved myself a whole lotta trouble and heartache.

Chapter 3

ON RACIAL STUPIDITY IN THE OBAMA ERA

I mean, you got the first mainstream African American who is articulate and bright and clean and a nice-looking guy.

—JOE BIDEN[1]

I didn't know shit about domestic or international politics when I landed a gig as a spokesperson for Barack Obama's presidential campaign in spring 2008. I was twenty-six years old, approximately twenty pounds lighter than I am now, and living what I thought to be my very best life in Paris. I'd moved to France six months prior to work on my doctoral thesis on the legacies of French colonial slavery. Aside from my womanly charms and youthful good looks, I had a string of fancy affiliations to help open doors for me. There was the Harvard thing, of course, and also the fact that I was a Ford Foundation fellow with a visiting position at the Institut d'Etudes Politiques (colloquially known as Sciences Po). An African American professor hooked me up with a ridiculously tiny—but *chic*—apartment in the elegant Montparnasse neighborhood of the 14th arrondissement, only a short walk from the French Senate and the gorgeous Luxembourg gardens. Very quickly, I fell in with an exclusive network of African American expats, some of whom were wealthy and almost all of whom were involved with an organization I'd never previously heard of: Democrats Abroad.

Before delving into Democrats Abroad, let me back up a bit and contextualize my relationship with Barack Obama during the heady days of that first campaign. I had no relationship whatsoever with Barack, except the fantasy relationship that existed in my mind. Although I was a student at Harvard, I had no connections to his inner or outer circle. I was not kickin' it with Dr. Henry Louis Gates Jr., of Beer Summit fame, who, to this day, probably doesn't know my name. I was not from a well-to-do family and had not yet vacationed on Martha's Vineyard with Democratic Party elites. As a Wellesley alumna, I wasn't even supposed to be interested in Obama—not with Hillary still in the race. But by December of 2007, I'd changed my email signature to this gem from one of Obama's speeches: "We have a stake in one another. . . . What binds us together is greater than what drives us apart, and . . . if enough people believe in the truth of that proposition and act on it, then we might not solve every problem, but we can get something meaningful done for the people with whom we share this Earth."[2]

Little by little, I felt myself beguiled by the promise of a black president and soon succumbed to what would become known in France as *Obamania*, the technical term for the intoxicating, hypnotic state of madness that results from sipping Barack's neoliberal, color-blind Kool-Aid.

As far as I can ascertain, I made my first donation to Senator Barack Obama's campaign—probably my first donation to any presidential campaign—in January of 2008. The very next month, I attended one of my first political rallies during a short trip back to the United States on February 4, 2008, at the Seaport World Trade Center, in Boston. I still vividly recall that night and the rock-star frenzy that surrounded it. Like thousands of people, I stood in line for hours to get into the auditorium, fueled by a combination of adrenaline and jubilation. The crowd was multiracial, multigenerational, and full of good, hippy vibes. Inside, the Seaport Center was a sea of red and blue "CHANGE WE CAN BELIEVE IN" signs. I remember feeling like I was a part of something beautiful. At some point past 10 p.m., as U2's "City of Blinding Lights" blared from the speakers, Senator Obama—bright, clean, good-looking Obama—took the stage at the precise moment Bono crooned *"Oh! You! Look! So beauuuuuutiful tonight!"* Wearing a perfectly tailored black suit and the aura of a man destined for greatness, the senator from Illinois entered to a tsunami of applause—and, in what must have been an impeccably orchestrated set of gestures, immediately embraced (in this exact order) an Asian American woman, a white man, an African American man, a white woman, and another white man. I, along with everyone else as far as the eye could see, chanted *"Obama! Obama! Obama!"* with all of the sincerity and ecstasy of the naive, poorly educated fools that so many of us were in the rapturous spring of 2008.

I tried my best to remain sober and skeptical, but as soon as Obama began speaking, I was under his spell and mesmerized. Cue Biggie's "Hypnotize." You just knew this man was gonna be president. The electricity of his charisma was unbelievable. And he was *fine*. Bruh looked so good. Sounded so good. Made you feel so good. When Obama smiled and said, *"I love you guys! I love ya!"* I could have sworn he was talking directly to me. "I decided to run because of what Dr. King called the fierce urgency of now," he told us. "Our nation is at war, our planet is in peril, and the dream that so many generations fought for feels like it's slowly slipping away."[3] I felt myself mmm-hmm'ing and nodding along. "We cannot afford to wait to end global warming. We cannot wait to bring this war in Iraq to a close. We cannot wait!" With his signature message of hope, Obama preached to his adoring devotees:

> There is a time in the life of every generation where that spirit, that hope, has to shine through. When we cast aside the fear and the doubt and the cynicism, and we turn to each other and we join hands and we remake this country block by block, county by county, state by state—this is one of those moments.

> This is our moment. This is our time. And if you're willing to join with me, if you are willing to vote for me, if you are willing to organize with me and mobilize with me, if you are willing to reach for what you know is possible and not settle for what the cynics tell you you have to accept—then I promise you this: *We will not just win an election, we will not just win the primary, we will win the general election! And you and I together, we will transform this country! And we will transform the world!*

And with this climax of collective euphoria, Stevie Wonder's "Signed, Sealed, Delivered" filled the stadium. Obama was our drug and we were all high as fuck.

After the Boston event, any reservations I had about joining the International Church of Obama dissipated. By March, I'd already updated my email signature from the three-liner to a paragraph-long Obama quote that began "*In the unlikely story that is America, there has never been anything false about hope . . .*" The very next month, I began regularly appearing on TV as a campaign spokesperson, praising Obama in French and English. Things were moving very, very quickly indeed.

Founded in 1964, Democrats Abroad describes itself as "the official Democratic Party arm for the millions of Americans living outside the United States."[4] Representing American expats in 190 countries on multiple continents, the group is actually treated as a state by the Democratic National Committee and sends both delegates and so-called superdelegates (party elites) to participate in the national conference. Republicans Abroad, a similar group for US expats on the Right, was established in 1978 and continued until 2013.[5] Practically speaking, such organizations exist to gather expats' votes and, more important, their valuable dollars. They also "inform" Americans about politics abroad—by pushing the party line. Like most Americans, I hadn't the slightest idea that Democrats or Republicans Abroad even existed, therefore, I was pretty surprised to learn about the intense political activities of these groups during the primary season of 2008.

One day while I was enjoying the Paris springtime, I received a phone call from my landlady, Velma, a beautiful, glamorous African American expat who'd been living in France since marrying a famous Belgian sculptor in the 1960s. Velma and I were becoming friendly, and she'd occasionally invite me to a cocktail party or an event and introduce me to members of the expat community. (I have to pause here and take a moment to explain to you what a singular, spectacular person Velma truly is. Imagine an ageless, perpetually fashionable, witty, black woman with a café au lait complexion and an infectious, sophisticated laugh, who always looks like she's on her way to a soirée featured in *The Great Gatsby*. The kind of woman who regularly jaunts between Paris, Normandy, Cannes, and Brussels and has met everyone from James Baldwin to Prince Charles. *That's Velma.*)

So, Velma calls and to my relief, it has nothing to do with the rent. She's going to Belgium for an art show next week, and it so happens that she has an extra ticket to a pricey Obama campaign event that she can no longer attend. Oh, and a superdelegate will be there and a campaign strategist will speak. Would I go in her stead? Uhh, of course I would? And *voila*: a few days later I found my broke-student self surrounded by rich, white American expats and a sprinkling of African Americans in the marble-and-chandelier environs of an opulent law firm in a bougie part of Paris. I'd never been to anything like this: high-powered Democrat donors and party officials chatting with one of Obama's campaign strategists. Afterwards, a friendly superdelegate struck up a conversation with me. She'd just gotten off the phone with a French television station who wanted to interview her about the campaign—something she did quite often. But this week, her schedule was packed. Would I be willing to go on TV to talk about Obama in her place?

Uhh . . . Would I . . . like to go on *television* . . . to talk about ~~my husband~~ Barack Obama, the next president of these United States? *Would I ever!*

There was just one small problem: The interview would be in English *and* French.

"I'm not sure my French is good enough," I said. "I've only been here a few months. You really think I can do this?"

"Sure you can," she insisted, then picked up her cell phone to tell the French television station that I would be speaking on behalf of the Obama campaign. "*Sure I can?*" I was entirely unconvinced, but my youthful ambition wouldn't let me turn this opportunity down. "Yes we can!" *was* the campaign slogan after all. About a week or so later, I was picked up by a black Mercedes sent by the television station, met by a friendly producer, escorted past security to a professional makeup artist, and seated under the studio's bright lights for a live broadcast on the US presidential election.

On April 4, 2008, I made my international television debut on France 24, the bilingual news network.[6] It was the fortieth anniversary of Martin Luther King Jr.'s assassination, and Barack Obama had recently delivered what was widely considered a landmark speech on race in Philadelphia. It would take me years—many years—to realize what a problematic speech it really was. The show's intention was to draw parallels between the senator's political rise and MLK's call for racial justice. It turned out that the superdelegate was right: I somehow managed to make my way through the interview with good-enough French to be invited back again and again.

In the French portion of the interview, the white host asked if white Americans were enthusiastic about Obama due to feelings of white guilt. If you understand French, you'll hear me argue that Obama's white supporters were motivated by hope rather than (or in addition to) guilt. Though I was certainly drinking the Democrats' Kool-Aid and spouting some racial stupidity in that interview, I did get a few things right. For example, I said that some of Obama's supporters thought they could "get over race" by voting for him—and that they were clearly wrong. I also said that racial progress was not promised simply with the election of Obama, because it might prove more difficult for a black president to directly address racism. In 2008, I had a racial critique of Obama's liberal voters, but I had no critique of the Democrats' complicity in whitewashing white supremacy. Though I knew Obama would not—and could not—be a racial savior, I did not see clearly that he was already downplaying racism and pushing postracial denial.

That appearance would be the first of many television and radio shows—first on behalf of Obama's campaign and then, after the primary, on behalf of Democrats Abroad. Without any media training whatsoever, I began doing interviews for all the major French TV and radio stations to push the Democrats' agenda. I became accustomed to those black Mercedes, makeup artists, and bright lights. I was invited everywhere. At one point I even costarred with Gwyneth Paltrow and other expats in a "Get Out the Vote" video produced by Democrats Abroad.[7] It was to the point where I'd sometimes get recognized in the streets of Paris—while I was a student! Shit was wild.

The level of frenzied interest in Obama throughout Europe was unlike anything I'd ever seen, but in France it was especially acute. Obama represented so many things for the French: a fresh face in US politics, an attractive "outsider," an outspoken critic of the hugely unpopular Iraq war, and, of course, the beloved African American. As many people know, France has had a love affair with African Americans since at least the twentieth century. From World War II soldiers to entertainers such as Josephine Baker and Nina Simone, to writers including Langston Hughes, James Baldwin, and, more recently, Ta-Nehisi Coates, African Americans have a very long history of exceptional reception in France broadly and the City of Lights specifically. In my own experience, living and conducting research in France during Obama's election magnified the peculiar phenomenon I refer to as African American Privilege.[8] Its peculiarity lies in the fact that it only exists outside the United States—and it usually involves the oppression of another nation's own racialized population. In the French case, African American Privilege means benefitting from friendly relations, access, and resources denied to French people of color. Though it's easy to get caught up in the rapture of being treated like a human being (or like a celebrity, as the case may be), the sad reality is that African Americans are typically used by the French to minimize or outright deny their own racism. This is so because French white people love to portray their country as a racial haven (a narrative that African American expats have, unfortunately, been drawn into) while depicting the United States as an international racial boogeyman. In this way, France makes itself look good by comparison, telling its minorities that "things could be worse"—that is, they could be damned to live in that racial hellhole on the other side of the Atlantic.

The problem with this narrative, of course, is that France has racially oppressed people of color for centuries, both on its mainland and in its overseas colonies. If I hadn't been in France for the express purpose of studying the country's history of colonial slavery and present-day racism, perhaps I, too, would have been seduced into parroting tropes that minimize French racism. But though I felt warmly embraced by French people and lavished with thrilling access for both my research and political campaigning, I was also continually confronted with the stunning violence of France's disregard for its minority populations. Over the course of my nearly two and a half years in Paris, I interviewed more than a hundred people, most of whom were of Caribbean and African descent. In cafés, university classrooms, and private residences throughout the region, French minorities (some of whom were biracial) told me what it was like to be called racial slurs, forced to stand in a trash can in elementary school, denied employment opportunities, targeted for housing discrimination, and even brutally shunned by white family members. Some of the anecdotes were so disturbing that one of my transcriptionists—a white French woman—confided in me that she broke down in tears typing up the interviews. They also reported being taught very little about the history of racism, colonialism, and slavery at school—histories that explained their very presence on French soil.

So, no, I could not, in good conscience, interpret my own exceptional treatment in France as evidence of some kind of profoundly enlightened, postracial society. Misreading African American Privilege in this way is a terribly myopic, selfish, and deeply stupid thing to do.

Aside from media appearances (which I admittedly found terribly exciting), being affiliated with Democrats Abroad also meant being invited to campaign events. Soon, I was hobnobbing with millionaires at invitation-only occasions for wealthy Democratic donors in Paris. But, I wasn't really hobnobbing with wealthy Democrats so much as I was . . . serving them. I was quite literally the help. In lieu of paying the pricey admission fee, the price of my ticket was my willingness to serve crowds of well-heeled, mostly white people fancy hors d'oeuvres and champagne. To be honest, I ate a lot of the hors d'oeuvres and drank a hell of a lot of the champagne too. When I worried about the optics of being a black woman serving rich white folk, I consoled myself with bacon-wrapped figs and petits fours, as well as the fact that some of the other volunteers were white millennials.

That spring, I emailed an acquaintance back in the States:

> On my way to a bougie Obama fundraiser tonight in Paris. Should be interesting. Everyone paid $1000 to attend. I got a "free" ticket from a friend, but as a result, I was asked [to] volunteer to help with things, along with some other free-riders. At first I was a little offended (i.e., am I going to be the black servant mammie at this fundraiser of mostly upper class rich white folks??). And then I was like "hmm well, these people are donating money to elect the first black president." . . . So I guess I'll take this one for the team.

As I'd later write that same acquaintance—a black academic—the fund-raiser was "a sort of out of body experience," in which I found myself in this group of uber-rich white American expats in this Parisian equivalent of a mansion immediately after the Jeremiah Wright controversy. (We'll come back to this later in the chapter.) The event included several viewings of Obama's Philadelphia speech. I kind of felt like an intruder: the only black person in these semiprivate events. It was, in retrospect, a bit like a scene from Jordan Peele's film *Get Out.* I saw a fifty-something DNC official crying while listening to Obama speak and middle-aged white men half smiling in approval as they heard Obama's carefully chosen words, words I would realize, years later, were precisely designed to put these wealthy white Democrats at ease. "I guess they liked me," I typed in a Gmail message, "as they've asked that I attend and 'help out' at the next few rounds of big ticket fundraisers. The next one is gonna have one of Obama's chief strategists, so that should be interesting." I was very clearly stuck in the sunken place.[9]

When I ponder what that superdelegate from Democrats Abroad saw in me, I suspect it was a naive, twenty-something black girl from Harvard who'd make a great tool for the Democratic Party. I had many of the qualities both major parties look for in minorities: respectability, ambition, a thirst for access and a thorough lack of political education. I had no serious critique of the Democratic Party's implication in systematic racism, nor did I have a serious critique of the role of the media in whitewashing destructive US policies at home and abroad. I'd not yet read Noam Chomsky's *Manufacturing Consent*, a devastating indictment of the propaganda function of mainstream news. Looking back, I didn't *feel* like a tool of party or state propaganda. In fact, I was given remarkable leeway to say whatever I found appropriate on international TV and radio. On one occasion early in my fifteen minutes of French fame, I asked a party official for "talking points" but was told to simply refer to Obama's webpage. DNC officials never made me check in with them in advance before a media appearance. Sometimes I formulated my political analysis in the cab on my way to the studio. But then again, as Chomsky astutely points out, the propaganda function of the media doesn't need to be overt in order to toe the party (or the state's) line. No one had to force me to do the party's bidding. I *wanted* Obama to win, and so I was personally motivated to defend his statements and proposed policies in ways that also implicitly legitimated the United States. Although I was careful to acknowledge the nation's ongoing history of racism—and spoke against the notion that Obama's election would usher in a color-blind era—I nonetheless adopted rhetoric and arguments that closely matched the candidate's. This meant emphasizing a kind of naive belief in "hope" as well as a narrative of racial progress that minimized contemporary racial oppression.

On election night in 2008, I joined a lavish gala for Republicans and Democrats at the Cinéaqua Paris, a beautiful aquarium near the Place du Trocadéro with stunning views of the Eiffel Tower. I wore a gold dress and a euphoric smile. The music was poppin'. The champagne was flowing. In between festivities, I dipped in and out of interviews with the major French networks, sharing my reflections on the increasing likelihood that the previously unthinkable was about to become quite thinkable indeed. Well past midnight Paris time, as the final results came in, Velma and I sat together, holding hands, watching Wolf Blitzer scream at the top of his lungs, as he is wont to do. Suddenly, the chyron on the bottom of the screen read:

CNN PROJECTION: BARACK OBAMA ELECTED PRESIDENT.

I read the words over and over again.

Barack Obama Elected President.

Barack Obama Elected President.

Barack Obama Elected President.

Time stood still.

I thought about my mother, watching the results from her apartment in Delaware. I thought about her mother, Betty-Ann, who raised six children, worked as a substitute teacher, and also cleaned white folks' homes in the Deep South. I thought about my family in Chicago—my aunt Tracey would be standing in Grant Park when Obama delivered his victory speech. I looked at Velma, who by now had become a cherished friend, a woman who had left the United States in the middle of the civil rights movement but remained deeply connected to political activism in her home country, a woman who had lived through Jim Crow segregation and indignities that I could only imagine.

Velma's face was in her hands. She was sobbing softly. And so was I.

The party at the Cinéaqua lasted until sunrise. As we, the Democrats, savored our unimaginable victory, a red-faced man came up to me and the Frenchman I was then dating. I immediately recognized him as a representative of Republicans Abroad. We'd crossed paths many times before during various events and televised debates. Tonight, he looked rather sullen—and a bit drunk. We were all holding glasses of champagne, so I extended mine for a toast.

"You're full of shit," he said, as he clinked my glass, then turned and walked away.

I was shocked—and embarrassed.

But, looking back, he wasn't wrong.

Many people have asked when I began to finally shift from being an Obama-bot to a critic of Barack, the Democrats, and US racism. One year stands out: 2013. But the seeds of change were planted earlier. There was a slow dissipating of my Obamania during the first administration, but to be honest, I had stopped paying close attention to politics. After Obama won in '08, I remained in France for another year to finish the interviews and data collection for my dissertation. When I returned to the US, I dropped my role as a spokesperson for the Democratic Party and focused on writing my thesis, which I completed in 2011. I was not especially politically active during this time. I was, however, beginning to learn a bit more about Obama's foreign policy, especially his disastrous use of drones. This worried me, given his soaring antiwar discourse during the campaign.

During the first Obama administration, I was also still reveling in the deranged psychological euphoria of living through a black presidency, which was a rather easy thing to do from the ivory tower—especially when that ivory tower was Harvard University. I was narrowly focused on my own success during this time: finishing graduate school, getting a tenure-track job. I didn't really begin to think seriously about racial politics in the United States again until the aftermath of Obama's reelection. It was around this time that the gap between his policies and my ideals became absolutely glaring.

Over the course of the 2012 campaign, I was still #TeamObama (quite literally—I actually used that hashtag) and uncritically embraced views that were pro-American. In one tweet, I thought I was throwing shade when I wrote: "Romney's strategy is to pooh-pooh on America." In another, I observed: "Obama looks super presidential." On October 23 of that year, @BarackObama tweeted: "RT if you're #ProudofObama as our commander in chief." Of course, I retweeted.

But soon after the election, I finally began to listen to progressive voices I'd once dismissed, including Cornel West, a longtime Obama critic whom I'd previously viewed as simply bitter. That fall, I tweeted: "@CornelWest is slowly convincing me in his progressive and provocative criticism of Obama," noting that West's "escalating Obama critique is killing me softly." Eventually, I began speaking up about my opposition to Obama's rampant militarism and unprecedented assassination program. Making a mockery of his Nobel Peace Prize, Obama authorized 563 drone strikes in Pakistan, Yemen, and Somalia—ten times more than his Republican predecessor—killing hundreds and possibly thousands of innocent people, children included.[10] This bloody number doesn't even encompass other drone strikes authorized by Obama in Libya, Afghanistan, and the Philippines.[11] And in one of the most terrifying abuses of executive power in modern history, Obama used the office of the presidency to justify killing US citizens in Yemen without trial by remote control.[12] *War crimes we can believe in.*

George Zimmerman's unpunished killing of Trayvon Martin was also a turning point for me. On July 14, 2013—Bastille Day in France—and one day after the not-guilty verdict was announced, I wrote an essay on my blog entitled "Dear America: It's Not You. It's Me." The post, which went semiviral, accurately reflects where my thinking was only four years ago.

> Dear America,
>
> We need to talk.
>
> You see, tonight Trayvon Martin's unremorseful killer was acquitted. Tonight, I fell silent with a dear friend when we heard the news. Our eyes closed. Our heads fell into our hands. There were no words.
>
> Tonight, I heard my mother's voice crack and tremble under the weight of her grief as she expressed her shock and sadness at seeing an unapologetic black-child-stalker-and-killer walk free.
>
> And tonight I realized, more than ever, that as much as I love your potential, as much as I love the good that I know is in your heart, as much as I appreciate and see the beauty of your highest calling, the truth is that I feel like this relationship—our relationship—is becoming abusive and toxic on a level that nearly boggles the mind.
>
> I'm a student of history, so I knew our relationship would be challenging. But for reasons that defy all logic, I always thought we could find a way. Yet tonight I find myself shell-shocked and worried that we're simply incompatible. On paper, we have so many core values in common. In practice? Not so much. I know what you're going to say—No, it's not just the Zimmerman verdict. It's the absurd Supreme Court

ruling on the voters' rights act. It's the profound stupidity and prejudice exemplified in Mayor Michael Bloomberg's defense of stop and frisk in New York, an official policy of harassment and profiling primarily directed toward people of color. It's the insanity occurring right now in Texas, where women are stopped and frisked for tampons as they enter the legislature to stand up for reproductive rights—even as guns are freely allowed. It's the fact we do not have a federal ban on the death penalty, despite the fact that we know innocent people—American citizens—have been killed by our imperfect justice system. It's the inability of this President to keep his campaign promise to close Guantanamo, despite the human rights abuses that continue to take place there. It's the robust indifference so many of my fellow citizens have to poverty in this country, even the plight of poor whites. It's the widening of the black/white wealth gap under a black President. It's also having a black President who doesn't talk about race. It's the prison industrial complex and its marginalization of poor, working class people and people of color. It's the Republican party's war on women. It's the crisis in Chicago. It's the Democratic party's complicity in establishing mass surveillance and the unconstitutionally invasive practices of the NSA's PRISM program. It's the drones. It's the drones. It's the drones. It's the legal, corporate buyout of our political process. It's the pathetic excuse for "progressive" television known as MSNBC. And—my God, that's just a few of the distressing issues happening now. I haven't even begun to talk about our history. The history of black women, men and children being murdered without consequence—a practice so old and institutionalized that it's become an American tradition. I'll stop talking about history now, though, because I see your eyes glazing over. Yes, I know, you're always telling me to let it go, since you think we've magically solved those wily problems of the past.

You know you're in a horrible relationship when you find yourself making those "pro's" and "con's" lists, trying to decide whether to stay or go. Maybe leaving has never really felt like an option—because, well, where *would* I go? Yes, I dated France for a few years and played the field in a few different countries, but I know there's no paradise down here. Where would I go where there is no injustice? Where would I go where sexism and classism and racism and queer-phobia aren't salient dimensions of social life? Where would I go where I would not be disgusted by daily forms of micro and macro aggression and oppression?

And then there's another inconvenient truth: I'm kind of in love with you. It's that irrational kind of love that loves in the face of ugliness, pain, and dysfunction. It is this irrational love that has made me hold out hope for so long. Love that made me listen, against my better judgment, when you sweet-talked me with "change" I could believe in. Love that has made me—and continues to make me—want to see what is beautiful about you despite your flaws. Because God knows we are all flawed.

Our destinies are intertwined. I'm not saying that we can't be together, but I am saying that I might need to see—and live among—other people. Other people who do not have a death penalty. Other people who have boldly legalized gay marriage. Other people who do not have a program of mass incarceration. Other people who do not promote a religion of gun ownership and cultural violence. Other people who protect women's rights. Other people who have laws against hate speech.

Yes, I know no country is perfect and every society has its baggage. I'm not wearing rose-colored glasses. But I am wearing tears—and not just my own. I'm wearing my mother's tears. My community's tears. My allies' tears. And the worst thing of all is that there is nothing new about this. We've been crying these tears for many lifetimes, for many generations. Here, in my sadness and pain, it would be easy to blame you, to say that you are the problem. But that would also be a lie. I am part of the problem. And I am also part of the solution.

What I know for sure is that it is the ego that ails us. What I know for sure is that the only hope we have of building a more perfect union is spiritual healing. And I know for sure that transcending the bullshit, hypocrisy and violence of it all begins with me.

So, listen America. I'm not saying it's over. And I have no idea where we go from here. But I know for sure that love is not supposed to feel like this.

Love is certainly not supposed to feel like this. But this sad soliloquy begs the question: *Why in God's name did I ever think the United States could love, or has ever loved, black people?* The love affair in question wasn't simply my devotion to the Church of Obama—it was my pathetic devotion to a revisionist, ahistorical version of the American Dream. More specifically, it was my inability to see that what had been sold and repackaged as an inclusive dream was actually a nightmare. Looking back, it's easy, now, to see how and why I got so caught up with Obama's empty promises of hope and change. What did I know? I was blinded by propaganda . . . and the human need to believe you have a homeland . . . and to love it, no matter how wretched it is. It's kind of like when you realize, after many years of abuse, that your beloved is, and always was, a jerk who treated you like shit from day one. You're angry at that asshole. But you're also angry with yourself. How could you have been so gullible? Why didn't you see the signs?

Not long after I published my post, the Black Lives Matter movement took the world by storm. Driven by their own despair over Trayvon's death, cofounders Alicia Garza, Opal Tometi, and Patrisse Cullors birthed the most recent iteration of a centuries' long freedom movement, one oriented toward critiquing the fundamental myth upon which this country was built: that black lives don't matter. I was skeptical of the uprisings and the hashtag in the early days. Could publicly affirming the value of black life actually make our lives matter more in a racist society? Would the movements take root? Despite my doubts, I was personally moved by the mantra *Black Lives Matter! Black Lives Matter! Black Lives Matter!* The more I heard the phrase, the more I realized that I'd been trained my whole life to disregard the fact that black lives were made not to matter in these United States. I began to draw connections between my research on the legacies of slavery in France and the establishment of global white supremacy.

And, increasingly, I was filled with rage at the inability, or unwillingness, of the nation's first black president to stand up for justice. It is now well known that Obama deported more undocumented people (most of whom are of Latino descent) than any other president in US history.[13] Despite the sustained uprisings and political mobilizing of activists in Ferguson and throughout the country, Obama never acknowledged or condemned systematic racism and unchecked police violence. Instead, he protected the racial status quo (and the state's monopoly on violence) by misrepresenting police killing and brutalization of vulnerable people as the result of a "few bad apples." And though Obama made sure to tell freedom fighters that there is "no excuse" for damaging property, he never gave a speech proclaiming that there is no excuse for officers raping and sexually assaulting black women.[14] Given Obama's enthusiastic embrace of state violence, particularly against black and brown people on the other side of the world, I shouldn't have been surprised.

The stunning contrast between Obama's patronizing speeches to black communities and his conciliatory response to violent police officers was as painful to witness as it was galvanizing.

I was not one of the prescient, principled voices speaking out against what was sure to come under an Obama presidency. Anyone with a modicum of political insight would have known that Obama was committed to covering white supremacy and capitalist violence with the veneer of multiculturalism long before his campaign began. But this is not a truth I cared to know. And the more difficult truth—the one that many Democrats are still not ready to accept—is that their beloved political party was also committed to the same agenda: maintaining the hegemony of white male capitalists with the help of superficial identity politics and a rainbow coalition of historically illiterate fools. This is what is generally meant by *neoliberalism*: pushing free-market capitalism, deregulation, competition, and individualism for the purpose of enriching the 1 percent.[15] The Democratic Party has been married to a neoliberal agenda since at least the 1980s, an agenda that prioritizes the interests of multinational corporations over the interests of working-class and poor people. To be perfectly honest, the very word "neoliberalism" bored me to tears until fairly recently. And this is the case even though I collaborated on research with scholars, such as the Harvard sociologist Michele Lamont, who have actively criticized inequalities in the neoliberal era. It's a word that, to my ear, sounded dry and abstract and made me want to put on a set of onesie pajamas and go directly to sleep.

But the more I listened to some of Obama's most vocal critics—including Cornel West but also folks such as Princeton's Eddie Glaude, the more I began to understand just why progressives were so disgusted by the president's embrace of neoliberalism. To put it simply: neoliberals elevate the economic interests of corporations and billionaires over marginalized people. The main difference between neoliberals in the Republican and Democratic Parties is that the former capitulate to private interests proudly, whereas the latter pretend to care about working-class families while supporting laws and macroeconomic policies that favor the super-rich. Another difference is that Republicans typically mislead working-class whites into supporting a neoliberal agenda that undermines their economic security by using overt and covert racism to draw attention away from the enrichment of the capitalist class. Republicans accomplish this by using racial stereotypes and appeals to white racial resentment to blame brown and black people—instead of white elites—for their plight. Commenting on the predicament of the white working class, Kirk Noden observed in the *Nation*: "Corporate Democrats have never advanced their interests—and at least Republicans offer a basic, if misleading, story about why they are getting screwed."[16]

Learning about and critiquing the bipartisan embrace of neoliberalism is, quite simply, one of the most important things we can do to become less stupid about racial politics. The expansive allure of neoliberalism explains so much about the contemporary political situation, including the use of identity politics to distract from structural inequality. As political scientist Adolph Reed Jr. observed in a searing essay published in *Harper's*, "Nothing Left:

The Long, Slow Retreat of American Liberals," the Democrats' capitulation to neoliberalism in the 1980s and 1990s involved the dismantling of vibrant political alliances between labor movements and progressive politics, as well as a retreat from policy reforms that could significantly help poor and working-class people of all backgrounds.[17] These generative, leftist movements were displaced by the rise of superficial identity politics celebrating minority tokenism and equal-opportunity-access to the ruling elite.

But as sociologists Jonah Birch and Paul Heideman have argued in the *Jacobin*, antiracist activism and class mobilizations are not—and have never been—dichotomous choices. "In fact," they write, "the history of the American left and labor movement since the 1920s suggests the opposite is true. Insofar as struggles for racial equality have gained traction, they have generated momentum for a politics geared toward the demand for 'social equality.'"[18] Today, as in the past, robust critiques of racial oppression necessarily involve a confrontation with class oppression too.

These caveats notwithstanding, there *is* a seed of truth in Reed's critique of certain activists who claim to speak on behalf of black lives. Even if contemporary antiracist movements involve an implicit (and, at times, explicit) challenge to class inequality, the reality is that some of the most prominent and well-funded minority voices representing themselves as "voices for racial justice" are, in fact, voices for private interests. This kind of neoliberal tokenism functions to cover the naked greed of the capitalist class with a rainbow coalition of clean, good-looking minorities willing to sell out the masses for their own "inclusion" in society's upper ranks.

In this regard, Barack Obama is the king of neoliberal tokenism *par excellence*. It's almost as if he's competing for the title of the Most Sold-Out Sell-Out of All Time or the Unclest of Uncle Toms. The reality, though, is that Obama never lied about his neoliberal bona fides—which is precisely why true progressives critiqued him from the left during his first campaign. While the rest of us were caught up in the madness of Obama's feel-good racial rhetoric, others were unpacking the implications of his economic agenda. In the *New York Times Magazine*, the senator from Illinois was described in a headline as a "Free-Market-Loving, Big-Spending, Fiscally Conservative Wealth Redistributionist" who embraces both neoliberalism (free-market deregulation) and European-style social democracy.[19] In other words, Obama would aggressively pursue the interests of the private sector while also advocating for some degree of redistribution of resources from the wealthy to the disadvantaged. But though Obama's administration certainly capitulated to capitalists—not only by providing Wall Street executives with golden parachutes but also by gifting the insurance industry with the neoliberal health plan known as "Obamacare"—his populist rhetoric proved to be little more than lip service and empty promises.

In a 2011 op-ed in the *Wall Street Journal* (no shit), Obama defended free-market capitalism in glowing terms: "For two centuries, America's free market has not only been the source of dazzling ideas and path-breaking products, it has also been the greatest force for prosperity the world has ever known. That vibrant entrepreneurialism is the key to our continued global leadership and the success of our people." He went on to defend an executive order designed "to remove outdated regulations that stifle job creation and make our economy less competitive."[20] If you think this advocacy for deregulation sounds an awful lot like President Trump's, you would not be wrong. By 2016, Obama was floating the idea of becoming a "venture capitalist" after leaving office (as though he wasn't already doing that work from the Oval Office). And only a few months after returning to private (sector) life, reports surfaced of Obama being paid $400,000 for a speech to Wall Street executives.[21] But though Obama might be the king of neoliberal tokenism, he certainly is not alone. Hillary Clinton's 2008 and 2016 presidential campaigns weaponized imperial feminism for the purpose of misrepresenting the nepotistic rise of one wealthy white woman as the collective empowerment of women everywhere.

The neoliberal policies favoring market capitalism appeal to wealthy Democrats just as much, if not more, than they appeal to wealthy Republicans. When Democrats repackage neoliberal policies as "Hope and Change" or a "Progressive Agenda," their lies are in fact harming the working class, the poor, and communities of color. There is nothing hopeful or progressive about bailing out Wall Street executives and corporate industries while decimating the social safety net, destroying public schools, and sending jobs overseas. Over the last few decades, the two major parties have increasingly aligned themselves with the dictates of the multinational corporations that control our economy—and our politics. This strategic alignment has occurred during precisely the same time period as the widening wealth gap between the super-rich and the rest of us. Party affiliation is no longer any indicator of whether a candidate supports elite interests. This might explain why, for example, presidential candidate Senator Bernie Sanders, with his populist message, never had a chance of winning the Democratic Party's nomination—and why so many establishment Republicans lined up behind Hillary Clinton's candidacy (and neoliberal agenda) in 2016. The oligarchs and billionaires are "Stronger Together," indeed.

In the middle of the '08 campaign, I was invited to "debate" a white American expat representing the now-defunct Republicans Abroad. The exchange was easy—almost too easy—and I defended Obama and the Democrats like a pro. Despite my practically destroying the Republican expat on international television, she took a liking to me and kept in touch. In June of that year, she asked if I'd attend an exclusive event at the US ambassador's residence as her guest. And there was a bonus: she wanted to meet for tea beforehand at her private club. I'd never before been to an ambassador's residence nor to a private club, so of course I said yes. The club was absolutely stunning, a lavish mansion in one of those gorgeous Parisian neighborhoods reserved mainly for white elites. We made small talk over tea, which was served in fine china. The Republican was very pleasant, but I struggled to understand why she would give me the time of day.

We continued to correspond. From time to time, she'd send me information about an NGO or an upcoming art exhibit. Her notes were always very friendly and, to my surprise, supportive of the president-elect. Many years later, she confided in me that she'd actually voted for Obama—twice. Of course she did. I've met many Republicans, over the years, who told me that they supported Obama. Most of them were well-to-do. Though I initially assumed their decision to bat for the other team had to do with Obama's highest ideals and postracial rhetoric, I began to suspect that they also saw in him the same thing Wall Street executives and other white elites saw in the senator from Illinois: an ambitious minority ready and willing to make rich white people comfortable. Perhaps they saw something similar in me.

I find it odd when the US is compared to other nations and portrayed as a society that values diversity. In fact, this country's majority population has proven to be highly resistant to racial and ethnic equality *for centuries*. And that's putting it mildly. The majority of the majority population has remained mired in white nationalism for many, many generations. At most, you could say the US superficially values diversity—as long as it doesn't challenge political and socioeconomic white supremacy. Many whites value toothless, token diversity: the kind that accommodates white supremacy. The Booker T. Washingtons and Obamas of the world.

By the way, this is also why it's a mistake to blindly extol the virtue of "diversity"; the neoliberal critique shows us that superficial diversity and tokenism can perfectly coexist with white supremacy. Black and brown individuals are not existentially threatening to most whites, as long as they remain in a subordinate *group position*. The "group position" part is key and explains why some whites voted for a nonthreatening black POTUS, hoping he'd serve white interests.

Obama went out of his way to prove his "non-threatening Negro" bona fides in 2008 when he distanced himself from Jeremiah Wright, then pastor of his church, Trinity United, in that famous Philadelphia speech, the one that moved wealthy white Democrats to tears. This is also why, by the way, I disagree with sociologist Tressie McMillan Cottom, who portrays Obama as a naive, optimistic simpleton who "didn't know his whites."[22] Obama was no racial simpleton, and despite his own account of having warm, trusting relations with whites, he was no stranger to the realities of systematic racism. In fact, Barack Obama may be the first president in history who formally studied racism from an explicitly antiracist perspective. Unlike most people who study the general topic of "race" (already a relatively small number), Obama actually learned about white supremacy as a law student at Harvard University. Later, as a law professor at the University of Chicago, he taught the work of critical race theorists, including his mentor and former professor Derrick Bell, one of the most strident and outspoken academic opponents of white racism and white supremacy.[23] Yet, despite his antiracist education, Obama made a political decision to embrace neoliberal policies that ultimately accommodate white supremacy. Yet, some Obama sympathizers and defenders still portray his racial politics as the result of ignorance or optimism.

Take, for example, Ta-Nehisi Coates's melodramatic article "My President Was Black" published in the *Atlantic*. After chatting extensively with the president on Air Force One, Coates concludes that Obama's optimism about racism derives, in part, from the "decency" of his loving white family:

> Obama's early positive interactions with his white family members gave him a fundamentally different outlook toward the wider world than most blacks of the 1960s had. Obama told me he rarely had "the working assumption of discrimination, the working assumption that white people would not treat me

> right or give me an opportunity or judge me [other than] on the basis of merit." He continued, "The kind of working assumption" that white people would discriminate against him or treat him poorly "is less embedded in my psyche than it is, say, with Michelle."[24]

Though it may be true that Obama does not have a "working assumption" of white discrimination, he was well acquainted with the social and historical realities of white racism. Is it possible that Obama was exposed to antiracist and radical critiques of white racism but could not fully embrace those positions due to his warm relations with white family members and friends? Sure, but it's also possible that Obama distanced himself from critics of white racism in order to win white voters. In other words, Obama might have trusted whites more than the average African American due to his upbringing and white family, but he also became a calculating politician. It does not take a genius to know Obama was aware of racism and white supremacy but actively chose access and power anyway. This calculus was on public display when Obama consciously decided to slam Jeremiah Wright in that Philadelphia speech, not because Obama was racially hopeful or naive but because he was a determined and ruthless politician. It was in that same speech that the presidential hopeful, after having spent years in Wright's church and nodding at his criticisms of white racism, decided to sing a different tune. On Wright's infamous remark "God damn America," Obama replied:

> They weren't simply a religious leader's efforts to speak out against perceived injustice. Instead, they expressed a profoundly distorted view of this country—a view that sees white racism as endemic and that elevates what is wrong with America above all that we know is right with America; a view that sees the conflicts in the Middle East as rooted primarily in the actions of stalwart allies like Israel, instead of emanating from the perverse and hateful ideologies of radical Islam. As such,

> Reverend Wright's comments were not only wrong but divisive, divisive at a time when we need unity, racially charged at a time when we need to come together to solve a set of monumental problems.[25]

But Obama knew quite well that racism is endemic and systematic in the United States. He also knew quite well that white people would never vote for him if he said such a thing. So Jeremiah Wright, the man who officiated Obama's wedding, the preacher whose sermons he'd listened to for years, found himself discarded and thrown away.

It's completely plausible that some whites who embrace racist views (consciously or unconsciously) felt sufficiently comforted by Obama's tap-dance routine. It's also plausible that some whites with racist views felt the need to prove their moral goodness by voting for an "exceptional black." I imagine many whites with racist views in the Republican and Democratic Parties voted for Obama for precisely this reason: he'd proven to be nonthreatening, a "black" who would not destabilize white supremacy. For many whites, voting for Obama became proof of moral virtue.

This moral virtue matters in the context of the post–civil rights era, when overt racism was increasingly (though not entirely) stigmatized. Many whites were (still are) hungry to prove that they can have their racist cake (beliefs) and eat it too (be a good person). Voting for Obama met that need for many whites, and it was an emotional need that Obama was all too happy to exploit on his way to the White House. So, yes, Obama knew "his whites." He knew they wouldn't tolerate a threatening Negro, and he did everything in his power to allay their fears.

This is also why #BlackLivesMatter was such a problem for Obama: he wanted to ingratiate white voters, and he knew how they'd interpret protests. Of course, Obama has never been a radical. And yet, at the same time, he could not completely distance himself from Black Lives Matter without revealing himself as an Uncle Tom to the black masses. Black Lives Matter caught

Obama between a rock and a familiar hard place: the competing needs to calm white fears and signal black authenticity. You will notice, though, a few things that suggest how Obama probably "really feels" about race, activism, and white power. Obama *never* condemned police officers who murdered unarmed black people with the same tenor as he condemned black fathers and protesters. Obama never lectured (white) law enforcement with the same patronizing and moralizing tone he used to lecture black audiences. Not once.

As president, Obama never acknowledged, much less criticized, white supremacy, because he picked a side a long, long time ago. I suspect Obama chose the side of white supremacy and neoliberalism for the same reasons other minorities make this choice: internalized oppression and naked self-interest. In *Stamped from the Beginning*, Ibram X. Kendi highlights one of the most important and devastating facts about Obama's rhetoric: his crafty combination of antiracist *and* racist ideas. Obama's shifts between language embracing racial justice and language embracing the racial status quo—sometimes within the same speech or even the same breath—fly in the face of conventional wisdom, which suggests that a politician is either racist or nonracist, a devil or an angel. Nothing could be further from the truth. Returning, once again, to Obama's "race speech" in Philadelphia, Kendi notes that

> Obama uttered quite a few antiracist words in the speech—most profoundly, his analysis of how for "at least a generation" politicians had used "resentments," fears, and anger over welfare, affirmative action, and crime to distract White voters "from the real culprits of the middle class squeeze." . . . But then, ever the politician, he refused to classify White "resentments" as "misguided or event racist"; amazingly, he "grounded" them "in legitimate concerns." Obama ended up following in the racist footsteps of every president since Richard Nixon: legitimating racist resentments, saying those resentments were not racist, and redirecting those resentments toward political opponents.[26]

Being less stupid about racial politics means understanding that politicians—yes, even people of color—combine racist and antiracist ideas, mainly for the purpose of appealing to racists *and* their victims.

After I finally woke up to the Democrats' complicity with state violence and white supremacy, I began to feel an ongoing state of horror watching Obama-bots praise the president as he raised hell abroad and denied racism at home. But as they say: *There but for the grace of God, go I.* I *was* that Obama-bot for so many years—the Democrat who was too lazy and complacent to take responsibility for informing myself about sins of the party. I'm still working on forgiving myself for my own ignorance, but at the very least, I *did* wake up. The sad reality is that Obama's warmongering and accommodation of white supremacy still has not caused a scandal for the vast majority of so-called liberals. Some say they "didn't know" about Obama's war crimes, his kill list of people he ordered assassinated, or the growing racial wealth gap on his watch. The same way, I suppose, that Trump supporters "don't know" (or don't care to know, or simply don't care) about his racism, sexism, and lies.

I've been criticized for calling Obama what he is: a highly strategic, ruthlessly ambitious Uncle Tom. When I tweeted precisely this in response to the news that Obama would be paid $400,000 for a Wall Street speech, someone replied: "*Sheesh! Harsh!*" Nah, homie. Harsh is selling poor people out to Wall Street capitalists, accommodating white supremacy, and bombing brown children with a smile. That's harsh.

It wasn't until after Obama's presidency that I discovered, thanks to a tip from one of my Twitter followers that Obama actually laid a wreath at a Confederate monument at Arlington National Cemetery every Memorial Day, despite protests from antiracists and progressives. To be quite honest with you, I'm *still* wrapping my head around the reality that only a few months after being sworn into office, the nation's first black president *honored the Confederacy.* Like, what the hell even was that?

When you think about it, "Uncle Tom" is a fairly mild term for a man who was so weak on white supremacy that he publicly honored men who died to keep people like him in chains. And the fact that the president tried to "offset" honoring the antiblack Confederacy by *also* sending a wreath to a monument for black soldiers is beyond craven. Imagine if Obama gave an award to white supremacist terrorists but then *also* gave an award to the NAACP. I mean, if this display of cowardice and immorality doesn't make you an Uncle Tom, what the hell does?

For some of us, it took Obama's election to demonstrate that a black president could collude with white supremacy. But there really is no excuse for not knowing that black political leaders very often capitulate to the interests of leaders of white supremacy and multinational corporations, a point made by the economist William Darity Jr. in an article in the *Atlantic* appropriately titled "How Obama Failed Black Americans."[27]

So, for the millions of us who missed the memo, let's all come together, hold hands, and admit how very stupid we were to get caught up in Obama's bullshit. As Malcolm X would say: We were hoodwinked and bamboozled. We were lost in the sauce. The black and brown voices that expressed critique of Barack Obama in the lead up to the 2008 election were branded "haters." Warnings from white and minority progressives were largely swept aside and ignored. Most Obama-bots weren't looking for critical perspectives on the man or his policies during that first presidential campaign. Personally speaking, I was looking for reasons to *believe*. And ten years later, I now know that my naive faith in the politics of racial hope was as misguided as it was genuine.

Those of us who care about improving this world can't afford to treat our politicians like religious figures. Critical thinking—especially about our political candidates and elected officials—is vital to becoming less stupid about racial politics. It means, at the very least, giving up religious devotion to charismatic leaders pushing forward-thinking "Hope and Change" or revisionist nostalgia like "Make America Great Again." Being critical about our racial politics requires being painfully honest about how political parties and corporate interests prey on our own racialized emotions, wishes, hopes, and dreams to enrich the 1 percent. Whether those dreams seem hopeful or whether they're grounded in fear, the reality is that both the Democrats and the Republicans regularly manipulate voters' racial imaginations while perpetuating systematic racism.

Chapter 4

TRUMP COUNTRY

The specific dissonance of Trumpism—advocacy for discriminatory, even cruel, policies combined with vehement denials that such policies are racially motivated—provides the emotional core of its appeal. It is the most recent manifestation of a contradiction as old as the United States, a society founded by slaveholders on the principle that all men are created equal.

—ADAM SERWER[1]

The phrase "*THIS IS NOT NORMAL!!!*" has been a nearly ubiquitous battle cry and primal scream on the Left since the orange man with tiny hands was elected in 2016. Some have criticized the media for "normalizing" Donald Trump (a theme we will come back to in the next chapter), while others condemn Trump for his "abnormal" political behavior (like getting into Twitter fights with the former president of Mexico) or mainstreaming white nationalism, fascism, and far-right extremism. It's undoubtedly true that Trump's lack of basic dignity and attack-dog politics appear to have made him an outlier in the modern era. Even newscaster Dan Rather felt compelled to emerge from retirement to warn the American people that Trump is a monstrous abnormality. In an appearance on Conan O'Brien's late-night talk show, Rather pushed back against the idea that there might be continuity between Trump's presidency and prior administrations:

CONAN O'BRIEN: We're living through a time right now where people are obsessed with our president. A lot of young people—well, people of all ages—don't know, one day to the next, what this man's gonna do, what he's gonna say. You have the perspective of having been in the news business, pretty much, my entire life. . . . You have interviewed every president, I believe, since Eisenhower. . . . You knew them all, and so, I don't know if that gives you a calm perspective about . . . Donald Trump . . . having talked to so many different presidents, does it give you any sense of some kind of continuity or has everything gone haywire?

DAN RATHER: Well it certainly doesn't give you a sense of calmness. Um, secondly, it's important for us to remember: this is not normal. There's never been anything like this before.

CONAN O'BRIEN: This kind of president?

DAN RATHER: No. We've certainly had presidents, for example, who didn't like the press. We've never had one who, steadily out of his own mouth, waged such an unrelenting campaign against the press. But this is something brand new in American history. That's first of all. It is not normal. There is a campaign to convince people—and I think particularly young people [that], "Oh well, this is just the way presidencies go." That is not true. Look. Many things about the age of Trump will make the stomach sicker than bad oysters. Everything from what he says to the way he says it. For example, trying to strike some equivalency between neo-Nazis—*neo-Nazis*—and other people who are trying to protest. The signals he's sent to outfits such as the Ku Klux Klan—the racist outfit—I mean, this is unprecedented in American history. And, therefore, it's a dangerous time.[2]

Listen, I'm not gonna sit here and act like Donald Trump is normal in the conventional sense of the word. Setting aside the fact that he's a billionaire—which materially sets him apart from the vast majority of people on the planet—he is clearly a strange, erratic, contemptible, and dangerous human being with access to enormous economic resources, political influence, and military power. But exaggerating Trump's political abnormality has its own dangers, like, you know, historical and sociological inaccuracy. Portraying his belligerence toward the media as some kind of unprecedented war, based mainly on the man's tweets and verbal harangues, would be laughable if it wasn't so misleading, particularly given that his direct predecessor, Barack Obama, led the most successful and devastating presidential attack on journalists and whistleblowers in modern history. It is well known among legal scholars and advocates for the free press alike that Barack Obama launched a horrifying campaign to criminalize journalistic activities, undermine First Amendment protections, and shroud government activities behind a veil of unprecedented secrecy. As a *Washington Post* headline declared: "Trump Rages About Leakers. Obama Quietly Prosecuted Them."[3] And though Obama didn't make it a daily habit to issue deranged public attacks against the press on Twitter, his administration "prosecuted more leak cases than all previous administrations combined."[4] In 2013, James C. Goodale, the First Amendment expert and attorney who defended the *New York Times* in the Pentagon Papers case, declared that Obama was well along the path to becoming "the worst president ever on issues of national security and press freedom."[5] Three years later, James Risen, the Pulitzer Prize–winning journalist, summarized Obama's extraordinary attacks on civil liberties as "the legal destruction of a reporter's privilege."[6] But we're supposed to clutch our pearls because Trump blubbers on about the "lying media" and clumsily retaliates against reporters for disparaging coverage.

The second half of Dan Rather's description of Trump as an abnormal president revolves around Trump's racial politics, and this claim deserves our close attention. Despite the cowardice of (white) media professionals and political pundits who couldn't bring themselves to acknowledge Trump's racism, the president's proclivity for white supremacy is not a new phenomenon. In the early 1970s, Trump, his father, and their real estate company were sued by the federal government for systematically discriminating against African Americans. Undercover federal agents documented evidence of widespread bias against black prospective tenants and favoritism for whites throughout Trump's properties. Former employees testified that they'd been instructed to restrict certain rentals to Jewish people and "executives" while they were "discouraged" from renting to African Americans.[7] By 1989, Trump was taking out full-page ads in four different New York newspapers publicly calling for the execution of the Central Park Five—four African Americans and one Latino falsely accused of raping a white woman. Though the men were later exonerated by DNA evidence and paid $41 million by New York City for wrongful imprisonment, Trump still insists—to this day—that they're guilty.[8]

It's worth noting that Trump's long history of racial animus did not prevent him from embracing wealthy people of color, from Oprah to Jennifer Hudson, or from landing a gig as a reality-TV host on NBC's *The Apprentice.* His racism, sexism, and all-around lack of decency didn't seem to be much of a concern for Bill and Hillary Clinton, who maintained a friendly, if transactional, relationship with The Donald for many years.[9] By the time Trump informally launched his political career by inventing the racist birther mythology that accused Barack Obama of being a noncitizen, he'd already established himself as a despicable human being. As David Leonhardt tweeted, "Donald Trump has been obsessed with race the entire time that's he's been a public figure."[10]

Attempts by journalists to compile "definitive" lists of examples of Trump's racism have to be updated almost daily. We're talking about a man who *began* his presidential campaign by stigmatizing Mexican immigrants with every racist trope imaginable, smearing them as "drug dealers, rapists, killers, and murderers."[11] Not only did he draw a moral equivalency between racist and antiracist protesters in Charlottesville, but he also referred to white supremacists as "very fine people."[12] He campaigned for Roy Moore, proslavery Alabaman accused of sexually assaulting teenaged girls, and he pardoned Sheriff Joe Arpaio, a lawless white supremacist who racially profiled and brutally tortured people of color, including women of color, in Arizona. We haven't even gotten to Trump's Muslim ban or his reprehensible "shithole" comments. Representative Frederica Wilson of Florida was right to describe Trump's White House as "full of white supremacists."[13] He's hired multiple racists and fascist sympathizers in his administration, including Steve Bannon, his former chief advisor. In addition to his previous stint at the helm of Breitbart News Network, an established cesspool of anti-Semitism, white supremacist racism, antiblackness, and Islamophobia, Bannon has repeatedly declared his admiration for anti-Semites and white supremacists.[14] And under Trump's presidency, the United States became one of only 3 countries in the world to vote *against* a UN resolution signed by 131 nations denouncing Nazism.[15]

All of this cozying up to white supremacist thugs and neo-Nazis is obviously alarming and reprehensible to anyone with a functioning moral compass. But is it really, as Dan Rather suggests, *unprecedented in American history*? Only in your dreams. The history of the United States actively recruiting, employing, and arming everyone from actual Nazis and perpetrators of the Holocaust to dictators, war criminals, and terrorists across the globe is harrowing. It's also a history that is essentially unknown to the vast majority of US citizens.

Consider Operation Paperclip, the formerly classified program in which the United States violated its own official policy of denying citizenship to Nazis and instead welcomed more than 1,500 German scientists and their family members—including people directly responsible for war crimes during the Holocaust—and hired them to work on government projects in the aftermath of World War II.[16] In addition to hiring Nazis for their expertise, US officials helped whitewash their war crimes, create new identities, and revive their reputations. Perhaps the most famous German scientist recruited by the United States was Dr. Wernher Von Braun, a committed member of the SS, the Nazi paramilitary organization; a weapons producer for Hitler; and a "card carrying Nazi who built the world's first ballistic missile with slave labor from concentration camps."[17] Von Braun went on to become a celebrated rocket scientist for the US Army and the first director of the Marshall Space Flight Center at the National Aeronautics and Space Administration. Authorized by Harry Truman, Operation Paperclip stretched from 1945 until at least 1990, meaning that no less than *nine presidential administrations* were involved in the government's secret partnership with Nazi researchers, engineers, and scientists. Let me say this again: *nine different US presidents* quite literally facilitated the normalization of Nazis.

But wait—there's more! While our (white, male) political leaders were happy to hire Nazis at the end of the war, they refused entry to thousands of European Jews fleeing the Nazi regime.[18] To take just one example, in 1939, President Franklin Delano Roosevelt declined to take action and allow the *St. Louis*, a ship carrying more than nine hundred Jewish refugees, to land in the United States. The desperate passengers were forced to return to wartime Europe—and 278 of those aboard were murdered in the Holocaust.[19]

But wait—there's more! Just three years after rejecting Holocaust refugees, FDR signed Executive Order 9066 in February 1942, thereby initiating the racist policy euphemistically known as the "internment" of Japanese Americans.[20] As a result of white supremacist hysteria, more than a hundred thousand Japanese Americans, children included, were rounded up without legal hearings or trials, forcibly removed from their homes, and relocated to ten different concentration camps scattered throughout California, Colorado, Wyoming, Utah, Idaho, and Arkansas.[21] More than 60 percent of those incarcerated were born in the United States. Historian Roger Daniels has described the racially motivated incarceration as an "attempt at ethnic cleansing."[22] Officially, Roosevelt and military officials rationalized their racist policy with the now familiar excuse of national security.[23] Japanese Americans were described as an enemy race and an existential threat to the nation's wartime effort—despite the lack of any evidence whatsoever of disloyalty or espionage among Japanese Americans. Of course, German Americans and Italian Americans were not treated similarly or sequestered in concentration camps. Gee, I wonder why.

But wait—you guessed it—there's more! We don't actually have to wonder why FDR, political elites, and military officials thought it was okay to subject Japanese Americans to state violence. The late-nineteenth and early-twentieth centuries saw the rise of anti-Asian racism (against what was popularly known as the "Yellow Peril") among the white majority, as well as the implementation of xenophobic policies designed to prevent Asian ethnic groups from entering the United States. White politicians, journalists, novelists, and scholars regularly described Asians as racially inferior to whites, and increasingly hostile immigration policies reinforced their subordinate status. The Chinese Exclusion Act of 1882, signed by President Chester Arthur, not only restricted Chinese immigration but also denied citizenship rights to people of Chinese origin. In 1907, FDR's cousin, President Theodore Roosevelt, established a so-called "gentleman's agreement" between the United States and Japan that severely limited Japanese immigration. As for FDR himself, he made his white supremacist views known early in his political career. In 1923, he penned an article for *Asia*, an international affairs magazine, and attempted to include a racist epithet—"the Japs"—in the title. The editors objected to the epithet but published the essay as "Shall We Trust Japan?" While framing his racial attitudes as moderate and enlightened—we're supposed to care that he mentioned the "dignity and integrity" of the Asian "races"—FDR nonetheless defended the eugenicist notion of racial purity, drawing upon white supremacist ideology to justify excluding people of Japanese descent from intermixing and sharing resources with white Americans: "[The] mingling of white with oriental blood on an extensive scale is harmful to our future citizenship. . . . As a corollary of this conviction, Americans object to the holding of large amounts of real property of land, by aliens or those descended from mixed marriages. Frankly, they do not want non-assimilable immigrants as citizens."[24]

In FDR's mind—and in the minds of most white Americans—the United States was, and should remain, a white country. Then, as now, the "economic insecurity" of white laborers (who were increasingly competing with Asian immigrants for work) was used to justify the racist exclusion of people of color. It was in this overtly nativist and white nationalist climate that President Calvin Coolidge signed the 1924 Immigration Act, a racist policy that essentially banned all immigration from Asian countries. That same year, FDR published more white supremacist screed in a series of essays collected as *Roosevelt Says*, in which he asserted the view that Japanese people could never be assimilated into the United States.[25]

But wait—there's even more! President Andrew Jackson was a slave trader, enthusiast of settler-colonialism, an advocate of ethnic cleansing, and a proud murderer of indigenous people. His white supremacist policy positions included the Indian Removal Act of 1830, which systematically cheated and forced indigenous people out of their own land and included the "outright endorsement of killing Natives."[26] I could go on and on, chronicling presidents who not only owned slaves but sexually assaulted them too. We could have a conversation about Thomas Jefferson, a white supremacist, enslaver, and rapist who believed that black people should be enslaved because he viewed them as "inferior to the whites in the endowments both of body and mind" and, accordingly, asserted that blacks should only be incorporated in the United States as slaves, never as free persons.[27] We could time travel closer to the present day and revisit the virulent racism of modern presidents from Dwight Eisenhower, who proclaimed that Southern racists were "not bad people," to Lyndon Johnson, who referred to civil rights legislation as "nigger bills."[28] And then, of course, we could chat about Bill Clinton, our so-called "first black president," who managed to play the saxophone on *The Arsenio Hall Show* while simultaneously facilitating the racist mass incarceration of African Americans and other people of color.

Focusing on the racism of individual presidents, whether it's Donald Trump or Richard Nixon, obscures the bigger, more ominous picture: the systematically racist society from which they emerged. Trump is not some kind of alien creature that came here from outer space. His brand of crude white supremacy resonates with tens of millions of US citizens (as well as white nationalists and neo-Nazis across the globe) because his views align with many of the foundational principles upon which Western colonial expansion broadly, and the United States specifically, were established. And the issue here is not just that our nation's founding principles were explicitly white supremacist, xenophobic, and imperialist. It's that these principles have been actively maintained, institutionalized, and normalized for generations.[29] The white supremacist in chief is a uniquely ugly and unseemly politician, but in many ways, we have always lived in Trump country.

On an October evening in 2016, I tuned into WNYC, the local NPR station, during my commute from Stony Brook University back home to New York City. The night's programming included a podcast featuring interviews with Trump supporters on Long Island, home to my university. As I drove westward, across the island, I listened to a journalist interview Patty Dwyer, a respiratory therapist, as they watched a television broadcast of Trump speaking at a campaign event. In the background, I could hear Trump launching invectives against political correctness—and, of course, against the Democrats. Soon, Patty began to choke up and apparently weep. She told the interviewer:

> Oh my gosh. Seems like I been waitin' for this since the eighties . . . when the political correctness started, when Bill Clinton was, y'know, with the "*What the definition of is, is?*" . . . I hear it

> as if I heard it yesterday. And that was the beginning of political correctness. . . . I'm emotional . . . about this, to hear someone actually say things we've been saying for decades and not feeling we were heard, you know what I mean? Nobody to speak up for us. It's pretty amazing.[30]

Like many white Long Islanders, Patty expressed concerns about immigration. She claimed to have previously voted for Obama, saying that she thought his presidency would represent the end of racism. But here she was now, seemingly breaking down in tears at the prospect of a white racist misogynist *speaking for her*.[31] Pretty amazing, indeed. While I was stupefied to hear an adult woman crying tears of joy for a man who was on the record as bragging about sexual assault, Patty's emotional response to Trump gave me a deep appreciation for how hungry white voters were for a politician who would speak their language, someone willing to trade the elitist posturing and respectability demanded of political correctness for the blunt, straight-talking, no-bullshit strongman persona that many disaffected and frustrated whites had been longing for.

Trump is often described by his supporters as someone who "tells it like it is" and says what people think. What this really means is that Trump says what many *white people think*, including the white supremacist views that are usually expressed behind closed doors. Patty's white tears for Donald Trump made me realize that there are generations of white people who have been socialized to believe that what we now call "racism" is just "the way it is"—the way it should be. Of course law enforcement should be supported, even as officers murder unarmed black people for simply existing. Of course brown immigrants should be kept out—they don't belong here. "*This land is my land*," the white fable goes, and it was never meant to apply to people from Mexico and Central America, even though they, and those indigenous to what we now call the United States, are quite literally the original Americans. No matter the fact that the United States gobbled up more than five hundred thousand square miles of Mexican territory in 1848 through imperialist violence. *Build that wall.* For centuries, the political and economic leadership of the US was openly, explicitly, and officially white-male supremacist. And though white women were disadvantaged by certain aspects of white-male supremacy, they also participated in the oppression of nonwhites, except they weren't taught that slavery, lynching, Jim Crow, or discrimination constituted "oppression." The nation—their nation—framed these things as perfectly moral. But the upheavals of the 1960s were eventually translated into political correctness, wherein the racist values of the nation were superficially disavowed but maintained in fact. This deeply hypocritical situation must feel awfully oppressive and exhausting to people who were trained to believe that their interests and well-being should come first but who were also trained to pretend to be color-blind, even as they worked obsessively to insulate their private lives from people of color.

As I made my way across Long Island to the city, I thought of the other white women scattered from sea to shining sea who felt genuine affection for the most openly racist presidential candidate in at least a generation. I imagined these white women—53 percent of whom would eventually cast their vote for Trump—feeling betrayed by the lying media, lying politicians, and their own lying country, a country that officially and proudly oppressed nonwhites for centuries, only to suddenly grant rights and resources to those once considered chattel. I imagined these white women reacting to the hypocrisy of a nation that pretends to be racially progressive when everyone knows (but won't admit) that white supremacist values are still dominant. I imagined these internally oppressed women crying because someone finally *(finally!)* was telling the truth about this country and its values—their values. How relieved they must have felt to hear a politician who was ready and willing to put white America first.

When Trump slandered African and Caribbean nations as "shithole" countries nearly a year into his presidency, another white woman came to his defense. Responding to the controversy,

White House press secretary Sarah Huckabee Sanders praised the president for his frankness: "No one here is going to pretend like the president is always politically correct. He isn't. I think that's one of the reasons the American people love him. One of the reasons that he won and is sitting in the Oval Office today is because he isn't a scripted robot. He's somebody who tells things like they are sometimes, and sometimes he does use tough language."[32]

Tough language. Telling it like it is. People of color know exactly what this means. In an interview with CNN's Van Jones, Jay-Z gave his take on Shithole Gate: "It's like, it's disappointing and it's hurtful. . . . But this has been going on. This is how people talk—this is how they talk behind closed doors."[33] Yes, this is how they talk. It's no secret that many white people and Westerners more generally view African and Caribbean nations as "shithole" countries. But what was interesting to me is that Trump was verbalizing what has long been US policy vis-à-vis Afro-Caribbean people, a policy of racist exclusion, white supremacist imperialism, and domination. And his base loves him for this honesty. Were his comments racist? Not according to Sanders and the white Americans she represents. For millions of white people, "being racist" is somehow completely unrelated to articulating racist views and supporting racist policies.

Trump speaks for so many white Americans because he centers what sociologist Joe Feagin has called the *white racial frame*, a wide range of racist "stereotypes, prejudices, ideologies, images, interpretations . . . narratives, emotions and . . . inclinations to discriminate" that whites mobilize to justify and maintain the racial order.[34] Unsurprisingly, this way of framing the social world consists of a "strong positive orientation to whites and whiteness" and hostility toward people of color generally and black people in particular.[35] The racist framings produced by and for the white majority have been constructed and reinforced over the course of centuries. As a result, white folks' commonly held beliefs and racialized feelings and biases have become deeply embedded in our society and woven into the fabric of our institutions.

Racist humor, so central to Trump's persona, also features prominently in the white racial frame.[36] Take, for example, this account from a white male college student, cited by Feagin and his colleague Leslie Picca:

> When any two of us are together, no racial comments or jokes are ever made. However, with the full group membership present, anti-Semitic jokes abound, as do racial slurs and vastly derogatory statements. . . . Various jokes concerning stereotypes . . . were also swapped around the gaming table, everything from "How many Hebes [an anti-Semitic slur] fit in a VW beetle?" to "Why did the Jews wander the desert for forty years?" In each case, the punch lines were offensive, even though I'm not Jewish. The answers were "One million (in the ashtray) and four (in the seats)" and "because someone dropped a quarter," respectively. These jokes degraded into a rendition of the song "Yellow," which was re-done to represent the Hiroshima and Nagasaki bombings. It contained lines about the shadows of the people being flash-burned into the walls ("and it was all yellow" as the chorus goes in the song). . . . Of course, no group is particularly safe from the group's scathing wit, and the people of Mexico were next to bear the brunt of the jokes. A comment was made about Mexicans driving low-riding cars so they can drive and pick lettuce at the same time. Comments were made about the influx of illegal aliens from Mexico and how fast they produce offspring.[37]

As shocked and disgusted as I feel reading about young people making Holocaust jokes or laughing about the deaths of hundreds of thousands of human beings in Hiroshima and Nagasaki, the harsh truth is that there is nothing at all unusual about the trivialization, and even celebration, of violence against people of color and religious minorities. Other empirical studies have repeatedly shown that white supremacist "joking" is common across the ideological spectrum, with liberal and conservative whites alike admitting to the routine practice of denigrating nonwhite minorities and using racial slurs. Remarkably, most people who engage in this kind of behavior—Trump among them—doggedly insist that their vile attempts at humor and use of racist epithets are magically nonracist.[38]

The key to understanding whites' insistence that they are always already nonracist (even when caught in the act of perpetrating racism) is the rise of what sociologist Eduardo Bonilla-Silva calls "colorblind racism" in the mid-twentieth century. One of the major consequences of the civil rights movement was the emergence of a new way of talking about race, an ostensibly kinder, gentler form of white supremacy that eschewed the biological essentialism of the past yet still denied white racism and blamed minorities for racial disparities. Instead of coming straight out and saying that black and brown people are inherently inferior, this "new" white racism defended white dominance with subtler forms of signaling, called dog-whistle racism in which coded terms and imagery are used in lieu of overt racial discourse. The gains of the civil rights movement and the introduction of equal protection laws changed the racial climate of the US. These new, fragile norms had the effect of officially framing white racism as a "bad thing" for the first time in the history of the United States. The norms and ideals of color blindness meant that white supremacist beliefs—the literal law of the land for generations—could no longer be easily expressed in public without the risk of criticism and even legal sanction. As a result, many whites "developed a concealed way of voicing" racist ideas while also pretending not to see race.[39] In other words, whites began attempting to be viewed as "politically correct."

But crude, politically "incorrect" racism, long embedded in white American culture, did not disappear. Instead, it was largely, though not entirely, pushed behind closed doors in all white, or predominately white, settings. This is what Leslie Picca and Joe Feagin mean by "two-faced racism": white folks' public, and hypocritical, posturing as "non-racist" even as they practice racist behavior in the comfort of all-white settings. For almost fifty years, the white "backstage," maintained by segregation and protected from the eyes and ears of people of color, allowed millions of whites to privately express their rage and hostility toward minorities while portraying white supremacy as a thing of the past. For many whites and people of color alike, Obama's election (and reelection) concealed the underbelly of racist beliefs and practices that were brewing under the surface of our society. That is, until Trumpism brought the ugliness and ordinariness of white racism back into public view.

Interestingly, Bonilla-Silva has argued that even Trump has had to strategically present himself as color-blind to win the presidency. "Trump's racial rhetoric," he writes, "is certainly inflammatory, but he constantly has to genuflect to the color-blind norms of the period. . . . A color-blind regime demanded that Trump maintain he was not racist."[40] Trump's weak efforts to frame himself as a friend to "the blacks" and other minorities includes photo-ops with people of color, from Kanye West to the National Hispanic Advisory Council to the presidents of historically black colleges and universities (HBCU), whom he invited to the White House. Color blindness also involves lapses of memory and habitual denial. Despite being on the record as knowing exactly who David Duke is, Trump feigned ignorance about the former grand master of the KKK when he earned his endorsement.[41] And to the surprise of no one at all, Trump has also made ample use of black enablers, from Kanye West to Omarosa Manigault Newman, former presidential aide, and Ben Carson, his secretary of housing and urban development, to provide cover from the charge of racism. Even after being fired from her role in Trump's administration, Omarosa maintained the color-blind party line, reassuring a journalist on ABC's *Nightline* with the nonsensical statement: "Donald Trump is racial, but he is not a racist."[42] And I can personally attest that Trump trolls on Twitter, or Russian bots, as the case may be, frequently post pictures of him smiling with people of color from Rosa Parks to Don King, to reassure themselves that he "doesn't have a racist bone" in his body.[43] "I'm not a racist. I am the least racist person you have ever interviewed," Trump told a reporter, albeit impotently, when news broke of his "shithole" slur against African and Caribbean nations. Trump may have violated a whole host of political norms, but claiming (against all evidence) to be color-blind and nonracist are not among them. And, given white folks' eagerness to ignore and excuse other white folks' racism, Trump's superficial performance of racial inclusivity has been largely effective for his target demographic. The WNYC podcast mentioned earlier also featured an interview with a white woman referred to as "Mrs. Johnson," who thought Trump wasn't prejudiced against minorities because "he's friends with them" and "hires them."[44] Mrs. Johnson would be shocked—shocked, I say!—to learn that lots of racist white people have minority friends and employees. I suspect that Trump could give a speech dressed in full KKK regalia and his supporters would still describe him as the next coming of Martin Luther King Jr. In this respect, Trump's ridiculous hypocrisy, duplicity, and denial make him like tens of millions of other white Americans across the political spectrum.

There has been a lot of handwringing over whether it's appropriate to call Trump voters racist. Bernie Sanders famously claimed that Trump voters were neither racist nor sexist. Though I am critical of Democrats' pathetic attempts to blame racism on Republicans, we need to be able to hold multiple truths simultaneously: racism is systematic and infiltrates our entire political system, and yes, voting for an overt racist and supporting his racist agenda is a racist thing to do. Political scientist Michael Tesler has run the numbers and the verdict is clear: Trump's appeal was bolstered by the increasing salience of the kind of old-fashioned racism that was once openly embraced before the civil rights era.[45] You might be wondering where old-fashioned racism went—and why so many of us were caught by surprise when it once again reared its ugly head in presidential politics. Tesler argues that white supremacist extremism declined among many individual whites and was officially disavowed by both major parties between the 1960s and the 1990s. As a result, for several decades, those old-fashioned racist views no longer served as a predictor for partisan political behavior. In other words, adhering to white supremacist ideology did not determine whether a white voter supported the Republican or Democratic Parties—hard-core racists were just about as likely to vote either way.

But something happened when a black man became the face of the Democratic Party. CNN's Van Jones called it a "whitelash." Suddenly, many whites, particularly those without a college degree, began to think that the Democrats were biased toward helping African Americans. Whereas college-educated whites traditionally associated the Democratic Party with more supportive policies for African Americans, working-class whites viewed the parties as having similar racial politics—that is, until Obama's election.[46] Tesler's data suggests that white adherents of old-fashioned racism (particularly those without a college degree) began fleeing the Democratic Party during Obama's presidency. The visible association between blackness and Democratic politics led to the perception, particularly among working-class whites, that the racial politics of the two parties were starkly different. For the first time in decades, white supremacist views became a factor in partisan politics, thus creating a political opportunity for an enterprising demagogue to use racism to win the support of angry white racists. Although I certainly didn't see Trump coming, Tesler seems to have had his finger on the pulse of white supremacy. Writing in 2013, he correctly predicted that white hostility toward Obama's presidency might culminate in the return of overt racism to the political scene.[47]

But make no mistake: working-class whites should not be blamed solely for Trump's victory. It is, by now, well known, that the Republican nominee won almost every white demographic group, irrespective of income, occupation, or age. As Ta-Nehisi Coates pointedly observes in his essay "The First White President":

> Trump won whites making less than $50,000 by 20 points, whites making $50,000 to $99,999 by 28 points, and whites making $100,000 or more by 14 points. This shows that Trump assembled a broad white coalition that ran the gamut from Joe the Dishwasher to Joe the Plumber to Joe the Banker. . . . Trump won white women (+9) and white men (+31). He won white people with college degrees (+3) and white people without them (+37). He won whites ages 18–29 (+4), 30–44 (+17), 45–64 (+28), and 65 and older (+19). . . . From the beer track to the wine track, from soccer moms to NASCAR dads, Trump's performance among whites was dominant.[48]

Trump garnered the support of wealthy and working-class whites alike while issuing vicious attacks against vulnerable minorities—women, the disabled, Muslims, Native Americans, African Americans, and the entire #BlackLivesMatter movement. And despite the valiant efforts of white observers to blame the election on the economic anxiety of white workers, study after study has confirmed what people of color already knew: Trump's appeal to whites was primarily driven by race—and racism—not class.

Obama-Trump voters, these exotic creatures, have featured prominently in white folks' desperate attempt to deny racism on the left and the right alike. Christian Parenti, an economist, pushed the discredited "class not race" line in *Jacobin.* "If Trump's victory were merely the result of racism," he asks, "how could it be that many white blue-collar, rust-belt areas voted for Obama by wide margins in 2008 and 2012 but then voted Trump?"[49] The idea that Obama-Trump voters could not be racist simply because they once voted for a black man is a strange and persistent delusion, one connected to the broader fantasy that liberals, and Democrats specifically, are somehow immune to racial animus.[50] But quiet as it's kept, there really are millions of Democrats who oppose racial equality and embrace racist beliefs. Though white Republicans express racist views at a higher rate than white Democrats, nearly one in four white Democrats believe that African Americans are lazier than whites and about one-fifth of white Democrats view African Americans as less intelligent.[51] One-third of Obama's white voters in 2008 actually *opposed* efforts to eliminate racial discrimination in the labor market.[52] *Slate* columnist Jamelle Bouie points out that some of the whites who "supported" Obama matter-of-factly referred to him as a nigger. As in, "*We're voting for the nigger.*"[53] Is it really so difficult to imagine that some of these fools would swing right for a white supremacist demagogue?[54]

If, for some odd reason, you're still having a hard time grasping the reality that some white racists voted for a black president, it helps to remember how Obama ran his campaign. Political scientist Vincent Hutchings reminds us that Obama specialized in "conciliatory racial politics," meaning that he deliberately crafted a political identity and watered-down racial agenda that would put millions of white people at ease.[55] As explored in chapter 3, Obama distanced himself from black radicals, including his own pastor, and positioned himself as an "exceptional Negro." Obama's conciliatory approach never advocated the redistribution of resources or the dismantling of white supremacy. He didn't campaign on a platform of reparations or racial grievance. Given his largely successful efforts to pitch his politics as nonthreatening to the white establishment, it becomes easier to see why some whites—hungry for absolution from racism—could vote for him while also holding racist beliefs.

But many liberals still cleave to the fairytale that membership in the Democratic Party provides immunity from racism. In fact, the myth that voting for the nation's first African American president is a "get out of racism free" card is so pervasive that it actually functioned as a major plot point in Jordan Peele's hit racial horror flick, *Get Out*. When Dean Armitage, a creepy and presumably liberal white neurosurgeon, tells his daughter's black boyfriend, "*I voted for Obama—twice,*" he's attempting to situate himself as a "good white person," which, in turn, is meant to signal "not racist." Time for another spoiler alert, because voting for Obama twice didn't prevent Armitage and his wife from luring black people to the family home for the purpose of violently enslaving their bodies and exploiting their brains. And that's exactly the point. Peele's brilliant political critique works at multiple levels: whites can (and generally do) claim to be nonracist while in the process of perpetrating antiblackness; liberal racism exists; and, yes, some liberal racists voted for an African American president. Peele's skewering of racist liberals for playing the Obama card is also backed up by empirical evidence. Experimental studies by social psychologist Daniel Effron and colleagues have shown that whites who express support for Obama actually give themselves permission (!!!) to subsequently engage in white favoritism. The researchers found that whites framed their support for Obama as a "moral credential" and evidence of nonracism, which then allowed them to discriminate against people of color with a clear conscience.[56]

We've already established that Trump's support came from whites regardless of class background and that it cannot be reduced to suffering of the white working class. But while we're here, let's also dispense with the absurd idea that economic insecurity is a legitimate reason for white people to vote for a racist. Any conversation about "economic anxiety" needs to examine why the vulnerabilities of black and brown working-class and poor people never seem to attract the concerns of either major party. And we also need to ask hard questions about why, exactly, white people of all classes feel justified in laying claim to lands and resources that don't belong to them while simultaneously excluding nonwhites. Indeed, the basic premise of manifest destiny in the United States, and Western imperialism more broadly, is the presumption of white entitlement, or what W. E. B. Du Bois referred to as "the doctrine of the divine right of white people to steal."[57]

There is nothing new about white racism being unjustly paired with and rationalized by economic concerns. In fact, as mentioned earlier in this book, economic and material interests were the driving forces behind the rise of modern racism. The original European settlers who established Jamestown in 1607 were motivated by economic anxiety, greed, and the desire to generate wealth for people who were fleeing ghastly conditions and religious persecution in Europe. Moreover, the dictates of racial capitalism are such that even well-to-do whites have justified their racial hostility toward and exploitation of people of color by emphasizing their need for economic security. What about the economic needs of people of color—and the poor?

In *Black Reconstruction in America*, W. E. B. Du Bois examined how white elites shored up their power by stoking racial animus among poor and working-class whites in the wake of the Civil War.[58] Du Bois argued that white elites sabotaged both labor movements and black advancement during the Reconstruction era by offering poor and working-class whites the "psychological wages" of feeling included in the so-called "master race"—even as they were being exploited and paid low wages by the white ruling class. In this way, wealthy whites used racism to generate conflict between white workers and workers of color, who might otherwise have joined forces to challenge the power structure that marginalizes them. Blaming newly freed slaves for the economic precarity of the white working class laid the groundwork for the establishment of Jim Crow laws, as well as the dismantling of federal protections for African Americans. All of this served, as Du Bois makes clear, to ensure that the white ruling class maintained their dominance. These tactics are still used by white elites to maintain their control over economic and political resources today. As critical race scholar Cheryl Harris points out in her 1993 essay, "The wages of whiteness are available to all whites regardless of class position, even to those whites who are without power, money, or influence. . . . It is the relative political advantages extended to whites, rather than actual economic gains, that are crucial to white workers."[59] It is a testament to the enduring drug-like powers of white supremacist thinking that a billionaire like

Trump seems more "relatable" to working-class and poor whites than black and brown laborers who, like them, are being economically exploited by white billionaires.

We've covered a lot of ground here—from history and economics to political analysis, social psychology, and pop culture—and I want to make sure I haven't lost you. All of these complexities notwithstanding, what I want to emphasize, once again, is that our entire society is built on white supremacy. So, the election of a white supremacist—even a vulgar, idiotic one—shouldn't surprise us: it's completely logical from a historical perspective. But I can't lie; it took me many months of stunned grieving to finally accept that a walking asshat won the presidency. I thought there was a bottom to our politics, and perhaps that was my continued naiveté. Trump's victory taught me that the bottom is beneath the floor.

The 2016 election also took my disdain with the Democrats to the supernova level, which is why I ultimately left the party. I was especially repulsed by Hillary Clinton's partisan framing of racism, which has made it all the more difficult for US citizens to come to grips with systemic white supremacy. The MAGA-hat-wearing white supremacist, usually conceived as some combination of neo-Nazi, working-class hick, or aggrieved coal miner, has become a popular whipping boy for many on the left—perhaps especially college-educated middle- and upper-middle-class whites who are not yet ready to sit with the reality that millions of college-educated middle- and upper-middle-class whites hold racist views. This caricature of the Racist Trump Voter, who Clinton, of all people, derided as "deplorable," serves multiple political functions: situating the Democratic Party and its leadership as "antiracist," allowing white elitists on the left to reassure themselves that the real racists are people very much not like them, and erasing the antiracism of poor and working-class whites.

Most of all, liberals' intellectually dishonest conflation of white supremacy with Trumpism prevents us all from having a rigorous conversation about how deeply rooted white supremacist racism is throughout our major institutions and in both major parties. To quote Eduardo Bonilla-Silva once more: "The more we assume that the problem of racism is limited to the Klan, the birthers, the tea party or to the Republican Party, the less we understand that racial domination is a collective process and we are all in this game."[60] Trump's election is a travesty, but then again so is the genocidal white supremacist racism upon which our entire nation is based.

I'd like to believe that Trump's election represented the final death throes of white supremacy—the darkest night before the dawn. But history suggests otherwise. I've had a lot of conversations, before and after the 2016 election, with white liberals trying to tell me how much progress "we've" made. The day before the election, a well-meaning white academic reacted to my pessimism by reassuring me that "things aren't so bad" and referring to improved data points. I had to explain that I'm also a data person, but that the data I see are the everyday lives of people of color who experience ongoing racial terror. To my surprise, thirty minutes later, this colleague knocked on my office door and said: "*You're right.*" He'd re-thought the racial progress narrative. Not only this, but he actually thanked me for pushing him to think beyond the liberal trope of progress.

The thing about white supremacy is that it socializes all of us to minimize its terror, to systematically deny or underestimate the harm. "*We've come so far,*" "*Things are getting better,*" "*It could be worse*"—all of these tropes minimize racial terror. Americans have been socialized to look on the bright side despite centuries of colonial and racial violence, torture, and the oppression of minorities. Our problem is not and has never been overreacting to racial terror. Our problem is the hegemony of under-reaction, denial, minimization. Ours is a society that has always socialized white folks to live in the midst of racial oppression but go on with their lives like normal. At every turn, those who oppose white supremacy have been met with denial, violence, "race card" accusations, or magnificent claims about progress. It seems that in the minds of many white liberals, we should all be celebrating the fact that most of us are not physically in chains.

White supremacy wants you to look at four hundred years of uninterrupted racial terror and conclude *"Things aren't so bad."* White supremacy wants you to look at the election of a KKK-endorsed POTUS and deny that we are in the midst of an ongoing state of emergency. White supremacy wants you to look on the bright side, to unify behind an unapologetic racist, to move on with your life as usual. And, perhaps especially, to keep buying into things that enrich the 1 percent. The daily whitewashing of Trump's racism and sexism we're seeing right now? The cowardly journalists who can't bring themselves to describe Trump as the white supremacist that he is? Or the journalists who admit that Trump is a racist, misogynist, pathological liar—but grant him credibility anyway? This is normal, business as usual for these United States. Putting lipstick on a corrupt, racist, sexist, colonizing pig is the American way. It certainly didn't start with Donald Trump.

Have you ever wondered how people lived with slavery, Jim Crow, and lynching but looked the other way? Look around right now. This is how they did it. They did it by going on with their lives. They did it by being polite, not rocking the boat. They did it by surrendering their critical thinking. They did it by cowering to demagogues and bullies. If the election of a man endorsed by a white supremacist terror group isn't enough to wake you the hell up, then I'm afraid that nothing will.

Chapter 5

FAKE RACIAL NEWS

It becomes a painful duty of the Negro to reproduce a record which shows that a large portion of the American people avow anarchy, condone murder and defy the contempt of civilization.

—IDA B. WELLS[1]

The United States has consistently treated white supremacist terrorists with more sympathy, respect, and leniency than it has treated civil rights activists. And nowhere is this pathological proclivity for coddling racists more evident than in the reporting of the news. It is now commonplace for liberal observers—and even some Republicans—to decry the "normalization" of white supremacy. Generally, this "normalization" is described as a shocking, recent phenomenon tied specifically to the rise of Trump and the public reemergence of the white nationalist movement. Proponents of this Normalization Thesis suggest that we've entered a fundamentally new era in which it has suddenly become acceptable to embrace white supremacist views. This new mainstreaming of white supremacy, we are told, is the result of an unholy alliance between Trump, nefarious dark money, and neo-Nazis branding themselves as the "alt-right." Very often, right-wing media trolls such as Breitbart News, as well as the mainstream press, are singled out for their role in facilitating this normalization process.

Soon after a 2016 speech in which Hillary Clinton criticized Trump for his racist dogma and refusal to disavow Nazi supporters, the journalist Soledad O'Brien called out CNN and other media outlets for giving airtime to self-identified white supremacists: "I've seen on-air, white supremacists being interviewed because they are Trump delegates . . . [and] they do a five-minute segment, the first minute or so talking about what they believe as white supremacists. So you have normalized that."[2]

In an article published the following year entitled "The Media Must Stop Normalizing the Nazis," Eric Alterman blasted the press for publishing glowing portraits of white supremacists: "That the *Times*, the networks, and other mainstream media outlets have been unable to communicate the degree to which our institutions are threatened by this Nazi-friendly administration is part of the reason that Trump and company can get away with what they do—aided by their own media cheerleaders at *Breitbart*, the Rupert Murdoch empire, and elsewhere."

Yes, the media's breathless, continual coverage of Trump and his overtly racist supporters has certainly disseminated and popularized white supremacist dogma. But in almost every respect, the Normalization Thesis is nonsense.

As a friendly reminder, there is nothing new about the normalization of white supremacy in the United States. White supremacy is the air we breathe—or don't breathe. It's embedded within our major institutions, our political economy, definitions of citizenship, our cultural codes and expectations, the way resources are distributed, and our psychological biases. White supremacist social arrangements and beliefs are woven into the fabric of our everyday lives. White supremacy is, in fact, so normal, so systemic, pervasive, and taken for granted that it is almost never acknowledged, much less opposed, by members of the majority population. Thus, the idea that white supremacy ceased to exist in the distant past but then suddenly became normalized in the last few years is, on its face, a lie—one sustained, primarily, by the KKK Fallacy, as well as the Political Fallacy, outlined previously.

The Normalization Thesis also rests upon the enduring fiction that white political, social, and economic domination had become a Very Bad Thing in the eyes of most white Americans. But the main lesson most whites absorbed from the civil rights era wasn't that they have a personal responsibility to fight systemic racism but, rather, that they have a responsibility to maintain a public appearance of being "nonracist" even as racism pervades their lives. As shown in chapter 4, empirical research convincingly demonstrates that though white attitudes toward certain issues like interracial marriage have changed over time, white people did not suddenly become antiracist or radically alter their views after the 1960s.[3] And of course, we know that the overall racial hierarchy did not change, despite the end of state-sanctioned apartheid and the selective incorporation of some people of color into positions of power. In truth, the vast majority of whites successfully arranged to exclude people of color from their neighborhoods, families, friendship networks, and intimate spaces while pretending to be nonracist in public.

Anyone who knows me knows that I'm a bit obsessed with the study on "two-faced racism" by Leslie Picca and Joe Feagin—I talk about it *all* the time—simply because it's such a devastating indictment of the lie that white supremacist views and behavior are somehow anomalous or abnormal. Drawing upon the accounts of more than six hundred white college students across the country, the researchers pored over journal accounts of thousands of events that the students defined as "racial incidents" in their everyday interactions. The considerable volume and content of the student reports (collected over a period of several weeks) provide stunning insight into the sheer frequency and normality of racist behavior and comments in the lives of white Americans. Some of the most interesting findings pertain to whites' reactions to other whites who criticize their racism. Significantly, when whites censure each other for racist behavior or remarks, Picca and Feagin show it is often the *public* nature of the racist performance that's framed as a problem, not white racism itself. The same racist comments and behavior that many whites tolerate or participate in themselves behind closed doors become problematic and inappropriate in public. Thus, the problem, for many whites, isn't white racism or systemic dominance; it's a failed public performance of being nonracist. From this perspective, it becomes easier to understand why Trump's public racism is frequently framed as shocking and abnormal, even though whites routinely express racist views and engage in discriminatory behavior behind closed doors.

Social norms are maintained through sanctions and rewards. The *Two-Faced Racism* study reveals the mechanisms that help sustain white supremacist norms in whites' private interactions. The authors note that whites typically ignored, tolerated, or encouraged each other's racism and sometimes admitted (in the privacy of their journals) to participating in racist behavior themselves. Moreover, on the rare occasions when the students said they called out white racism, they were frequently censured and socially punished. According to the student reports, whites frequently accuse other whites who criticize their racism of being "offensive" or ridicule their sensitivity or lack of humor. When whites respond to white critique of their racism with apologies, they also typically issue denials (*"I didn't mean anything by it"*). Picca and Feagin also show that the small minority of whites who called out white racism behind closed doors reported having to "work up the courage," as they knew their critique would disrupt the white comfort their peers are accustomed to maintaining in the absence of people of color. The prevailing need to maintain white comfort in all-white (or predominately white) spaces is a recurring theme in the text.

I want to underscore here that whites' unwillingness to take a stand against racism in their private lives spills over into white-dominated institutions, including corporate media. In other words, interpersonal and institutional racism are connected. Despite the slogans of "diversity and inclusion," the leadership groups of white-owned media companies did not suddenly decide to hold themselves accountable for confronting and ending their complicity with white supremacy. Instead, they've carefully cultivated the public appearance of nonracism. Observers who blame Trump and the profit-driven twenty-four-hour news cycle for mainstreaming white supremacy are missing the point. *White supremacy was already mainstream.* And the press, overwhelmingly owned and operated by white men, has been aiding and abetting the cause of white domination for centuries. How do newspapers, TV and radio stations, websites, and other media outlets normalize white supremacy on an everyday basis? They do it by circulating racist myths, images, and stereotypes; subtly (and, at times, not so subtly) portraying minorities in denigrating terms; implicitly justifying white violence toward people of color; and promoting white-centered perspectives and privileging the views of other white-dominated institutions, such as the police. In the past, they did it by explicitly describing people of color as biologically, culturally, and intellectually inferior and deserving of death and exclusion. As Stuart Hall notes, "The media are not only a powerful source of ideas about race. They are also a place where these ideas are articulated, worked on, transformed and elaborated."[4] And, importantly, media representations often mix racist ideas with putatively "inclusive" or even antiracist ideas. As I'll argue later, this "both sides" approach to racism is a common (and deplorable) feature of media narratives and images about race.

Of course, the prevalence of racial stereotypes in the news reflects patterns of bias in popular culture more generally. From the history of minstrel shows to the racist use of "yellowface" to depict Asians in Hollywood films, the historical record shows us that white supremacy remains thoroughly infused in the images and messages we consume from mass media. And these dynamics are still in effect today.[5] The (white) British director Ridley Scott was unapologetic about casting a whites-only list of actors and actresses to depict Middle Eastern and African characters in the film *Exodus: Gods and Kings.*[6] The #OscarSoWhite campaign, created by April Reign, a black writer and activist, brought attention to the lack of diversity among Oscar nominees. Asian roles are still being depicted with "yellowface" or played by white actors and actresses. Maggie Q, an Asian American actress, spoke to the ongoing discrimination she faces in the profession: "Nothing can be more frustrating than the fact that there aren't enough roles that [Hollywood] allows us, and then to take a role that is written Asian and turn it into one that you can no longer be considered for is adding insult to complete injury. . . . You already have a community of people fighting to be taken seriously."[7]

Almost five million people viewed a viral video that appeared on John Oliver's *Last Week Tonight* on HBO, which asked how Hollywood whitewashing is still "a thing."[8] Well, whitewashing is still a thing because white supremacy is still a thing.

Despite the appearance of more diverse images and "woke" representations, research has shown that stereotyped images of people of color have not drastically changed or improved over time. Sociologist Elizabeth Monk and her colleagues argue that Latinos are the most negatively portrayed ethnoracial group on prime-time television, typically portrayed as criminals and foreigners with heavy accents, while white characters are generally shown as "solidly middle income, fair with regard to skin and hair color, devoid of a heavy accent, articulate, respected" and "viewed as moral and admirable characters."[9] This routinized association between whiteness and moral goodness is also evident in the images that appear on the news. Think, for example, of Brock Turner, the white Stanford University student accused of rape and convicted of sexual assault in 2016. Local police refused to release his mug shot to the public until the end of his trial, which meant that media outlets used his respectable yearbook photo (complete with suit and tie) to depict a sexual offender. In this way, the intersections of racial, gender, and class privilege converged to whitewash a white man's crimes.[10]

Today, news organizations and media outlets participate in the normalization of white supremacy by taking a "both sides" approach to racism, a trend that is especially noticeable in the wake of the civil rights movement. But, as with individual people, white-dominated institutions have been more interested in appearing nonracist than in admitting or confronting their racism. Far from eliminating white supremacist bias from reporting, news outlets have continued to center white perspectives and prejudices. Perhaps most important, the press has been able to accomplish this by actively excluding and marginalizing the perspectives of people of color—and using the few minorities they do hire as proof of their nonracism—all while presenting themselves as objective arbiters of the news. Though journalists and media professionals would like to believe that their employers are somehow removed from the dynamics of systemic racism, the news is produced *within* contexts of white supremacy—not beyond it.

It can certainly be argued that Trump and his media acolytes have emboldened, amplified, and encouraged white supremacists, but this was only possible because we live in a society where systemic racism has been the well-established and widely institutionalized norm for generations. Coddling and normalizing bigots is as American as apple pie. And the media? It, too, has a very long history of aiding and abetting white supremacy. There is nothing new about the press, and mass media more broadly, participating in the normalization of white domination, racist beliefs, and discriminatory practices.

Steve Bannon, the virulent racist, unrepentant misogynist, and proud enabler of neo-Nazi fascists, has become a prominent target for liberal accusations of racism, but major outlets such as the *New York Times* and the *Washington Post* were for Bannon before they were against him. According to 2016 reports featured on *Politico* and *Think Progress*, both papers joined Fox News (yes, Fox News) to arrange exclusive deals with Bannon, as well as Breitbart's Peter Schweizer, to publish "oppositional research" targeting Hillary Clinton.[11] One year later, the editorial boards of the *Times* and the *Post* condemned Trump's decision to name Bannon as his chief advisor. In a stunning about-face, both boards expressed outrage (or, at least, mild concern) over Bannon and Breitbart's white nationalism, anti-Semitism, Islamophobia, xenophobia, and antiblack racism. But naturally, neither paper thought it newsworthy to mention their own, very recent, complicity. Which begs the question: If Steve Bannon deserves condemnation for providing a platform for the alt-right, and Trump deserves condemnation for providing a platform for Bannon, what, pray tell, do the *New York Times* and the *Washington Post* deserve for providing a platform for Breitbart, Bannon, *and* Trump?

Another egregious example of media complicity occurred when *The Huffington Post* removed its editor's note from Trump articles. The note, which correctly pointed out that Trump is a racist, misogynist, and serial liar was *immediately* removed after his election. *HuffPo*'s (then) Washington bureau chief, Ryan Grim, said he wanted to give the racist, misogynist, lying president a "fresh start."[12] He hastened to add: "If he governs in a racist, misogynistic way we reserve the right to add it back on." They never did, of course.

On the extremely rare occasions when news organizations admit their implication with racism, the matter is treated as a thing of the past. Take, for example, Connecticut's *Hartford Courant*, which made headlines across the country in the summer of 2000 for acknowledging its racial hypocrisy. After running numerous articles urging the US Congress to apologize for slavery and blasting the Connecticut-based insurance company Aetna for its involvement in the slave trade, the *Courant* was eventually forced to acknowledge that it, too, had a history of supporting and profiting from enslavement. Like many other newspapers, the *Courant* received revenue for publishing ads for the sale and capture of enslaved African Americans. In a revelatory article entitled "Courant Complicity in an Old Wrong," the paper issued its own apology:

> From its founding in 1764 well into the 19th century, The Courant ran many ads for the sale and capture of human beings. . . . In effect, Courant publishers, including founder Thomas Green, profited from the slave trade. . . . Unfortunately, the practice of advertising for slaves was commonplace in newspapers prior to abolition. . . . We are not proud of that part of our history and apologize for any involvement by our predecessors at The Courant in the terrible practice of buying and selling human beings that took place in previous centuries.[13]

It would be a mistake, though, to limit the concept of "complicity" to the placement of ads. Given the hegemony of white supremacist ideology, most news organizations from the colonial period through the mid-twentieth century implicitly or explicitly normalized white supremacist rule. Sociologist Joe Feagin argues that print media helped ensure the hegemony of white supremacist views by circulating racist images and inculcating racist ideas among new waves of European immigrants. "In newspapers and magazines," he notes, "highly racist cartoons and drawings, coupled with written portrayals framing African Americans negatively, taught whites of all nationalities, ages, and classes the white racial framing of African Americans."[14] It's important to remember that white supremacist racism in the media also involved the stigmatization of European ethnic groups that were considered racially inferior—including the Irish, Italians, Poles, and Jews.[15] The scientific racism common among white elites who owned and operated the media trickled down to the wider public through biased framings, harmful stereotypes, and racist caricatures. In this way, newspapers fed white Americans a daily diet of propaganda that solidified their hatred of people of color and bolstered their belief in their own "biological, cultural and social supremacy."[16]

Members of stigmatized European ethnic groups who wanted to make it in this racist culture eventually found ways of assimilating into white supremacy. Though there were white dissenters who opposed the racial orthodoxy, abolitionist and antiracist publications were (and still are) a very small minority.

After the Civil War, journalists continued normalizing white domination by stoking white fears of non-European immigrants and promoting anti-Asian sentiment.[17] When the Chinese Exclusion Act was passed by Congress in 1882, effectively barring immigration from China, newspapers across the nation had already thoroughly poisoned the public mind with denigrating depictions of Chinese, Japanese, and other Asian people, who were typically portrayed as subhuman "yellow hordes" threatening national security as well as the job opportunities and well-being of working-class whites.[18] Then, as now, news organizations and print media helped racist lawmakers amplify their white supremacist messages, paving the way for restrictive policies designed to protect the racial, political, and economic order.

When Ida B. Wells, the great civil rights leader, educator, and investigative journalist, published an editorial that would later become the book *Southern Horrors: Lynch Law in All Its Phases*, she included a section aptly titled and in all caps "THE MALICIOUS AND UNTRUTHFUL WHITE PRESS."[19] Written in 1892, *Southern Horrors* was the first comprehensive study of lynching, a groundbreaking and courageous achievement that marked the beginning of Wells's lifelong commitment to combatting the racist lies and propaganda used to instigate and justify the grotesque and barbaric violence of white vigilantes.[20] As co-owner of the Memphis-based newspaper *Free Speech*, Wells used her platform to debunk the many falsehoods fabricated in order to defend the lawless murder of African Americans—and to unveil the role of the white journalists, many of whom encouraged white vigilante violence.

Many proponents of lynching argued that black men must be killed in order to guard against an epidemic of sexual violence inflicted upon white women and girls. Wells began to question this master narrative as she became aware of innocent black men who'd been lynched, including one of her own friends, who was murdered after a dispute that had nothing to do with white women or rape. The trauma of this loss, and the knowledge that it was completely unrelated to the rationale being used to defend lynching, led Wells to investigate other mob killings and report her findings in editorials.[21] On May 21, 1892, she published an editorial in the *Free Speech* that would definitively change the course of her life:

> Eight Negroes lynched since last issue of the Free Speech, one at Little Rock, Ark., last Saturday morning where the citizens broke . . . into the penitentiary and got their man; three near Anniston, Ala., one near New Orleans; and three at Clarksville, Ga., the last three for killing a white man, and five on the same old racket—the new alarm about raping white women. The same programme of hanging, then shooting bullets into the lifeless bodies was carried out to the letter. If Southern white men are not careful, they will overreach themselves and public sentiment will have a reaction; a conclusion will then be reached which will be very damaging to the moral reputation of their women.[22]

The conclusion Wells was intimating here was the plain fact that at least some white women were having consensual sex with black men. The local white community was so enraged by the truth of her words that members burned the offices of her newspaper to the ground and threatened to murder her if she ever returned to Memphis. At the time, there was no massive network of activists to protect her, and the National Association for the Advancement of Colored People did not yet exist. And when the organization was eventually formed, in 1909, nearly two decades later, *she* was one of the founders.

Undeterred and unbowed, Wells continued her advocacy and political activism in exile, expounding upon the same historical and sociological observations that earned her death threats. Through her pamphlets and essays in the dissident black press, she meticulously countered white supremacist inventions that included, among other things, the calumny that blacks were subhuman, immoral monsters; the claim that every black man who had sex with a white woman must have raped her; the pretension that whites who carried out extrajudicial murder of black people and sexually violated black women and girls were legitimate arbiters of morality; that white women were morally "pure" beings who needed patriarchal protection from the scourge of black male predation; and that whites had not just the right but a moral duty to assassinate blacks and mutilate their bodies beyond recognition. Wells insisted that white men's claims of protecting white womanhood were farcical, not only because of their refusal to admit the consensual nature of sex between some black men and white women but also because of white men's systematic crimes against black women and girls: "To justify their own barbarism they assume a chivalry which they do not possess. True chivalry respects all womanhood, and no one who reads the record, as it is written in the faces of the million mulattoes in the South, will for a minute conceive that the southern white man had a very chivalrous regard for the honor due the women of his own race or respect for the womanhood which circumstances placed in his power."[23]

Needless to say, in the eyes of many white racists, including those highly positioned within the US government, Ida B. Wells became public enemy number one. According to historian Paula Giddings, the US Military Intelligence Division covertly monitored Wells throughout her career, conducting surveillance through the use of black spies and even labeled her "a far more dangerous agitator than Marcus Garvey."[24] In the parlance of today's state-sponsored white supremacists, she would have certainly been called a "black identity extremist."

In her crusade to tell the truth about lynching and white supremacy, Wells castigated the fake news produced by whites—and amplified in the press—that was used to encourage white crimes against black people. A journalist and news professional herself, Wells was strongly positioned to critique the role of the white press in misrepresenting the facts surrounding lynching. Then, as now, the complicity of the white (supremacist) press had deadly consequences, as she explains below:

> In a county in Mississippi during the month of July the Associated Press dispatches sent out a report that the sheriff's eight-year-old daughter had been assaulted by a big, black, burly brute who had been promptly lynched. The facts which have since been investigated show that the girl was more than eighteen years old and that she was discovered by her father in this young man's room who was a servant on the place. But these facts the Associated Press has not given to the world, nor did the same agency acquaint the world with the fact that a Negro youth who was lynched in Tuscumbia, Ala., the same year on the same charge told the white girl who accused him before the mob, that he had met her in the woods often by appointment.[25]

Southern Horrors cites numerous examples of white journalists circulating the rape charge to falsely criminalize blacks and absolve white crimes. Take, for example, the *Daily Commercial*, a Memphis-based paper, which described black men as sexual monsters on the hunt for white women, despite the fact that no black men had been charged with rape in Memphis:

> The lynching of three Negro scoundrels reported in our dispatches from Anniston, Ala., for a brutal outrage committed upon a white woman will be a text for much comment on "Southern barbarism" by Northern newspapers; but we fancy

> it will hardly prove effective for campaign purposes among intelligent people. The frequency of these lynchings calls attention to the frequency of the crimes which causes lynching. The "Southern barbarism" which deserves the serious attention of all people North and South, is the barbarism which preys upon weak and defenseless women. Nothing but the most prompt, speedy and extreme punishment can hold in check the horrible and beastial [*sic*] propensities of the Negro race. . . . The generation of Negroes which have grown up since the war have lost in large measure the traditional and wholesome awe of the white race which kept the Negroes in subjection, even when their masters were in the army, and their families left unprotected except by the slaves themselves. There is no longer a restraint upon the brute passion of the Negro.[26]

But Wells pointed out the absurdity of this latter point—the implausible notion that black men suddenly became rapists after the abolition of slavery but left white women untouched during the Civil War. "[The] world knows," she wrote, "that the crime of rape was unknown during four years of civil war, when the white women of the South were at the mercy of the race which is all at once charged with being a bestial one." More importantly, she began to uncover the real story: white lynch mobs were targeting successful, upwardly mobile African Americans in order to violently maintain white supremacy. Her friend Thomas Moss was one of three black men, coowners of a grocery store, who were lynched and brutally dismembered by white mobs after being harassed and threatened at their place of business. The case, like the vast majority of lynchings, had nothing to do with claims of rape.

Both Wells's *Southern Horrors* and her *A Red Record: Tabulated Statistics and Alleged Causes of Lynching in the United States* (1895) examined instances in which black men were jailed or murdered on the basis of white women's lies—and the bloodthirsty instigation of the white journalists.[27] One incident involved a married white woman of Ohio, J. C. Underwood, who accused

William Offett, a black man with whom she had a consensual affair, of rape. Although Offett maintained his innocence, he was found guilty and sentenced to fifteen years' imprisonment. After having served four years, Underwood confessed to having lied about the rape and admitted that she had, in fact, initiated the relationship:

> I met Offett at the Post Office. It was raining. He was polite to me, and as I had several bundles in my arms he offered to carry them home for me, which he did. He had a strange fascination for me, and I invited him to call on me. He called, bringing chestnuts and candy for the children. By this means we got them to leave us alone in the room. Then I sat on his lap. He made a proposal to me and I readily consented. Why I did so I do not know, but that I did is true. He visited me several times after that and each time I was indiscreet. I did not care after the first time. In fact I could not have resisted, and had no desire to resist.[28]

Wells suggested that Offett would have been slaughtered in a Southern state without any judicial process whatsoever. "There have been many such cases throughout the South," she pointedly wrote, "with the difference that the Southern white men in insensate fury wreak their vengeance without intervention of law upon the Negro who consorts with their women." Her investigative reporting revealed how ridiculous it was to believe that the same white people who had the entire apparatus of state and local violence at their disposal for maintaining white supremacy, who wrote the laws—then broke them with impunity—who continually forgave each other for heinous crimes against black men, women, and children, needed protection from the existential threat posed by black people simply breathing, and not the other way around.

Ida B. Wells's oeuvre was a radical acknowledgement and repudiation of white supremacy. She understood that the mainstream news was produced by the same population that benefitted from the maintenance of the racial status quo. It's rather unfortunate that most journalists haven't followed in her footsteps, acknowledging the systemic biases and inequalities that reliably shape the news. Instead, many media professionals continue to view racism as an external topic they can cover neutrally, rather than a system of power that shapes how they view the world and write about it. Of course, the fiction of white objectivity is easier to maintain in the absence of racial minorities from positions of power in the corporate media news industry. Although minorities currently compose nearly a quarter of the population, they are either underrepresented or absent altogether in organizations that produce the news. Here's a number for you: six. That would be the number of corporations that control 90 percent of all mass-produced media.[29] Last I checked, the CEO of every single one of these companies (Time Warner, Disney, Comcast, News Corp, CBS, and Viacom) was a white man.[30] The same can be said of major newspapers: from the *Wall Street Journal* (owned by Rupert Murdoch) to the *New York Times* (owned by the Ochs-Sulzberger family) and the *Washington Post* (owned by Amazon billionaire Jeff Bezos). One exception that proves the rule is Dr. Patrick Soon-Shiong, a South African–born medical researcher and pharmaceutical mogul of Chinese descent, who in 2018 purchased the *Los Angeles Times* and several other newspapers for $500 million. He also happens to be a billionaire, the richest doctor in the country, and a man, so that helps.[31]

Aside from the executive suite, whites dominate every step in the production of the news, from marketing and advertising, to layout and design, and, of course, editing and writing. A 2017 survey conducted by the American Society of News Editors found that US newsrooms remain overwhelmingly staffed by whites. Across 661 print and online news organizations, only 16.6 percent of journalists and other employees are people of color.

Accordingly, whites also dominate editorial decisions: 86.5 percent of news editors are white and an astonishing three-fourths of news organizations have *no* minority representation among their top three editors.[32] Remarkably, the ASNE framed these abysmal findings in optimistic terms, though their own data indicated that 19 percent of newsrooms were actually *less* diverse in 2017 than they were in 2001. No matter that whites are still overrepresented at all of the nation's leading daily newspapers or that some news organizations (including *thirteen* out of thirty newspapers in the state of New York) are Whites Only. We are supposed to be impressed and encouraged. The authors reassure us that news organizations are "still more diverse than they were during the two decades prior to 2016 when diversity figures essentially plateaued and minorities consistently accounted for between 12 and 13 percent of newsroom employees." Over a twenty-year period, US newsrooms diversified by an average of just *three* percentage points toward census parity. Three. Percentage. Points. Let's break out the champagne.

Whites are overrepresented as reporters and editors even in metropolitan areas with relatively large minority populations. According to the last US census, my hometown of Chattanooga, Tennessee, is 58 percent white and 42 percent nonwhite. But the staff over at the *Chattanooga Times Free Press* is a whopping 93 percent white. Even more disheartening is that the pattern of white domination holds for cities where whites are a numerical minority. In San Francisco, where whites compose only 36 percent of the population, the *San Francisco Chronicle* somehow managed to hire a staff that's 76 percent white. The population of New York City is 44 percent white, but that didn't stop the *New York Times* from ensuring that 81 percent of its staff is—you guessed it!—white. Demographics be damned, white supremacy will find a way.

By now, it should be clear that there is a cyclical, self-reinforcing relationship between structures of white domination (laws, economic relations, and power dynamics within institutions) and the collective representations that help maintain the system. But perhaps you think I'm being too hard on media professionals. Are they really at fault for the proliferation of racist ideas? Could it be that news outlets are simply presenting a mirror of our racist society—reflecting racial dynamics that are already there?

Lucky for us, media scholars and advocacy groups have already examined these questions. The results are as conclusive as they are disheartening. Decades of empirical data indicate that news depictions regularly exaggerate negative depictions of people of color far beyond statistical realities. In a 1996 study assessing the representation of poverty in mainstream media, scholar Martin Gilens found that news accounts heavily distort the racialization of the poor, overrepresenting blacks and underrepresenting whites.[33] Media descriptions across the major television broadcast networks (NBC, ABC, and CBS), as well as magazines (*Time*, *Newsweek*, and *US News and World Report*) systematically misrepresented the intersections of class and race. While blacks constituted 29 percent of the poor when the study was conducted, they were represented in 62 percent of magazine stories and 65.2 percent of evening news programs about poverty. In other words, mainstream media *blackened* the portrayal of poverty, depicting African Americans as impoverished more than twice as often as we would expect given their actual representation among the poor. Tellingly, Gilens also found that magazine stories about the "underclass" focused *exclusively* on the black poor.[34] The overrepresentation of black poverty and the underrepresentation of white poverty have clear implications for public support for social safety nets and poverty programs. Polling data has demonstrated that whites are less likely to support policies to help the poor when they associate poverty with blackness.[35] Given that whites do, as a rule, chronically overestimate the percentage of blacks in poverty and grossly underestimate the number of white folks in poverty, media distortions that are repeated day after day, year after year, are clearly implicated in the reproduction of racist stereotypes and the miseducation of the public.

Beyond (mis)representing poverty, news reports also maintain the racial order by continuing the same tradition Ida B. Wells observed in her fight against lynching: the widespread and systemic production of exaggerated images of black criminality and the underreporting of white misconduct. A 2015 study by Color of Change, an advocacy group, found that every single news network in New York City overrepresented African Americans as criminal offenders—by an average of 24 percent above their actual arrest rate.[36] While blacks represented 51 percent of all arrested New Yorkers, they were 75 percent of the criminal perpetrators shown on the local news. Incidentally, the worst offender of all was WABC, ironically owned by the same Walt Disney company that helped Shonda Rhimes build an empire of diverse dramas such as *Scandal*, *Grey's Anatomy*, and *How to Get Away with Murder*. As the study notes, the network portrayed a stunning 82 percent of criminal perpetrators as black, thus "reinforcing dangerous stereotypes by exaggerating the image of black people as criminals."[37] To make an already abysmal situation exponentially worse, *none* of the news programs examined provided *any* context whatsoever for viewers to acknowledge, much less understand, the biases and inequalities embedded within the criminal injustice system. The study further concluded: "Coverage of crime consistently lacks discussion of factors such as over-targeting of black people by police, discriminatory incarceration (e.g., black people receiving harsher sentences for the same crime compared to white people), and the impact of poverty, unemployment and discrimination on crime."[38] Given the prevalence of fake racial news and white supremacist reporting across the mainstream press, is it any wonder that Breitbart and other cesspools of white nationalist dogma have found eager audiences for falsified crime statistics depicting blacks and other people of color as natural born criminals?

Do journalists have a duty to inform the public about institutional racism within the judicial system or about the ineffectiveness of discriminatory policing practices like stop-and-frisk? I sure think so. But it appears that many reporters and news professionals believe their job is to distort racial reality, drive up the ratings, and cape for white supremacy. As many reporters have become little more than mouthpieces for police departments, they tend to amplify officers' accounts rather than question them. According to the Color of Change study, reporters "freely admit that the demands of delivering breaking news, which impacts both ratings and revenue for their stations, incentivizes their over-reliance on information and perspectives from police departments, which further introduces bias into the overall pattern of reporting."[39] White supremacist policies and practices ensure that people of color are disproportionately monitored, criminalized, policed, and incarcerated—and racist media coverage ensures that people of color are depicted in ways that justify those same policies and practices. As the study states clearly, officers "over target . . . [and] the news media exaggerate."[40] The end result? Millions of people go to sleep every night after being indoctrinated with police propaganda, inaccurate images of black criminality, and false portrayals of white innocence. And many of them wake up the next day proclaiming that they "don't see race." But we know from well-established research that the psychological consequences of being systematically exposed to racist ideas are wide-ranging. Lisa Wade, a sociologist, put it this way: "Each time we see a black person on TV who is linked with a violent crime or portrayed as a criminal, the neurons in our brain that link blackness with criminality fire. . . . The more often a link is triggered, the stronger it becomes."[41] Whether we like it or not, our implicit biases spill over into multiple spheres of social life, from hiring to housing, politics, and policing.[42]

The news industry isn't just a mirror reflecting society's racism. *It's a megaphone.*

The underrepresentation of white violence, white perpetrators, and white crime (past and present) means that generation after generation have been socialized to disassociate whiteness from negative traits. Unsurprisingly, news and images produced by white-controlled media tend to produce a flattering, and inaccurate, portrait of white folks vis á vis other groups. Clearly, white folks' delusions of grandeur have deadly consequences for the rest of us. This is why legal scholar Robert J. Smith and colleagues argue that we need to acknowledge "implicit white favoritism"—the obvious, though curiously underrecognized, flipside to bias against people of color.[43] Social psychological experiments have actually shown that it is more difficult for individuals to visually recognize weapons when they've been exposed to an image of a white face. In other words, linking nonwhiteness with criminality and whiteness with innocence makes us far less likely to accurately see what is happening right before our eyes.

Thirty years ago, Peggy McIntosh, a well-known white antiracist scholar, wrote an influential and powerful essay about the "invisible knapsack" of white privilege.[44] More recently, she updated her very long list of unearned advantages to include critical reflections on the media:

- The men of my race who took 400 billion dollars in the 1994 U.S. S & L (savings and loan) scandal are not branded as criminals or seen as enemies of the U.S. people, even though the money has never been returned.
- I am allowed to believe, and encouraged to believe, that people of my race are in general law-abiding rather than law-breaking.
- TV shows and films show people of my color as the main defenders of law and order; cleverest detectives, best lawyers and judges, and wiliest outlaws.
- Portrayals of white males on TV as criminals and violent individuals do not incriminate me as a Caucasian; these males, even the outlaws, are usually presented as strong men of a quintessentially American type.
- The voiceovers of criminals, shifty individuals, and villains in Disney films and in ads rarely sound like people of my racial/ethnic group.

- Illegal acts by the U.S. government, in the present and in the past, around the world, are not attributed by whites to Caucasian immorality and illegality.[45]

These reflexive insights provide a useful model of what antiracist media literacy can look like. Because awareness is the very first step, one of the most critical things we can do is take stock of the messages and images we absorb from the media we consume. What happens when we begin to acknowledge what is being said—and not being said—about our groups and others? What steps can we take to divest from and challenge the fake racial news and alternative facts of white supremacy? And how can we actively support organizations, writers, and publications seeking to shift the racial status quo?

Sometimes people ask why I (now) hate the *New York Times*. How much time do you have? My animus toward the *Times* runs so deep that I sometimes have to pray to God for forgiveness. It's to the point where all I want for my birthday is a "*Fuck the New York Times*" t-shirt—and matching mug. I sometimes dream of launching a start-up and finding angel investors to turn old issues of the *Times* into recycled toilet paper. If I ever got a tattoo, it would probably say . . . Well, you get the idea.

But for many years, I thought of the *Times* as a highly reputable publication. When I still identified as a run-of-the-mill liberal, I excitedly read *NYT* columns written by my former professors and writers I respected. For a while, I even subscribed to the paper. Like the *Atlantic*, *Harper's*, and the *Paris Review*, the *Times* was one of those publications I felt pressured to peruse, at least occasionally, in order to conform to the norms of the East Coast intelligentsia. At one point, I considered submitting an op-ed. But then, something changed. The same Black Lives Matter movement that pushed me to more fully acknowledge our nation's investment in antiblackness also pushed me to become a more critical consumer of the news. When the *New Yorker* published a "sit-down" interview with Darren Wilson—the police officer who killed Mike Brown—I canceled my subscription. Another turning point for me was the 2015 Charleston shooting, in which nine black people were assassinated by a white supremacist while they prayed in a South Carolina church. I saw media outlets putting the words "hate crime" in quotes—and half expected them to report that black "people" were killed. When terror attacks are carried out by people of color, or when the victims are primarily white, media outlets play sad, patriotic music. But I heard nothing of the sort for the victims in Charleston. I noticed that media pundits could barely mouth the words "racism" and "white supremacy" even when the murderer was openly racist and white supremacist. But most of all? It became crystal clear to me that an attack on black US citizens is almost never framed by the press or our politicians as an attack on the United States.

When it comes to the fine art of not giving a fuck about black people and other people of color, the *New York Times* really is in a league of its own. From an atrocious 2017 op-ed that asked "Is There a Case for Marine Le Pen?" (that would be the white nationalist who came in second place in the French election) to the aforementioned "partnership" with Steve Bannon all the way back to a 1967 editorial attacking Martin Luther King Jr. for his principled opposition to the Vietnam War and a 1922 article that essentially said "Don't Worry About Hitler," the *New York Times* has long been a venue for "gotta-see-both-sides-of-white-supremacy" bullshit. It publishes antiracist articles right alongside racist screed. And despite its inclusion of a sprinkling of minority writers and editors, the paper has a long record of throwing black and brown people under the bus while capitulating to white supremacy. In 2013, an intrepid and groundbreaking Latina reporter named Tanzina Vega created the first and only race beat at the *New York Times*. Just two years later—and only months after the murder of Eric Garner at the hands of the NYPD—the paper decided to shut down the column, effectively ending the only beat dedicated to the serious analysis of race, ethnicity, and racism.[46] You already know that their record on diversity is pretty abysmal, but it's probably even worse than you think. As of 2017, the *NYT* employed "no regular Arab American or Muslim American writers."[47]

And yet somehow, someway, the paper maintains a sterling reputation despite its liberal (in both senses of the term) racism. The same multiracial neoliberal elite clutching their woke pearls over the latest racist op-ed or essay in the *New York Times* will reliably return to fawning over the paper after the temporary "outrage" dies down. I was beyond done with the *Times* way before the paper published its infamous profile of Tony Hovater, also known as the "Heartland Nazi," which might as well have been titled "White Supremacists: They're Just Like Us!"[48] Observers rightly pointed out the rather significant contrast between the *Times*' efforts to normalize an advocate of ethnic cleansing and the paper's heartless denigration of Mike Brown. As the writer Sady Doyle noted: "Above and beyond anything else about this NYT thing: We already know that Nazis are people. We've covered the fact that Nazis are people. The people that Nazis want to kill are also people. That's what we seemingly haven't established yet."[49] Sean McElwee, a policy analyst, posted an iconic take down on Twitter, juxtaposing paragraphs from the two articles. One of these men is depicted as deserving of empathy. The other, as deserving of death:

> In Ohio, amid the row crops and rolling hills, the Olive Gardens and Steak 'n Shakes, Mr. Hovater's presence can hardly make a ripple. He is the Nazi sympathizer next door, polite and low-key at a time the old boundaries of accepted political activity can seem alarmingly in flux. Most Americans would be disgusted and baffled by his casually approving remarks about Hitler, disdain for democracy and belief that the races are better off separate. But his tattoos are innocuous pop-culture references: a slice of cherry pie adorns one arm, a [*sic*] homage to the TV show "Twin Peaks." He says he prefers to spread the gospel of white nationalism with satire. He is a big "Seinfeld" fan.

> Michael Brown, 18, due to be buried on Monday, was no angel, with public records and interviews with friends and family revealing both problems and promise in his young life. Shortly before his encounter with Officer Wilson, the police say he was caught on a security camera stealing a box of cigars, pushing the clerk of a convenience store into a display case. He lived in a community that had rough patches, and he dabbled in drugs and alcohol. He had taken to rapping in recent months, producing lyrics that were by turns contemplative and vulgar. He got into at least one scuffle with a neighbor.[50]

Would you be surprised to learn that the "No Angel" piece was actually written by a black man? Don't be. What kind of minority writers do you think are most likely to be hired at the *Times*? Initially, the whitewashing of the news was accomplished by excluding people of color altogether from white-owned publications (thus explaining the rise of the black press). But we've made so much racial progress that white newspapers can actually *hire people of color* to do their white supremacist reporting *for* them!

In his critique of the *Times*' Nazi-coddling, Eric Alterman, mentioned at the beginning of this chapter, actually defended the newspaper from accusations of racism: "The *Times* was tougher on a black victim of police murder than it was on a Nazi not because the paper is 'racist,'" he assures us. "Rather, it's because the *Times* is addicted to showing 'both sides' of any controversy, no matter how egregious and awful one of those sides might be."[51] What litmus test did Alterman use to absolve the *New York Times* of racism? He doesn't say. Are we really to believe the *NYT* "isn't racist" simply because a white man says so? If a news organization that has, for well over a century, normalized the white racial frame, privileged white perspectives and white writers, amplified racist ideas, normalized white nationalists, systematically excluded people of color from employment and leadership positions, attacked civil rights leaders, and provided propagandistic coverage for the state's racist imperial wars launched primarily against predominately black and brown populations isn't racist, then what the hell *is*?

It shouldn't be so difficult for liberals and left-of-center folk to admit that the *New York Times* is complicit with systemic racism. In this respect, it is like most other newspapers—only more egregious and harmful, given its Teflon reputation and global influence. What Alterman and so many other clueless white media analysts still refuse to accept is that providing a platform for white nationalists and presenting white supremacy as "just another side" *is really fucking racist.*

The existential question that white folks keep struggling with—"*Should we listen to the white supremacist side now??*"—only ever has one answer: *NO.*

Chapter 6

INTERRACIAL LOVE 101

I can't possibly be racist because my friend/lover/ child/coworker or random acquaintance I speak to once a year is a person of color.

—WHITE PROVERB

One of my biggest pet peeves is hearing people perpetuate the absurd idea that centuries of racial terrorism and systemic domination can be undone by holding hands or copulating across the color line and singing "Kumbaya." Why oh why do people *still* believe that interracial love (or sex) can end racism when thousands of years of heterosexual love and sex have quite obviously failed to end patriarchy? I hate to be the one to break it to you, but we're not going to end white supremacy by "hugging it out." And we're certainly not going to fuck our way out of racial oppression. That's not how power works.

In the interest of science, I just took a break from writing this chapter to enjoy a roll in the hay with my half-white, half-Japanese girlfriend. Despite our best efforts, our interracial, interethnic lovemaking was surprisingly unable to usher in the Age of Aquarius. Maybe if we just keep trying, we'll eliminate the racial wealth gap through the sheer power of our orgasms and loving-kindness. Or maybe not. ¯_(ツ)_/¯

The delusion that interracial love will save us from white supremacy just won't go away. It has even been parroted by people of color who should know better, but evidently don't. Appearing on *The Daily Show* in 2015, the rapper and actor Common shared his hot take on racism. In an apparent attempt to reflect on the power of reconciliation, he told Jon Stewart:

> If we've been bullied, we've been beat down and we don't want it anymore. We are not extending a fist and we are not saying, "You did us wrong." It's more like, "Hey, I'm extending my hand in love . . ." Let's forget about the past as much as we can and let's move from where we are now. . . . Me as a black man, I'm not sitting there like, *"Hey, white people, y'all did us wrong."* We know that existed. . . . I don't even have to keep bringing that up. It's like being in a relationship and continuing to bring up the person's issues. Now I'm saying, *"Hey, I love you. Let's move past this. Come on, baby, let's get past this."*[1]

There is so much wrong with this perspective that I hardly know where to begin. First of all, who is this "baby" that Common is referencing? Would that be Dylann Roof, the white supremacist who murdered nine black people attending church in 2015 just a few months after Common's call for minorities to extend a "hand in love"? Or maybe the "baby" in question is the Cleveland police officer who murdered twelve-year-old Tamir Rice in 2014 within seconds of seeing him?

In truth, what Common advocated on *The Daily Show* has nothing at all to do with love. What he encouraged was erasure and denial. Like too many well-meaning people, Common expressed the misconception that racism (1) is merely an interpersonal misunderstanding (and not a systematic and social reality); (2) only existed historically (and is not an ongoing feature of our society); and (3) can be solved by people of color loving white folks more intensely. The rapper's words also reinforced the obscene and persistent slander that people of color (not white racists!) are the ones who actually need to learn how to love. But no one who has even semi-seriously studied the matter would conclude that the history of racial oppression boils down to people of color having a love deficit. And yet, the fact remains that minorities who stand up against racism are routinely accused by actual racists of being "the real racists," of not "loving enough." Common's absurd comments reinforced this narrative and, in so doing, unintentionally minimized the racial violence that ordinary people of color experience on a daily basis.

It's difficult to reconcile such racial ignorance with the fact that Common is the same dude who costarred in the Ava DuVernay civil rights movie *Selma.* He helped usher in the golden era of socially "conscious" hip-hop. He hangs out with Chrissy Tiegen and her legendarily woke husband. And yet, unbelievably, he suggested that the cure to racism is a "hand in love" less than a year after the brutal, highly publicized murder of Eric Garner, who died a painful death while being suffocated by New York City police. Common must be well aware that racial oppression continued after the civil rights era. He witnesses the evidence of systemic racism in our nation and in his hometown of Chicago. He lived through the #BlackLivesMatter movement. He must have seen the haunting, unending stream of videos showing unarmed black people being slaughtered by police. And so I would ask our brother sincerely: *How can we extend a "hand in love" if we can't breathe?*

To be clear: I am not saying that interracial love is an impossibility. If that were the case, I wouldn't be with my current bae or have friends from a wide variety of backgrounds. But the first requirement of "interracial love" is that all involved must recognize the historical and present-day reality of racial oppression. It's not a "thing of the past" or something to simply "get over." We can't kiss and make up when racial terror is still an everyday occurrence. And if your "interracial love" leads you to lie to yourself about the ongoing reality of racism, then you need to rethink what love really means.

The second requirement of interracial love is acknowledging that love has never magically eradicated oppression anywhere at any time in the entire history of humanity. Instead of viewing interracial intimacy as an antidote to racism (or proof that one is not racist), we should consider the possibility of love as a resource for facing the difficult truth about the society we live in, and about the racial violence we all must live with. Love can help us cultivate compassion for our own suffering—and the suffering of others. Love can provide solace, strength, and even a sense of healing in the midst of oppression. Love can sustain us as we do the difficult work of transforming our societies. But ignorant, superficial love sho' ain't gonna end racism.

Loving across our racial differences involves learning about racism and taking a hard look at how prejudice and systemic discrimination continue to reproduce racial inequalities—not "a long time ago" but right now. *Today.* Racially ignorant "interracial love" isn't helpful. To the contrary, such misguided, honey-glazed postracialism only serves to placate white folks who don't want to acknowledge the ongoing atrocities of white supremacy—and people of color who want to turn away from painful truths. Challenging and dismantling oppression cannot be achieved by pretending it is not happening or by cultivating a nice warm and fuzzy "feeling." Real love, in the service of social justice, means having the ovaries to tell the hard truths, to face the depths of our individual and collective suffering, and to work together to reduce harm.

Thankfully, there are other black and brown voices in Hollywood that show it is, in fact, possible to win an Oscar and yet be aware that systemic racism is still "a thing." John Legend, who wrote the Academy Award–winning song "Glory," from *Selma*, with Common responded to the "hand in love" comments with a few of his own:

> I think it's not enough for us to extend the hand of love. I think it's important that that goes both ways. It's important also that we look at policies we need to change as well. It's important for

> us also to fight for certain changes that need to happen. . . . It's not enough to say we need to love each other, you have to go behind that and say we need to change these policies, we need to fight, we need to protest, we need to agitate for change.[2]

Chrissy Tiegen's husband is right. The love we need is the love of collective action. This is the kind of vigorous, informed love I see in the work of Thich Nhat Hanh, the Vietnamese monk who founded Engaged Buddhism. It's the kind of love I see in black feminists' invitation to make decolonizing a central feature of our efforts to build more just communities. This is the kind of love I'm trying to practice as I go about the difficult work of being vulnerable and honest about the dynamics of oppression in my public and private lives.

M. Scott Peck defines love as "the will to extend one's self for the purpose of nurturing one's own or another's spiritual growth."[3] Clearly, racism and all forms of oppression are the very opposite of love. To dominate another person—or an entire group of persons—is to deprive them of their power, to deny their inherent value, and to subject them to forms of abuse and exploitation. If love involves an active commitment to our mutual growth and fulfilment, then interracial love cannot be about mere sentimentality; it has to involve both recognizing and radically resisting the weaponry of terror that maintains white supremacy at the expense of racialized "others." What we need, quite desperately, is the willingness to cultivate revolutionary love, grounded in knowledge, compassion, courage, and collective action.

What we don't need is more kumbaya, postracial bullshit.

It's not difficult to understand why the topic of interracial sex and intimacy remains terribly fraught. For much of US history, white men maintained a system of racial and sexual violence that allowed them to savagely rape and sexually assault black women and women of color (as well as young girls) with impunity while simultaneously portraying black men and men of color as sexual savages.[4] In theorizing the afterlives of slavery, black studies scholar Christina Sharpe describes the interpenetration of racism with forms of sexual violation, harm, and terror as "monstrous intimacies."[5] In a similar vein, Sylviane Diouf, director of the Lapidus Center for the Historical Analysis of Transatlantic Slavery at the Schomburg Center for Research in Black Culture, speaks to the particular trauma of enslaved black women, whose bodies were often sexually objectified and brutally violated even as they were economically exploited and subjected to physical and psychological torture:

> But as slaves and as women, they and their daughters and granddaughters bore the brunt of oppression. Studies have shown that women were more likely to be subjected to excessive physical abuse than men. They were more vulnerable, less likely to respond with force. . . . They were the victims of sexual abuse, from harassment to forced prostitution, and from breeding to rape. Rape by sailors on the slave ships, and rape by overseers, slaveholders, and their sons in the Americas was a persistent threat to all, a horrific reality to many. Used, like it continues to be used today, as a weapon of terror, rape was meant to assert power over and demean not only the women, but also their fathers, brothers, husbands, and sons, who were reminded daily that they were considered less than men since they could not protect their womenfolk.[6]

Reflecting on the sexual terror imposed on enslaved black women by "the white male's sexual barbarity," Angela Davis astutely observed in 1971 that "in its political contours, the rape of the black woman was not exclusively an attack upon her. Indirectly, its target was also the slave community as a whole."[7] More recently, legal scholar Adrienne Davis has described US slavery as a system of "gender supremacy," which was "one of the first to institutionalize and perfect sexual harassment."[8] But, even as white men gave themselves permission to rape and sexually abuse enslaved black women, men, and children, they also developed policies prohibiting interracial marriage (known as "antimiscegenation laws") and crafted negative stereotypes portraying their victims as sexual deviants.[9]

Though it's been fifty years since *Loving vs. Virginia*, the 1967 Supreme Court decision that finally legalized interracial marriage, interracial relationships remain a charged topic. Very often, romance across racial boundaries is either demonized or idealized. When interracial love isn't being portrayed as the "solution" to racism, it's being depicted as the devil's handiwork—or a source of terror. Jordan Peele's brilliant and utterly terrifying 2017 film *Get Out* really fucked it up for those of us in non-horrific interracial relationships. But on the upside, we were all gifted with what is, by far, the best and most pithy description of internalized racism ever conceived: *being stuck in the sunken place.*

Back in 2010, Jill Scott infamously took to the pages of *Essence* magazine to write about her disdain for black men who partner with white women. Admitting to feeling a painful "wince" when she sees black men with white girlfriends and wives, she analyzes her own reaction as historically rooted in the oppression of black women—and the elevation of white women:

> When our people were enslaved, "Massa" placed his Caucasian woman on a pedestal. She was spoiled, revered and angelic, while the black slave woman was overworked, beaten, raped and farmed out like cattle to be mated. She was nothing and neither was our black man. As slavery died for the greater good of America, and the movement for equality sputtered to life, the White woman was on the cover of every American magazine. She was the dazzling jewel on every movie screen, the glory of every commercial and television show. . . . We daughters of the dust were seen as ugly, nappy mammies, good for day work and unwanted children, while our men were thought to be thieving, sex-hungry animals with limited brain capacity. We reflect on this awful past and recall that if a black man

even looked at a White woman, he would have been lynched, beaten, jailed or shot to death.[10]

Undoubtedly, Scott spoke for many black women when she acknowledged feeling "betrayed" by black men who partner with white women. In the interests of keeping it all the way real, I'll admit that even as a black woman partnered with a white-passing, non-black, biracial woman, I am occasionally still disappointed to see a black man partnered with a nonblack woman. In my case, I know that this feeling stems from my awareness of popular tropes of (some) black men's denigration of black women and stated "preference" for white women and nonblack women of color. Conversely, I have always been irrationally excited to see black women partnered with a nonblack boo—for the very same reasons. In my mind, I framed black women's interracial dating as a form of resistance. Despite knowing that this line of thinking is stupid, I still find myself throwing an imaginary fist in the air when I see another black woman dating interracially. And from talking to other black women, I know I'm not alone. Sociologist Chinyere Osuji found a similar dynamic in her research on interracial marriage in the United States and Brazil.[11] Black wives of white husbands in her study reported that their friends thought they were making the most out of a bad marriage market for black women by expanding their options and selecting white partners. In other words, their friends thought they were gaming the system—a system set up to devalue us. Before I tried interracial dating myself, I strongly encouraged my single, straight black girlfriends to stop waiting around for a black man and get themselves a white, Asian, or Latino boo. "Get your swirl on!" I told them, spreading the gospel of *Jungle Fever*, with zero experience of my own. Nine times out of ten, these ladies paid me no mind. "I prefer black men" was the typical, resolute response. And who could blame them? For most of my romantic and sexual life, I "preferred" beautiful black men (and women) too. The truth is, my people were, by far, the most likely to show me love.

And then I moved to Paris. In France, I found a nation that was both systematically racist and very eager to sexually objectify black women and women of color. For the first time in my life, I met more black women than I could count who were paired up with a white boo. And while some of these women recounted harrowing experiences of racism in the midst of these relationships, there were others who seemed very happy with their interracial *Love Jones.* But aside from a few casual flings with white dudes, most of my romantic encounters in the City of Lights revolved around black and brown love interests. When I returned to the United States, I was booed up with a black Frenchman. And when that shit show of a relationship mercifully came to an end, I was still almost exclusively sexually and emotionally seen by people of color. Despite my eager proselytization of interracial relationships for all of my black girlfriends, the idea that *I* would ever "end up" with a white man seemed improbable. White dudes weren't really checkin' for me. And the idea of partnering with a white or Asian woman (much less a white *and* Asian woman) was unthinkable. The thought never seriously crossed my mind.

Then I met my current bae and had to rethink my entire life.

Despite all of my prior pontification about interracial dating, I didn't really know what it might involve until I actually walked that path with her. I certainly didn't know that two people with such divergent backgrounds—I mean, it doesn't really get any more divergent than Tennessee and Tokyo—could find so much common ground, until it happened. I learned that it is possible to grow up certain you will end up with a black Prince Charming and then find yourself in love with a charming nonblack woman. Love can be unpredictable that way, and when the real thing comes along, you seize it.

Let's clear one thing up right now: *interracial love is not the same thing as antiracist love.* I know this comes as a shock to many, but being sexually attracted to someone of a different race doesn't earn you a Nobel Peace Prize or magically transform you into an antiracist. As we've established, racism exists at multiple levels of analysis, from the macro level of social structures to the micro level of interpersonal interactions. Power relations often play out within the contexts of intimate encounters. And if we think of interpersonal racism as a form of domination and abuse, it becomes easier to understand how and why racist oppression unfolds within intimate encounters. Simply being in a "relationship" with another human being has never in and of itself provided protection from emotional or physical abuse. Thus, it should go without saying that forming a friendship, romance, or sexual relationship with someone from a different "race" does not itself serve as some kind of a shield from racist ideas or racially abusive behavior. Racism and interracial desire can and do coexist, just as sexism and intergender desire coexist. It doesn't take a team of sociologists or rocket scientists to acknowledge the fact that sexual desire can also be dehumanizing. More broadly, what we may call "inegalitarian sex" is routine in patriarchal societies, where the most common sexual pairings take place between men and women who occupy unequal positions of power within society.[12] Have you heard of sexual harassment? Sexual assault? The #MeToo campaign? Patriarchal gender norms? Then it should come as no surprise that interracial sex and relationships are often ground zero for racist ideas and behavior. Take, for example, this vignette from Leslie Picca and Joe Feagin's study, published in *Two-Faced Racism*, in which white students were invited to keep track of "racial events" in their everyday lives. Here, a white girl named Abby (not her real name) recounts an incident that took place within a group of her friends:

> Five of us (all white) were at the apartment when one of the guys came over and joined us. On television was Arissa, one of the cast members of *Real World*. This guy says, "That was a good shit I just took." I then said, "Thanks for sharing that with us!" He then pointed out Arissa on the TV and said, "Well looking

> at her reminded me because she is black. She's black, my shit is black, she's a piece of shit." This guy is pretty weird and always said outrageous things. Everyone in the room is used to how he acts so no one gave him a response. The guy who said these things is white and has a fetish for girls of all other races. He always talks about wanting to have sex with them.[13]

Abby's white male friend expressed sexual desire for "girls of other races" while also describing those same girls in shockingly denigrating terms. Except no one in Abby's peer group seems to be especially shocked, as they didn't say anything to censure him. Picca and Feagin note that the "apparent contradiction of a white man desiring, perhaps in this case half-consciously, a sexual object that is also racially devalued is common in U.S. history and can be seen in old images constructed by white men of black women as tantalizing 'jungle nunnies' or 'jezebels.'"[14] In other words, there is nothing at all remarkable about racist white men expressing sexual desire for black women and women of color, even as they proclaim that these same women are undesirable.

Sometimes, interracial relationships are racially abusive. Sometimes interracial relationships are toxic. Sometimes people of color "stuck in the sunken place" excuse their white partner's racism. Consider, for example, the case of one Jason Holding, a racist white cop in Fort Lauderdale who was fired for sending racist text messages. His black girlfriend, Perpetua Michel, testified in his defense saying that he didn't use the N-word in a "hateful" way.[15] Apparently, in her mind, there is a "nice" way for white people to call black people niggers.

In some ways, the persistence of racism within intimate relationships and family units is even more depressing than racism within segregated contexts. For those who still *think* forming families across the color line can somehow eradicate racial violence, consider the fact that biological and familial attachments have never systematically prevented abuse or violence anywhere in the world at any time. Brazil is a vivid example of a white supremacist nation that actively promoted "race mixing." A few years ago, I was invited to an international workshop where I discussed my work on white supremacy. Over lunch, I had a chance to discuss the complexities of racism within intimate relationships with two experts on Brazil: one scholar who was actually Brazilian and another who was Danish. As we nibbled on grilled fish and salad, we talked about the similarities and differences between racialization in Brazil and the United States. For example, it is well known that Brazilians use a much wider repertoire of categories and colorful phrases to refer to what US citizens typically think of as "racial" differences. Family dynamics also came up, and the Danish scholar mentioned hearing Brazilians matter-of-factly refer to their light-skinned kids as "pretty" and matter-of-factly associate dark skin (of their own children) with ugliness. Of course colorism works similarly in the US and elsewhere—lighter children are often treated better than their darker siblings.[16] But what I pointed was something I always found interesting about Brazil: siblings born to the same parents can be different "races." That is, if two Brazilian kids are born to a mixed couple, the lighter child can be considered "white" and the darker child considered "black." One scholar pointed out that in Brazil, parents typically put all of their investments into the lighter, white kids. At this point, my eyes widened as I realized the implications of what this must mean for Brazilian families. Because it is *easier* for people with African ancestry to be viewed as white in Brazil than it is in the United States, it's also easier for families to "cash in" on their white investments. When I said this, both scholars agreed intensely, including the Brazilian colleague. In a way, each Brazilian family can sort of get a piece of the white supremacist pie, as long as they have "light-skinned" or, even better, "white" kids.

In fact, these observations find resonance in recent scholarship on racialization in Brazil. Elizabeth Hordge-Freeman's 2015 book *The Color of Love* examines intimacy in Afro-Brazilian families in Bahia, a region of the country with a significant black population.[17] Hordge-Freeman shows that colorism distorts family dynamics, as lighter-skinned children are framed as more aesthetically beautiful and receive preferential treatment. In his 2006 book *Race in Another America*, sociologist Edward Telles also reveals that lighter children in Brazilian families stay in school longer than their darker siblings, suggesting the broad implications of color-based discrimination for the reproduction of inequalities and systemic disadvantage.[18]

Unfortunately, as long as our societies systematically privilege lighter skin, people will try to survive (and increase their children's likelihood of surviving) by accommodating white supremacy. Parents deny their role in reproducing racism, selling out their kids; lighter siblings receive more resources. Darker, blacker family members experience systemic and interpersonal oppression that often goes unacknowledged (or is justified).

Which returns us to the global problem of racism: interracial intimacy isn't a panacea precisely because many mixed families and "I don't see color" couples reproduce racism.

Being in an interracial relationship within a racist society is always going to be a complicated affair. As sociologist Amy Steinbugler shows in her brilliant 2012 book *Beyond Loving: Intimate Racework in Lesbian, Gay, and Straight Interracial Relationships*, couples approach racial matters in a variety of ways. Some decide to avoid addressing racism while others attempt to confront racial oppression head-on. But the bottom line, according to Steinbugler, is that interracial couples exist in a matrix of domination. They are affected by the politics of the racial hierarchy in which we all live. This is the case whether the lovers involved want to face reality or not.

In my relationship with my girlfriend, intersectional oppression is something we talk about and deconstruct on a daily basis. She reads my Twitter rants against racial stupidity—and drafts of my scholarly manuscripts. I love the fact that she brings up white supremacy over coffee on a Saturday morning. Topics like "cultural appropriation" and "scientific racism" are literally pillow talk in our household. Sometimes we go to sleep discussing the history of eugenics or slavery, and then I wake up like "*According to Chomsky . . .*" We are really living this life. But there are other interracial "friendships" and relationships in which all involved sign a gentlemen's agreement to sweep racism under the rug. In the midst of Ferguson, Black Lives Matter, and uprisings in Baltimore, I often wondered how (or, really, if) interracial couples across the nation were discussing racial trauma. All too often, interracial couples don't even bother talking about how racism shapes their lives because they can't do that kind of intimate work. And sometimes the white partner intentionally or unintentionally subjects their non-white lover to interpersonal racism or fails to protect the person from the racist behavior and comments of their white friends and family members.

Increasingly, black women and women of color are using social media and blogs to speak up about their experiences of racism and sexism within interracial relationships. In the wake of Trump's election, a twenty-five-year-old black woman posted a Facebook video of her white (then) boyfriend saying, "What Trump should do, the second he's elected, give all you motherfuckers tickets back [to Africa]. You don't like it? Peace! Black Lives Matter? Go matter to fucking Ghana."[19] Writing in *The Establishment*, TaLynn Kel indicated that her white husband's "unconscious racism nearly destroyed" their marriage.[20] Their painful attempts to forge an antiracist path together has involved careful attention to the way they discuss race and racism. Noting that she tries to "keep our communication about racism as safe as it can be for him—without doing harm to myself," she explains what interracial intimacy involves in their relationship:

> [My] anger is accepted without my having to explain or justify it. He knows he is not an authority and that his ally work is in white spaces, not black ones. He is continually unlearning white supremacy and how to de-center himself in these conversations. It's no longer focused on his hurt feelings or fears

> that I hate all white people. Instead, it's about knowing that all white people in this country are racist until they take on the continuous task of unlearning what everyone and everything has taught them about race in America.

My girlfriend and I have had to think long and hard about how to address our different perspectives on racial oppression effectively and lovingly. In the beginning, this was difficult work. It isn't easy being vulnerable about the pain of antiblackness with someone who will never experience it, no matter how much that person loves you. Looking back, my apprehension made perfect sense. Racial vulnerability can't be shared with just anyone at any time; it requires trustworthiness and true intimacy. But, because I didn't know how to be vulnerable with my nonblack bae, sometimes our "conversations about race" turned into uncomfortable exchanges and, at times, gut-wrenching arguments. I had to learn how to teach her what I know about racism in a way that is loving and honors the sanctity of our relationship. And she had to learn how to listen and show support in a way that felt loving to me. When I talk about my experience of racial pain, I mostly desire her compassion, validation, and care. If I'm moved to tears reading the latest racially traumatic news or watching a film about slavery or civil rights, I want her to pass the tissues and show concern. With practice we've found ways to draw connections between different kinds of intersectional oppression—what we might think of as an "intersectional sensibility"—without pretending that our experiences are exactly "the same." They aren't.

Quite honestly, it took a skilled couples counselor to help us find ways to communicate authentically about racial oppression without hurting each other unnecessarily. And it took a great deal of commitment on both of our parts to do this intimate "race-work" without running away from each other—even when we wanted to. Over time, we deepened our friendship and began building true interracial intimacy. Because we trust each other and share the same racial politics, I can bring up concerns about her responses to antiblackness, unintended racism, or the dynamics of white privilege, and she can bring up concerns about how I express my views or talk about how she experiences the racial hierarchy. As a biracial woman, my girlfriend's racial and ethnic experiences are very different from mine. She's often perceived as "just" white. People generally react with surprise when they learn that her mother is Japanese and that she spent half her childhood in Tokyo. As someone racialized as a white woman, she acknowledges her white privilege. Her family's Japanese heritage has further sensitized me to anti-Asian racism and xenophobia. And her experiences living in black communities from Harlem to Senegal and working with marginalized populations as a social worker and therapist have sensitized her to the intertwined realities of racism and colonialism. We're both committed to acknowledging our differences and challenging our own biases. Neither one of us views interracial relationships as "the cure" to white supremacy.

In the first episode of the TV series *Dear White People*, Sam, a woke biracial student activist who previously spoke out about the dangers of "dating your oppressor," gets caught secretly dating a white boo. When confronted by her angry and incredulous best friend, she says: "I thought I knew what I wanted, but when I'm with him, I don't know. I . . . It's like a respite from everything. We're goofy. We reference obscure movies. We watch *Game of Thrones*. . . . I've tried to break it off before, but he sends one text, and I can't help but smile all day long."

The scene speaks to the pressure some people of color feel to explain why they fell in love with a white person. I've certainly been there. Some people still have the misconception that being pro-black means being antiwhite and thus react with surprise (or dismay) when they find out I'm dating a woman they perceive as white. There is also a history of internally oppressed black folk depicting white and non-black partners as more desirable than black lovers, and for this reason, minorities who date across racial boundaries are sometimes regarded as "sell outs." Clarence Thomas being married to a white woman doesn't help. But making assumptions about folks' racial politics based on the color of their partner is incredibly stupid. Even so, I would be lying if I said that I don't give the side-eye to other people of color in interracial relationships, wondering out loud if they've *ever* dated a member of their own racial or ethnic group.

I'm going to let you in on a dirty secret.

Back when news first broke of Prince Harry dating biracial actress Meghan Markle, I became quietly obsessed. I knew it made no sense whatsoever to get excited about a woman of African descent marrying into the decrepit, elitist, white supremacist British royal family. I mean, Harry was the same guy who once got caught wearing a Nazi costume at a Halloween party, for God's sake. I knew all of these things. And yet, every headline about Meghan Markle made me beam with racially problematic happiness. I'd never heard of her—or her show *Suits*—but I suddenly couldn't get enough of the headlines chronicling her romance with the prince. *How did they meet? What were his blonde exes saying? How did Meghan get into yoga? What did her black mother think of Harry? And OMG she's besties with the only queen I recognize—Serena Williams!*

There was just one thing: I couldn't publicly admit to being caught up in this madness. When I periodically updated my girlfriend about their romance, she rolled her eyes. She couldn't care less.

"Why are you interested in these people?"

"I can't explain it. I know it's wrong. I'm ashamed."

"I'm telling Twitter."

"Noooooooooo!"

And so we laughed and joked about my covert obsession. I knew my interest was racially stupid. For all I knew, Meghan was walking into a *Get Out* situation. (By the way, wouldn't that make a fire sequel? An interracial horror flick set in Buckingham Palace . . .) Every time another tidbit from Meghan and Harry's adventures hit the *Daily Mail* or *People*, I was here for it. I felt like the

GIF of Michael Jackson eating popcorn at the movie theatre—you know the one—from *Thriller*.

But I wouldn't dare admit any of this to my thirty thousand followers on Twitter. What could be more problematic than getting irrationally excited about a mixed girl dating a rich white dude who got caught "playfully" wearing a swastika at a party way back when? Of course their relationship didn't prove anything about the state of race relations in Britain or the "evolution" of his views on race. And yet I found myself quietly cheering for them—and judging myself accordingly.

It's indisputable that many things have changed since Sidney Poitier's groundbreaking role in the 1967 film *Guess Who's Coming to Dinner* or the "controversial" kiss between Captain Kirk and Lieutenant Uhura in a 1968 episode of *Star Trek*. Nicole Ari Parker's film debut was as a black woman in an interracial lesbian romance. From director Mira Nair's *Mississippi Masala*, depicting love between Denzel Washington's fine ass and the gorgeous Indian American actress Sarita Choudhury, to weekly depictions of scandalous interracial sex on ABC's *Scandal* and powerful black bisexual women characters like Annalise from *How to Get Away with Murder* who link up with whomever the fuck they want, there are more diverse representations of interracial romance than ever before. One of my favorite recent portrayals of interracial love was in the short-lived but brilliant series *Sense8*, directed and produced by the Wachowski sisters, in which a black cisgender queer woman falls in love with a white transgender lesbian.

But beyond the bedroom, interracial intimacy also extends to the formation of meaningful friendships. The sad reality is that hundreds of millions of US citizens go their entire lives without forming meaningful, authentic friendships with people of another race. In large part, this is due to white people's active efforts to insulate themselves from people of color (euphemistically known as "white flight"). White people's preference for segregated lives (remember they built an entire system of racial apartheid to avoid sharing space with people of color?) plays a significant role in perpetuating racial stupidity and helping whites maintain a quasi-monopoly on economic, political, and social resources. Also? Segregation allows whites to protect themselves from interracial intimacy of all kinds.

Polling data reported in the *Washington Post* suggests that a whopping 75 percent of whites have no non-white friends whatsoever.[21] Further, whites' friendship networks are exponentially more racially restrictive than the peer groups of African Americans. According to Christopher Ingraham, "blacks have ten times as many black friends as white friends. But white Americans have an astonishing *91 times as many* white friends as black friends." Even more disturbingly, sociological research indicates that whites typically use their sporadic and "casual acquaintances" with people of color to behave in a racist manner "with a clear conscience."[22] In other words, for many whites, the functional role of their black or brown "friends" is to give themselves even more permission to be racist without viewing themselves as such.

In this context, some have questioned whether true interracial friendship is even possible—or advisable. Writing in *Salon*, black feminist scholar Brittney Cooper spoke to the difficulties of practicing vulnerability with white people in a racist society:

> I believe deeply in the power of friendship to make us better human beings. But interracial friendships, especially in adulthood, require a level of risk and vulnerability that many of us would rather simply not deal with. And that is perhaps one of racism's biggest casualties: Beyond the level of systemic havoc that racism wreaks on the material lives of people of color, in a million and one ways every day, it reduces the opportunity of all people to be more human.[23]

To be sure, interracial intimacy has its challenges. But there can also be particular joys as well. I find that discovering common ground with someone of a different racial or ethnic identity can be a surprisingly delightful experience. I've had fascinating discussions with my white Jewish friends about our unexpected cultural similarities despite our otherwise divergent experiences. And with my lady, I've been astonished to learn that a black bi girl from Tennessee could have so much in common with a half-white, half-Japanese lesbian who grew up between two continents. We both feel like citizens of the world and know what it's like to live outside the United States. We've bonded over our shared experiences of social exclusion—even though the causes of our exclusions were different. We both love being outside in nature, have an interest in synchronicity, and listen to random music like Deep Forest. Our tastes in wine, food, aesthetics, and humor largely overlap. When we moved in together, we discovered that we had many of the same books. We've created our own shared language composed of broken Japanese, Franglais, and ridiculous inside jokes.

But what we have is unique to us and involves an ongoing, daily commitment to nurturing our personal growth and contributing to our communities. It also involves telling the hard truths about power and oppression—and finding ways to sustain the trust required to bridge our differences.

Looking back on my own experiences with interracial intimacy, I no longer blindly romanticize interracial or intraracial dating. That's just plain stupid. But I do recommend *antiracist* dating and friendship, regardless of the background of the folks involved.

This morning, as I slept-walked to the bathroom to brush my teeth, Bae called out:

"Are you awake?"

"Huh?" I stopped in the hallway and peered at her with half-open eyes. She paused and smiled at me like a Cheshire cat.

"Are you still sleeping?"

"I mean, I need my coffee. What's going on?"

"Have you read the news?"

"Why baby? *Why?* What's going on?"

"I'll let you check the headlines."

"No! Just tell me, dammit. I'm awake now. What's up?"

"Did you hear about Meghan Markle?"

"DID SOMETHING HAPPEN TO HER?"

"Well—"

"Oh man, I hope nothing—"

"She's engaged to Prince Harry!"

"Oh my god!"

Suddenly I was awake as fuck. I squealed with delight, jumped for joy, and starting clapping like a maniac. Then I walked over to Bae, who was laughing hysterically, and hugged her.

Chapter 7

BECOMING RACIALLY LITERATE

If you've made it this far in the book, then you've faced a lot of uncomfortable truths, and I want to thank you for taking this journey with me. I know from personal experience that studying oppression and confronting racial stupidity can be terribly demoralizing. Coming to terms with systemic racism and interrelated forms of domination is not an easy thing for any of us. You might have felt challenged, offended, or shocked by some of what you've read. If you're a person of color or a veteran of the antiracist struggle, you might feel that some of your experiences, frustrations, and observations have been validated. At this point, you might be wondering where we go from here. Is a better world possible? Will we ever be able to get over the racial divide?

Well, I've got some good news and some bad news. The bad news is that I can't tell you that racism will ever come to an end—because no one really knows. I wish I could reassure you that "*We can end racism in our lifetime!,*" but I actually think those kinds of promises are misleading at best and counterproductive at worst. When we take the long view of human oppression, we are reminded that the history of human beings brutally exploiting each other is quite long. Recall, from the introduction, that modern humans have been on this planet for a couple hundred thousand years. Look around right now. This is what two hundred thousand years of "progress" has produced. Clearly, we have a long way to go.

The good news is that we don't actually have to believe in the possibility of a utopia to know that change is possible. There is no reason, logically speaking, why we must believe a system of oppression will or can end in our lifetime (or at all) in order to fight and struggle against it. Patriarchy has been in existence for thousands of years—much longer than modern racism. As a woman, I must struggle against patriarchy and sexism whether or not these obstacles will disappear in my lifetime. Class oppression is an ancient phenomenon. We don't have to delude ourselves that class bigotry and domination will be eradicated in order to enjoin the struggle against it. Our ancestors include people who fought against oppressive systems knowing they would not live to see the end of those systems. We can celebrate freedom fighters and abolitionists who envisioned the end of chattel slavery and brought about changes that others said were "impossible" while also acknowledging that neither slavery nor racism, nor any other form of oppression, has actually come to an end. There are, after all, still thirty million people enslaved across the globe, and the practice remains both racialized and legal in the United States today.[1]

Is it possible for the United States to become a nonracist country? There are certainly experts and activists who embrace this vision. It is clear to me, however, that as long as the United States exists as a settler-colonial state, it will remain racist. The Native predicament—the continued victimization of indigenous people by ongoing colonial occupation, racist ethnic cleansing, and land theft—gives people of conscience ample reason to be skeptical about the possibilities of surgically removing racism from a country built on the violent and symbolic negation of racialized minorities. And even if it were possible to surgically remove racism from the United States (or from the planet), we would still be left with the thorny problem of human beings' desire to hoard resources and dominate others. In fact, the impulse to channel resources to narrowly defined in-groups goes above and beyond the human condition. Biological research has shown that plants—*plants!*—demonstrate favoritism for their own "siblings" and discriminate against "foreign" plants.[2] I'd like to think that humans can figure out how to be more generous and inclusive than organisms without brains, but clearly we're not there yet.

Despite these stark realities, I am optimistic about all that we can do to collectively transform ourselves and our communities for the better. Becoming aware of our individual and collective racial stupidity is possible. Antiracist mobilization is still possible. Resistance is possible. Harm reduction is still possible. Building coalitions for the cause of justice is still possible. Creating joy and opportunities for love and connection is still possible. There are many things we all can do as individuals, organizations, and institutions to not only become more knowledgeable about systems of oppression but also to leverage our knowledge to bring about some of the positive change we'd like to see.

I've attended and spoken at a whole lot of events about the racial divide over the years. Inevitably, someone raises a hand during the Q&A and asks the assembled panel of experts a logical question: "*What exactly should I do now?*" I vividly remember being the person standing up in the auditorium, voice shaking, asking the burning question. And of course, these days, the question is often directed to me. Being educated about inequality and oppression can feel as if the weight of the world has been placed on your shoulders and now you've got to DO! SOMETHING! ABOUT IT! It's a positive sign to want an action plan that will explain how to put your newfound knowledge into practice and make this world a better place.

But this is what I'd tell my younger self: *No one is going to be able to explain to you, in a sound bite, what you should do to challenge racism.* They simply can't. The answer is going to vary for each individual, depending on your personality and background, interests, talents, and inclinations. So, it's *your* job to figure out how you can best leverage your knowledge and skills to help humanity.

And if you don't know the answer to this question quite yet, that's absolutely fine and, in fact, even a good thing. Because answering this question requires self-interrogation and thoughtfulness. So, take your time but commit to answering it. No one can solve this riddle for you.

To help you construct your antiracist path, let's consider some concrete steps all of us can take to not only address our racial ignorance but also bring about some of the antiracist change we'd like to see in the world. I'm going to argue that our capacity for creating positive social change depends on developing our racial literacy, so some of these action items involve exercises designed to increase your awareness and insight about the role of race and racism in shaping your life experiences, your relationships, your ways of thinking, your privileges (or lack thereof), and your access to resources. Becoming racially literate—that is, becoming less stupid about race—involves developing our critical thinking, increasing our awareness of how race permeates our lives, forming meaningful relationships across difference, and using our knowledge to organize for antiracist transformations. And it requires brutal honesty.

Racial oppression is a vast and complex subject—clearly, we've only begun to scratch the surface in this short book. I don't pretend to have all the answers, and I'm also in a continual process of deepening my knowledge and becoming more aware of my own blind spots. As an educator, I'm also acutely aware that teaching and learning the realities of racism have never been enough to end it—a bitter lesson the scholar-activist W. E. B. Du Bois came to accept after decades of trying to end racial ignorance through research and education. Nevertheless, attaining racial literacy really is a major prerequisite to organizing for antiracist transformation, which is why I'm passionate about empowering people with the tools to understand and remedy their own racial ignorance. We can acknowledge the limits of consciousness-raising while also understanding its importance. Coming to terms with systemic racism provides us with a lens for understanding the influence of our racist society on our ways of thinking and behaving. This insight is key, I believe, for moving beyond useless debates over "white guilt" or whether all white people are racist. Once you realize that a racist society inevitably socializes its citizens to absorb racist ideas and behave in a discriminatory way, then you're less likely to be preoccupied with adjudicating whether an individual is or is not "a racist." We're dealing with collective problems and institutionalized inequalities. In order to address these systemic forces, we're going to need to become racially literate and become more comfortable telling unflattering truths about our society. So, while education is not enough, it certainly has its place. Power structures must be disrupted in order to be changed, but, to paraphrase James Baldwin, we can only change those things we are willing to face.

One of the recurring themes in this book is the complicity of Republicans and Democrats in the maintenance of systemic racism. As early as 1956, W. E. B. Du Bois rejected both major parties in a blunt repudiation of their common record of disenfranchising marginalized people and promoting endless war. In a scorching piece published in the *Nation* entitled "I Won't Vote," Du Bois denounced the farcical nature of "liberal democracy" in the United States.[3] "I believe," Du Bois wrote, ominously, "that democracy has so far disappeared in the United States [and] that no 'two evils' exist. There is but one evil party with two names, and it will be elected despite all I can do or say." It is worth noting, as Du Bois explains in his essay, that he reached this accurate and grim assessment of the United States after spending a lifetime arguing in favor of "the lesser evil" and agitating for civil rights here and abroad.

Du Bois's appraisal would be echoed, years later, by Martin Luther King Jr., not in the famous "I Have a Dream" speech," which he gave the day after Du Bois's death, but in the year leading up to his own. Toward the end of his life, the actual Martin Luther King Jr.—not the watered-down caricature created by the ruling elite—came to fiercely oppose US militarism, capitalist exploitation, and state violence, and was, predictably, opposed by a rainbow coalition of militarist "liberals," including the NAACP and Dr. Ralph Bunche, as well as the *New York Times*.

Speaking on April 4, 1967, at the famous Riverside Church in Harlem, a year to the day before his assassination, King launched a searing critique of the United States' role in perpetrating multiple forms of injustice, oppression, and terror at home and abroad. The speech, "Beyond Vietnam: A Time to Break Silence," has been largely silenced by the same ruling elites King courageously wig-snatched and excoriated. I would urge you to not only read the speech in its entirety but to actually listen to it and hear Dr. King's erudite condemnation of the United States' role in perpetuating systemic racism, militarism, poverty, and war crimes.

The lamentable truth of King's description of the United States as the "greatest purveyor of violence in the world" grows exponentially more devastating with each passing year. King denounced the warmongering of the United States military as "demonic" and inextricably linked to the oppression of the poor. Recounting his own political transformation as he observed the unfolding horrors of the Vietnam War, he said: "I knew that America would never invest the necessary funds or energies in rehabilitation of its poor so long as adventures like Vietnam continued to draw men and skills and money like some demonic destructive suction tube. So, I was increasingly compelled to see the war as an enemy of the poor and to attack it as such."[4]

This Martin Luther King Jr., who, a decade earlier was still waxing poetic about the American Dream, began speaking openly about the reality of the American nightmare. From the pulpit of the Riverside Church, Dr. King warned:

> This business of burning human beings with napalm, of filling our nation's homes with orphans and widows, of injecting poisonous drugs of hate into the veins of peoples normally humane, of sending men home from dark and bloody battlefields physically handicapped and psychologically deranged,

> cannot be reconciled with wisdom, justice, and love. A nation that continues year after year to spend more money on military defense than on programs of social uplift is approaching spiritual death.[5]

Approaching spiritual death. Those words were spoken fifty years ago.

The United States would continue murdering, torturing, and raping civilians, children included, in Vietnam for *eight years* after the Riverside speech—*seven long years* after his untimely death. Over two million innocent Vietnamese civilians were needlessly murdered during the Vietnam War.

Though much of this book has centered the United States, I hope it is clear to you that we must think beyond our own borders. Those of us who feel moved by the call of justice would do well to listen to Dr. King's prophetic voice. The vision he articulated toward the end of his life linked systemic racism to militarism and capitalism. And, quiet as it's kept, King also supported independence movements throughout Africa and even traveled to Ghana to witness the inauguration of Kwame Nkrumah.[6] Bringing his internationalist perspective into dialogue with intersectionality provides a more holistic and progressive account of how racism manifests, not only in the United States but also through imperial domination and warfare stretching across the globe. In order to oppose racism, we have to actually be concerned with oppression writ large. This means drawing critical connections between the plight of people of color and the poor in the United States and the broader struggle for freedom and tolerance on our small planet. It means fighting ethnic and religious bigotry throughout Asia and standing in solidarity with the Roma in Europe as well as African migrants. It means denouncing the immoral violence of anti-Semitism as well as Israel's immoral destruction of the Palestinian people. It means taking a stand against ethnocentrism and genocide in Rwanda and standing up against antiblack racism in Brazil, Latin America, and the Arab world. As antiracists, we have to cultivate concern and compassion for the suffering marginalized people in our own communities and on the other side of the world.

It's easy to see why people of color would benefit from dismantling white supremacy, but what incentive do whites have to join the struggle for racial justice? After all, why would anyone willingly give up hoarding ten to twelve times the wealth of people of color or maintaining a quasi-monopoly on political power? We've already examined how white elites use white supremacist racism to marginalize working-class and poor whites. But I would argue that even middle-class and wealthy whites are ultimately at risk in a system based on violence, immorality, greed, and exploitation. Some of the techniques of surveillance, policing, social control, eugenics, and dispossession used against indigenous people, enslaved Africans, and people of color throughout US history have also been wielded against members of the majority population. Poor whites, for example, have been the targets of forced sterilization.[7]

The cynic in me is very cognizant of the fact that dominant groups do not usually give up power. To quote Frederick Douglass: "Power concedes nothing without a demand." And, yet, I am also convinced, as we have seen both historically and in the present, that select members of a dominant group can transcend their narrow identities and recognize our interdependence. From this interconnected web-of-existence perspective, the fight for racial justice is not just something that will help people of color—it's vital for our collective well-being and maybe even for the survival of life on this planet. Some of the benefits of eradicating the racial hierarchy include

- Shared prosperity
- Improving our understanding of power relations
- Gaining insight into multiple forms of domination
- Heightening social and historical awareness

- Improving one's moral standing
- Promoting empathy and compassion
- Reducing social isolation
- Diffusing anxiety and fear of the "other"
- Building multicultural competence in an increasingly diverse world

And that's just for starters. What would you add to this list?

While each person's individual path will differ, here are ten suggestions for steps we can all take, right now, to build a less racist—and racially stupid—society. Most of these recommendations can also be implemented by organizations, communities of faith, businesses, and other groups that are ready to begin the hard work of undoing racism.

1. RELINQUISH MAGICAL THINKING.

This one's hard. Really hard. But it's so important that I'm listing it first. People often tell me things like "*You'd think our society would be over racism by now!*" I want to respond, "Why? Because you've been personally working to end it? Or because you thought someone else would do the work you're not doing?" Listen. I know it's tempting to wish racism away—to just sort of assume that there's an inevitability to progress. But if you want to be less stupid about race, you need to let that shit go right now. There is no quick fix for racism. Go back and read that sentence. Then tell a friend. *There's! No! Quick! Fix!* None. There are lots of reasons why people persist in believing, against all evidence, that racism can be magically erased. They may conclude that since racism doesn't look like it did four hundred years ago, that it will eventually disappear, like diseases we've eradicated. Alas, no.

Other reasons surely have to do with cognitive dissonance and mechanisms of denial; that is, racial oppression is so intrinsically violent, so ghastly and inhumane, that facing it in its full, catastrophic splendor is almost more than the mind can handle. And so, given that it's human nature to avoid what's unpleasant, many minds do not handle it at all. And then there are those who cling to the fantasy that racism can be easily eradicated simply because they've never studied it—and so they are unfamiliar with the scope of its historical, economic, psychological, sociological, environmental, and health dynamics.

But for the sake of a thought experiment, let's just pretend that we could, somehow, suddenly eradicate racial prejudice from the minds of every human being on the face of the planet. Imagine, for example, that Will Smith and Tommy Lee Jones came down from the heavens, à la *Men in Black*, flashed a bright white light and made us all forget every concept related to race or racism. (This would be every white liberal's dream—a world where we could say we "don't see race" and not be lying!) Well, I hate to break it to ya, but even the complete erasure of racial prejudice in the contemporary era would not be enough to undo the harm of racial injustice or disassociate resources from skin tone. As sociologists Dalton Conley, Devah Pager, and Hana Shepherd have already pointed out, the ongoing effects of past discrimination (such as racist policies, redlining, and restrictive housing covenants) would continue to reproduce the racial wealth gap (and related disparities) even in the absence of present-day discriminatory behavior.[8] It's also easy to see that the persistence of color-based disparities (and patterns of segregation) would very likely lead to the reemergence of color prejudice after the bright white light wore off. And even if material resources were somehow redistributed and patterns of segregation dismantled (through some combination of magic, reparations, or radical social reorganization), we would still be left with flawed human beings, the same folks who have been enslaving, dominating, raping, and murdering one another for millennia.

If you want to pursue the cause of social justice, *give up the need for quick fixes and gird your loins for a long struggle.* To sustain your work for the long haul, you'll have to build up your reserves of resilience, self-care, community care, and courage. You'll have to nurture your capacity for hope, humor, love, and connection, even, and especially, in the midst of oppression. What keeps me going, personally, is a deep and abiding commitment to spiritual practice and my experience of God's presence—not in a specific church, temple, or other place of worship but in every face and every situation I encounter in this life. Laughter helps too. As does friendship. And meditation. And spending time in nature. And really good wine.

2. CRITICALLY ASSESS YOUR RACIAL SOCIALIZATION.

If you want to be an antiracist change agent, you're going to have to think long and hard about your own racial socialization. Most of us were not taught to acknowledge the impact of racial ideas, scripts, and behavior on our upbringing and values, but that's the kind of internal work that's required for addressing racism. It's easier to pretend that racism is someone else's problem, but the truth is that none of us is immune. I like to joke that many whites, perhaps especially liberals, are prone to believing this myth: *I am magically untouched by the racist society that socialized me.* But there are also minorities who pretend to be exempt from the dynamics of internalized oppression or the scourge of colorism and prejudice. We have all been in the sunken place, and it does us no good to claim otherwise.

In chapter 2, we explored some of the insights of the groundbreaking black feminist text *All the Women Are White, All the Blacks Are Men, but Some of Us Are Brave*, edited by Akasha Hull, Patricia Bell Scott, and Barbara Smith. The volume includes an excellent chapter with practical guidelines for racial consciousness-raising that promote "personal sharing, risk taking and involvement" in order to create political change through personal awareness and transformation. The authors suggest spending time reflecting on and answering over thirty questions related to your childhood, early adult experiences, and involvement in activism. Although the questions are primarily geared toward white women's racial consciousness-raising, I think they could be useful to folks from a wide variety of backgrounds—including people of color. Examples include

- When were you first aware that there was such a thing as race and racial differences? How old were you? Recall an incident if you can.
- What kind of contact did you have with people of different races?
- How did you first experience racism? From whom did you learn it? How did it function in your perception of yourself?
- When were you first aware that there was such a thing as anti-Semitism?
- What kind of messages did you get about race as you entered adolescence? Did your group of friends change?
- When you were growing up, what kind of information did you get about Black people through the media? How much of it was specifically about Black men?[9]

The authors also suggest completing a weekly "homework" exercise to record racist incidents you see, hear, and observe in your daily life. You might also fruitfully expand the exercise to simply include "racial" incidents or events of any kind and also be mindful, and honest, about racist *thoughts* that you find yourself having. You could record your observations in a journal and share your reflections with trusted friends. This kind of racial consciousness-raising can also be revelatory for people who genuinely believe that racism is not relevant to their lives.[10]

In addition to answering the reflection questions mentioned above, I also recommend checking out Project Implicit, an online collaborative project developed by researchers at the University of Virginia, the University of Washington, and Harvard. I don't want to spoil it for you, but suffice it to say that the exercises in Project Implicit are designed to shed light on a wide variety of hidden biases. I use it as a teaching tool in my Ethnic and Race Relations course at Stony Brook and think everyone should give it a go.[11]

The more aware we are of our racial socialization, the more empowered we are to challenge our biases and our conditioning. This is life-long work, and I recommend using the tools of midfulness and meditation to cultivate compassion for yourself and others as you embark on this journey.

3. START OR JOIN AN ANTIRACIST STUDY GROUP AND SHARE WHAT YOU LEARN ABOUT SYSTEMIC RACISM.

Owning up to our racial stupidity already puts us ahead of the game vis à vis the vast majority of the population. But we can't just wallow in our ignorance. Making a long-term commitment to challenging racism also requires a lifetime of learning. Even as an educator and an expert on racism, I am constantly seeking out new information to address gaps in my knowledge and am humbled by how much more I have to learn. Just the other day I learned that the first Europeans were brown-skinned Africans who arrived from the motherland forty thousand years ago and that "white" or pale skin did not become widespread among Europeans until about eight thousand years ago.[12] This completely upends our conventional thinking about whiteness and Europeanness. Recent DNA analysis also indicates that the first British settlers had dark skin, dark curly hair—and blue eyes.[13] I mean, damn. *The more you know.*

If you have a leadership role in an organization, institution, or corporation you can help by investing in educational resources. As part of your antiracism curriculum, be sure to integrate an intersectional approach. As explained in chapter 2, antiracists must draw connections between systemic racism and other axes of domination (e.g., class oppression, (hetero)sexism, and ableism to name a few). As you commit to learning about systemic racism, you should also think critically about the links between racial injustice, capitalist oppression, and sexism—a recurring theme throughout this book.

Another topic of study includes your local history of racial oppression. Have you investigated the dynamics of racial oppression and segregation in your neighborhood and state? What about racist practices or policies at your place of employment or your educational institutions? You could take concrete steps toward challenging systemic racism by uncovering how it manifests within your own social spheres—and pushing for new practices and policies to redress disparities and injustice. What I'm suggesting here is a little different from examining your racial socialization and experiences. Instead, I'm urging you to start digging into history. I would recommend paying special attention to the history of the indigenous populations in your hometown or state and to the history of settler-colonialism, the latter of which has continually dispossessed native peoples from their land and exposed them to systemic state violence. Also, understand the connection between historical violence against indigenous people and present-day disparities. Here's a little-known fact for you. According to the Center on Juvenile and Criminal Justice, Native Americans are killed by police at a higher rate per capita than *any* other racial or ethnic group.[14] Given what we know about the inherent violence of settler-colonialism, do you really think this statistic is a coincidence?

Look into your local histories of slavery and abolitionism to get a sense of whether and to what extent racist violence, segregation, or restrictive covenants favored whites and excluded people of color in your town. Just as important? The history of antiracist struggles and mobilizations in your locality. Were there activists or rebellions that stood up against the racial power structure? Take a trip to your neighborhood library or bookstore (assuming it has not yet been put out of business by Amazon) and see what you can find out.

As we learn about systemic racism and the social construction of race, we should take the next step and share our knowledge with others. Have you heard the phrase “Each one, teach one”? Well, that “one” is you. The next time you hear someone claim that she “doesn’t see color,” understand that the person is really saying she doesn’t see racism. And, even better, *tell the person that this is what she is saying.* That is, it is impossible to overcome racism by issuing empty calls to “unify” or attempting to erase our differences. Challenging racial oppression requires acknowledging the divisions that are already there—and taking active steps to remedy these divisions. David Oppenheimer, a legal scholar and social justice advocate, puts it this way: “Racism-awareness requires us to be sensitive to the continuing effects of racism in our society.”[15] Whether we like it or not, racial prejudice and racist ideology have already “colored” the mental maps and lenses we use to navigate the social world. And, let’s face it: white supremacy is, by definition, divisive; it is a system of violence that unjustly divides our resources, routinely favors whites, and excludes people of color. While it would be lovely to live in a world where these divisions did not exist, that is not the world we live in now. If we are going to change this world, we are going to need people like you—yes, you—to see the dynamics of systemic racism clearly. We certainly don’t need more folks falsely claiming to be immune to the forces of racial prejudice and bigotry.

As you learn about systemic racism, you can begin to take an active role in combating racial denial by raising racial awareness (and most importantly, racism-awareness). Think about your own community and social connections and look for opportunities to share resources. We already know that large majorities of white people (and a smaller proportion of people of color) actively deny the existence of racial discrimination in a variety of spheres. To take just one example, nearly 70 percent of whites actually believe that blacks and whites are treated equally in the workplace, while only 34 percent of blacks hold this view.[16] It’s not especially surprising that lots of white folks are living in a racial fantasyland composed of alternate facts, but we also need to talk about the *one-third of African Americans* who fail to acknowledge racial discrimination and disadvantage in employment, despite decades of research and activism addressing the persistence of racial discrimination and disadvantage in employment. Do you know anyone in denial about the existence of systemic racism? Who could you help enlighten?

Consider bringing in antiracist experts and activists to educate members of organizations to which you belong. Through consciousness-raising, we can collectively move from an epistemology of racial ignorance to an epistemolgoy of racial awareness.

4. EMPOWER YOUNG PEOPLE TO UNDERSTAND SYSTEMIC RACISM.

Howard Stevenson, a clinical psychologist and expert on racial conflict, suggests that adults go about the work of raising their own racial awareness *before* attempting to discuss race and racism with children.[17] This makes sense on an intuitive level, right? Of course it is easier to talk about race and racism with young people if you've already begun the work of addressing your own racial socialization and feelings of awkwardness or even trauma. But you may have noticed that we humans typically dislike uncomfortable situations and topics, so, many parents, including parents of color, avoid directly discussing racial discrimination and injustice with their children. And in some cases, parents of color—like my mom—decide not to talk about race in an effort to protect their kids from exposure to racist ideas. There is, of course, empirical evidence to support these concerns. The risk of experiencing diminished performance and deflated feelings of self-efficacy as a result of being aware that members of your group are viewed negatively (e.g., as less intelligent) is known as *stereotype threat*, a concept coined by social psychologist Claude Steele. The phenomenon applies not only to racial minorities but to other kinds of stigmatized groups as well (women included). The question of whether and when to address the harsh realities of racism with children is a tricky matter, but many experts agree that it is important to provide young people with age-appropriate information about the existence of racism. In part, this is because research has demonstrated, time and time again, that children begin to pick up society's harmful prejudices at an early age. One of the most well-known studies in this genre was the famous "doll test," designed and conducted in the 1940s by Mamie and Kenneth Clark, two African American psychologists (and a married couple) who demonstrated that white and black children *as young as three years old* expressed preferences for white dolls and negative attitudes toward black dolls.[18] Some research has even indicated that *three-month-old infants* observe differences in skin tone and show evidence of racial bias.[19]

The bottom line is that living in a racist society involves being exposed to racial beliefs and discriminatory behavior very early in life—even before we are conscious of our own identities. As a result, we need to reflect on our own experiences, become more comfortable talking about our racial memories, and discuss the historical, social, and psychological dynamics of racism with young people. An actionable step in this direction might include seeking out educational resources for addressing racism with children. (Hint: Ask them questions about their own experiences and observations before launching into a history lesson!)[20] And, perhaps most importantly, help ensure that children and adolescents in your sphere of influence understand that race is not just about "skin color" or "seeing race." It's a systemic problem that's going to require collective mobilization to bring about enduring change—and youth have an important role to play in dismantling white supremacy.

5. RECOGNIZE AND REJECT FALSE EQUIVALENCIES.

One of the most dangerous—and pervasive—forms of racial ignorance is the insistence on drawing a false equivalency between being a member of the racial majority group and a member of a racial minority group. The myth of color blindness, which rose to prominence after the civil rights movement, relies on erasing the difference between those who benefit from white supremacy and those who suffer from its pathological effects. The most prominent form of this false equivalency is the dumbass idea of "reverse racism," the notion that people of color who hold prejudiced views or even behave in a discriminatory manner are "racist" in the same way that white people are racist.[21] James Baldwin already wig-snatched this foolishness in his 1972 book *No Name in the Street*, in which he writes: "The powerless, by definition, can never be 'racists,' for they can never make the world pay for what they feel or fear except by the suicidal endeavor that makes them fanatics or revolutionaries, or both; whereas, those in power can be urbane and charming and invite you to those houses which they know you will never own."[22] What Baldwin meant to convey here was the different positionality of the powerful and the powerless. While everyone socialized in a racist society is exposed to racist ideas and can decide to collude with the racial order, the fact remains that racism is not an equal opportunity affair. Only people who belong to a racially dominant group (or groups) can benefit from systemic racism.

Of course, anyone can be prejudiced. Anyone can be a jackass. But in a white supremacist society, only people socially defined as white—those who benefit from white supremacy—can occupy the structural position of a racist. With that said, it is absolutely true that nonwhites can perpetuate racist ideas, can cooperate with white supremacy, and can express prejudiced beliefs. Nonwhites can also exercise dominance and oppression along related axes of oppression (e.g., class, gender, sexuality, and ability). But nonwhites, at the present time, do not have the economic or political power to exercise or collectively benefit from systemic racism in the United States, and this, after all, is what it means to be racist. In order to promote the cause of racial justice, antiracists need to recognize and actively reject false equivalencies between dominant and dominated groups.

6. DISRUPT RACIST PRACTICES. GET COMFORTABLE CALLING SHIT OUT.

If you're not making powerful white people uncomforable, you're doing antiracism wrong. Many people of color are already accustomed to not only experiencing racism but also bearing the burden of calling the shit out. And quite frankly, we're tired of this shit. This is particularly true for those of us who study or work in predominately white institutions. Let the record reflect: white supremacy persists, to a great degree, because of white folks' refusal to aggressively challenge other whites on their racism. Because most whites live highly segregated lives, they typically face great social pressure to maintain smooth relations with white friends, family members, and coworkers—including those who routinely express racist views and behave in a discriminatory manner. What this means is that white folks' need to protect white comfort and help other whites save face poses a serious obstacle to racial justice. If you're white and you want to do more than pay lip service to dismantling racism, you're going to have to become more comfortable with difficult conversations and conflict—particularly with the white racists in your circle. You remember that study by sociologists Leslie Picca and Joe Feagin that I keep referring to in this book? Their research suggests that it is easier and more effective for whites to call out white racism when they are joined by even just one other white ally.

So, white people: y'all need to team up with your antiracist homies, leverage your social influence, stand up against racist behavior, and be willing to make your racist family members, friends, and/or colleagues uncomfortable. Even more to the point: white folks need to make a proactive decision to do this work, rather than rely on people of color (who are already subject to the terror of racial violence) to pick up your slack and carry the burden of dismantling oppression. Make heroes out of antiracists. Follow in the bold tradition of fierce critics of white supremacy like Jane Elliott, a white teacher from Iowa who was so devastated by the murder of Martin Luther King Jr. that she famously decided to teach her class of white third-grade students about racism by arbitrarily dividing them by the color of their eyes.[23] In very little time, Elliott saw her young students gleefully and almost immediately engage in discriminatory behavior against their classmates on the basis of made-up stereotypes about eye color. The effects were so strong that students' classroom performance actually decreased when they were told that their eye color made them less intelligent. Since 1968, Elliott's social experiment has been repeated across the globe among countless audiences, and for five decades, she has been on a campaign to raise awareness about white supremacy and systemic racism. A fierce advocate for social justice, Elliott is completely unafraid to tell it like it is:

> I think white people aren't aware that racism isn't just wearing white hoods and burning crosses. It's also fixing the system so that black votes don't get counted. It's refusing to open the polling places in precincts where most of the eligible voters are people of color. It's outlawing affirmative action at the state level even though it has proven successful. It's building more prisons than we build schools and guaranteeing that they will be filled by targeting young men of color with things like the "three strikes" legislation in California and the DWB—"driving while black." These are problems encountered by young black men all over this country. It's the fact that there are more children attending segregated schools in the US today than there were previous to *Brown v. Board of Education*. It's white flight and red-lining by financial institutions. It's television programming that portrays people of color as villains and white people as their victims. It's ballot-security systems, which are used to intimidate minority voters and so result in the very activities which they are supposedly designed to prevent.[24]

We need more white people like Jane Elliott.

7. GET ORGANIZED! SUPPORT THE WORK OF ANTIRACIST ORGANIZATIONS, EDUCATORS, AND ACTIVISTS.

We can all make a commitment to supporting groups and activists who are doing the work, day in and day out, to dismantle white supremacy and related forms of domination. One of the central lessons of this book is the deceptively simple, yet widely ignored, insight that racism is structural and systemic. The most intelligent way to address a systemic problem is to approach it *systematically*, which involves organizing and mobilizing collective action. It's important to know that we cannot effectively bring about racial transformation through individual action alone—we have to work together with like-minded people. Even if you aren't a big fan of joining groups, you can certainly learn about and support their work. I recommend identifying organizations that draw intersectional connections between racial oppression, class inequality, and other axes of domination, such as Project NIA (which works to radically reduce the detention and incarceration of young people), Black Lives Matter, the African American Policy Forum, and the Transgender Law Center. This year, 2018, is the fiftieth anniversary of Martin Luther King Jr.'s Poor People's Campaign, which sought to bridge civil rights activism with the cause of economic justice. You might consider joining efforts led by the Reverend Dr. William Barber II to revive King's campaign and galvanize a long overdue moral transformation in this country. You could send a donation to the Southern Poverty Law Center or UnidosUS (formerly known as the National Council of La Raza). White readers may want to specifically seek out a white antiracist organization, such as SURJ (Showing Up for Racial Justice). You might support the intellectual and political labor of freedom fighters and radical dreamers organizing to abolish capitalist oppression, prisons, and even the police. If all of this sounds extreme or naive to you (as it did to me, initially), at least take the time to learn more about why imagining a way of relating to each other and solving our social problems without economic parasitism, prisons, state violence, or policing is valuable.[25] The W. K. Kellogg Foundation maintains a racial equity resource guide and a list of organizations working to bring about antiracist change. Check it out.[26]

8. AMPLIFY THE VOICES OF BLACK WOMEN, INDIGENOUS WOMEN, AND WOMEN OF COLOR.

You may be wondering why I didn't just say "*Amplify the voices of black people and people of color.*" Well, the reality is that men's voices are (still) amplified over women as a matter of course. If we're going to get serious about disrupting racism, we're going to need to center intersectionality. This means lifting up and learning from nonwhite women and femmes, particularly disabled women, queer women, trans women, and working-class and poor women of color. It's two-thousand-fucking-eighteen, y'all. We can no longer afford to collectively treat the unique oppression of black women and women of color as a side issue or keep on crowning an uninterrupted series of black and brown men as the spokespeople for the Race Problem. It was generous, I suppose, of Toni Morrison to refer to Ta-Nehisi Coates as the "James Baldwin" of our generation, but every generation doesn't need a James Baldwin. We do not need black men and men of color to play the role of the latest White Liberal Whisperer. We can do better. We can actually listen to black women and women of color.

Read and support the work of a wide variety of racially marginalized women like Shailja Patel, Sara Ahmed, Janet Mock, Audre Lorde, Lorraine Hansberry, Kimberlé Crenshaw, Ijeoma Oluo, Issa Rae, Mona Eltahawy, and Rokhaya Diallo. Stop treating black women and women of color like afterthoughts. You can challenge a great deal of racial stupidity today simply by centering women's experiences in discussions about racial oppression. *Say our names.* We compose about half of the human species. Even if women were a tiny demographic minority, our erasure would still be a crime. And don't just gobble up our knowledge—pay black women and women of color appropriately.

9. SHIFT RESOURCES TO MARGINALIZED PEOPLE.

Over the course of several centuries, our society has become exceedingly accustomed to channeling social, economic, and political resources to people socially defined as white (and especially to white men). Favoring whites and withholding resources from nonwhites has long been a well-established cultural norm. If we're ever going to challenge systemic racism, we're going to change that norm, and that requires changing how we distribute a whole host of things—access to high quality education, health care, jobs, money, wealth, time, opportunities, citizenship, and, yes, respect. To put it bluntly, we will have to stop overvaluing whiteness and undervaluing people of color. Concretely, this requires collectively divesting from what Cheryl Harris calls the *property interest in whiteness* and working with antiracists to change our cultural heritage of normalizing white folks' economic, social, and political dominance. Together, we can do the hard work of establishing a new cultural norm—one of shared wealth, prosperity, and equity. It's not enough to talk about antiracism or reflect on our racial socialization. We have to commit to actively shifting resources to marginalized people—and not just people of color. Following in the footsteps of Combahee River Collective and Martin Luther King Jr., we have to link the struggles of the working class and poor to the exploitation of racialized minorities.

What does this look like in practice? Institutions, organizations, politicians, and everyday citizens can all make it a regular, ongoing practice to look for ways of disrupting the status quo by investing material, cultural, social, and political resources into vulnerable communities. This kind of transformation might take the form of reparations or innovative policy proposals like baby bonds.[27] But it can also look like creating opportunities to hire and increase the salaries of minorities, rolling back the excess greed that drives neoliberalism, expanding the safety net, providing Medicare for all, and ensuring that we invest more in education and our collective well-being than in warfare, policing, and mass incarceration. All too often, businesses, universities, and political groups content themselves with diversity at the lowest levels of power and normalize the continued dominance of white men at the top. This needs to change. Political and economic resources should be redistributed throughout our society—and this includes shifting away from the norm of white male hegemony to a new norm of shared prosperity and diverse leadership.

10. CHOOSE AN AREA OF IMPACT THAT LEVERAGES YOUR UNIQUE TALENTS.

Learning about any axis of oppression (much less multiple axes of oppression!) can feel overwhelming and daunting, to say the least. That's why it's so important to recognize that you cannot take on all the troubles of the world. No one can wave a magic wand and make human suffering disappear—and we're only on this planet for an infinitesimally short moment in time. When students ask me for direction, I try to convey to them the importance of choosing an area of impact that bridges their interests with their unique talents. But in order to do this, you have to invest some time and energy in self-exploration. No one can tell you what your purpose is (that's your job), but if you are having a hard time narrowing down your talents, you might ask friends, family members, and mentors to help you identify your gifts and strengths. Perhaps you have a knack for artistic expression, a facility with numbers, a photographic memory, or an interest in history. How can you leverage your set of skills and talents to help improve society? Answering this question can help you figure out what piece of the social justice puzzle you want to focus on, knowing that you can't do everything. You should also remember that your answer to this question can change over time. Maybe you get involved with political activism for a while and then move on to empowering communities of color through education or health-care advocacy. You don't have to be a "single-issue" antiracist, but I do recommend selecting a few areas to build your knowledge and maximize your impact.

Octavia Butler, the great science fiction writer, was once asked to comment on the possibility of a world without racism. Her initial response suggested that "nothing—nothing at all" could make human beings become more tolerant and let go of racist beliefs and behavior.[28] In constructing her argument, Butler pointed to certain problems at the core of the human experience—our proclivity for hierarchies and feelings of superiority, a toxic desire that stretches back as far as recorded history can reach. "Simple peck-order bullying," she says, "is only the beginning of the kind of hierarchical behavior that can lead to racism, sexism, ethnocentrism, classism, and all the other 'isms' that cause so much suffering in the world." Was Butler suggesting that we give up the fight against our baser instincts? Not quite.

> Of course, we can resist acting on our nastier hierarchical tendencies. Most of us do that most of the time already. And we can make a greater effort to teach children to resist their hierarchical impulses and beliefs. . . . Will this work? Well, it hasn't so far. Too many people will not, perhaps cannot, do it. There is, unfortunately, satisfaction to be enjoyed in feeling superior to other people. . . . Amid all this, does tolerance have a chance?
>
> Only if we want it to. Only when we want it to. Tolerance, like any aspect of peace, is forever a work in progress, never completed, and, if we're as intelligent as we like to think we are, never abandoned.

Butler's point here is that nothing can *force* human beings to turn away from hierarchical thinking and oppressive behavior. How do we know this to be true? The history books—and the evening news. And complete eradication of human hierarchies and systems of domination might not be possible either. But she calls for us to undertake a mission, to enjoin a very long struggle.

The outcome of this struggle is uncertain. Nothing is promised. But no matter how impossible the odds may seem, no matter how daunting the history of oppression feels, change is always possible. Although we can't wave a magic wand and make all the suffering in this world disappear, we do have options and agency. What we have right now is the capacity to act, to learn, and to grow beyond our limitations, to recognize that our fates are deeply intertwined. We can admit our ignorance. We can listen to people who experience forms of oppression we will never know. We can notice when we are tempted to look down on someone else—for any reason at all—and see in this ancient temptation the seeds of oppression. We can make better choices. We can call out injustice and disrupt oppressive systems. We can identify allies and mobilize for change. We can be courageous. We can generate compassion for ourselves and others, build community and nurture our well-being even in the midst of great suffering. We can imagine a less harmful world, one in which white supremacy and heteropatriarchy and class oppression no longer exist, where love and interdependence are valued above power and dominance. The amazing thing about being alive is that we can imagine this world, even if we never live to see it. And we can choose to commit ourselves, moment by moment, day after day, to the always unfinished work of overcoming.

Acknowledgments

This book, like all books, owes its existence to a community of supporters, friends, and loved ones who made it possible. I gratefully acknowledge Michael Bourret, my kickass agent, who found the absolute perfect home for this project. Thank you, Michael, for believing in my voice. I could not have asked for a more supportive team at Beacon Press, led by the brilliant Gayatri Patnaik along with Molly Velazquez-Brown and Maya Fernandez. I feel privileged to have written this book with the editorial support and guidance of three women of color from such diverse backgrounds. Your perspectives, suggestions, and questions were incredibly generative, and I'm still in awe of how often we were all on the same page.

The Critical Race and Intersectionality Reading Group at Stony Brook was a productive and helpful forum for me as I worked out some of the core ideas in this book. Warm gratitude to the graduate student coordinators, Caglar Cetin and Adam Safer, as well as to the participants, including Vanessa Lynn, Hewan Girma, Aida Nikou, Magdala Desgranges, and Jessie Daniels. Much appreciation to Terri Francis for pointing me to Nell Painter's book, *Sojourner Truth: A Life, a Symbol*, referenced in Chapter 2. Several invited talks (at Trinity College and Wellesley College) also allowed me to share some of the work in progress. Thank you to the friends and colleagues who made time to read portions of this manuscript, including Leah Perry, William Darity Jr., Chinyere Osuji, and Jessie Daniels. Of course, any errors or nonsense in these pages fall on my shoulders, not theirs.

Much love to my small but powerful tribe: Mom, Ainee, Anna, Isaac, Stan, Joy, Lori, and Jonathan. Thank you to my ancestors for existing and surviving. Deep gratitude to Mooji and Joel Goldsmith, my spiritual teachers, for deepening my conscious awareness of God's presence. My mother, Barbara Moore, pored over every single one of these chapters and offered honest, incisive feedback that drastically improved the manuscript. Much appreciation to Aldon Morris for being an inspiration and helping me believe that I have something important to say. Vilna has been encouraging me to write beyond the academy for years, and so I thank her for pushing me to conquer my fears and do the damn thing.

Given that portions of this book developed from reflections I first shared on Twitter, I would be remiss if I didn't thank all of y'all holding it down in these tweets. I learn so much from the thousands of people across the globe who interact with me on social media and appreciate your support, your engagement, and even your criticism. Thank you for snatching *my* wig when needed.

Last, but certainly not least, I gratefully acknowledge my partner, Kei Petersen, for her fierce and unshakeable belief in me and this project. Kei: You've been with me every step of the way, through all of the highs and the lows and all the working titles. You encouraged me (again and again) when I thought this thing would never see the light of day. You read every word, sometimes more than once. You sharpened my thinking with your questions, insights, and objections. You picked up my slack with the household chores while I got lost in the writing—and then held me accountable for getting my shit together and doing my fair share of our domestic labor. You've taught me what the daily action of love looks like. I'm so blessed to have you in my life. Thank you for the gifts of your wisdom, light, humor, and of course—your abiding hope.

Notes

INTRODUCTION: THE ORIGINS OF RACIAL STUPIDITY

Some material for the introduction was originally published as a blog on *Huffington Post*: "#RaceTogether and the Harm of Racial Ignorance," March 19, 2015, https://www.huffingtonpost.com/crystal-fleming/race together-and-the-harm-of-racial-ignorance_b_6895070.html.

1. Martin Luther King Jr., *Where Do We Go from Here: Chaos or Community?* (1967; Boston: Beacon Press, 2010).

2. Brennan Williams, "Common Says Black People Showing Love to White People Is the Cure to Racism," *Huffington Post*, March 18, 2015, https://www.huffingtonpost.com/2015/03/18/common-white-people-cure-to-racism_n_6895864.html.

3. On inaccuracies about race and racism within US textbooks, see James W. Loewen, *Lies My Teacher Told Me: Everything Your American History Textbook Got Wrong* (New York: New Press, 2008).

4. Lilly Workneh, "Starbucks CEO Howard Schultz Takes Powerful Step to Discuss Race with Employees," *Huffington Post, Black Voices*, December 17, 2014, http://www.huffingtonpost.com/2014/12/17/starbucks-howard-schultz-race_n_6344164.html.

5. Twitter post from Starbucks, March 17 2015, https://twitter.com/Starbucks/status/577920416238428160.

6. Michael Tanenbaum, "Protests over Controversial Arrests at Center City Starbucks; Police Commissioner Says Officers Did Nothing Wrong," *Philly Voice*, April 14, 2018, http://www.phillyvoice.com/starbucks-arrest-philadelphia-center-city-police-investigating/.

7. Jill Disis, "Starbucks Will Close 8,000 US Stores May 29 for Racial Bias Training," *CNN Money*, April 17, 2018, http://money.cnn.com/2018/04/17/news/companies/starbucks-store-closings-racial-bias-education/index.html.

8. On the dynamics of stereotype threat, see Claude Steele, *Whistling Vivaldi: And Other Clues to How Stereotypes Affect Us* (New York: W. W. Norton, 2011).

9. For insight into the social dynamics of the kind of Pentecostal church I grew up in, see Judith Casselberry, *The Labor of Faith: Gender and Power in Black Apostolic Pentecostalism*, (Durham, NC: Duke University Press, 2017).

While Casselberry's study examines the Church of Our Lord Jesus Christ of the Apostolic Faith, based in Harlem, New York, I attended a similar (and rival) denomination called the Church of the Lord Jesus Christ of the Apostolic Faith, headquartered in Philadelphia, Pennsylvania. On the bullying of Muslim girls in school, see Akinyi Ochieng, "Muslim Schoolchildren Bullied by Fellow Students and Teachers," *CodeSwitch*, NPR, March 29, 2017, http://www.npr.org/sections/codeswitch/2017/03/29/515451746/muslim-school children-bullied-by-fellow-students-and-teachers.

10. Ann Morning, "Toward a Sociology of Racial Conceptualization for the 21st Century," *Social Forces* 87, no. 3 (March 2009): 1167–92.

11. On the historical construction of whiteness, see Nell I. Painter, *The History of White People* (New York: W. W. Norton, 2010), and Noel Ignatiev, *How the Irish Became White* (New York: Routledge, 1995).

12. See Cheryl Harris, "Whiteness as Property," *Harvard Law Review* 106, no. 8 (1993): 1707–91; George M. Fredrickson, *White Supremacy: A Comparative Study of American and South African History* (New York: Oxford University Press, 1982); Charles W. Mills, *The Racial Contract* (Ithaca, NY: Cornell University Press, 1997). Fredrickson defines white supremacy as "attitudes, ideologies and policies associated with the rise of blatant forms of white or European dominance over 'nonwhite' populations." (xi) On global white supremacy and racial domination in France, see Crystal M. Fleming, *Resurrecting Slavery: Racial Legacies and White Supremacy in France* (Philadelphia: Temple University Press, 2017).

13. See Theodore W. Allen, *The Invention of the White Race, Vol. 1: Racial Oppression and Social Control* (London: Verso, 1994). In a widely cited formulation printed on the back of his book, Allen provocatively wrote, "When the first Africans arrived in Virginia in 1619, there were no 'white' people there. Nor, according to colonial records, would there be for another sixty years."

14. On the racialization of European ethnic groups, see David Roediger, *Working Toward Whiteness: How America's Immigrants Became White: The Strange Journey from Ellis Island to the Suburbs* (New York: Basic Books, 2006); Nell Irvin Painter, *The History of White People* (New York: W. W. Norton, 2011); and Vilna Bashi Treitler, *The Ethnic Project: Transforming Racial Fiction into Ethnic Factions* (Redwood City, CA: Stanford University Press, 2013). See also Eduardo Bonilla-Silva on structural racism and the emergence of 'racialized social systems' in the aftermath of European colonialism. Eduardo Bonilla-Silva, "Rethinking Racism: Toward a Structural Interpretation," *American Sociological Review* 62, no. 3 (1997): 465–80.

15. W. E. B. Du Bois was one of the first sociologists to denounce and draw connections between forms of racial violence directed toward multiple groups. Writing in *Dusk of Dawn* (1940), he observed: "Lynching was a continuing and recurrent horror during my college days: from 1885 through 1894, seventeen hundred Negroes were lynched in America. Each death was a scar upon my soul and led me to conceive the plight of other minority

groups for in my college days Italians were lynched in New Orleans, forcing the Federal government to pay $25,000 in indemnity, and the anti-Chinese riots in the West culminated in the Chinese Exclusion Act of 1892. Some echoes of Jewish segregation and pogroms in Russia came through the magazines; I followed the Dreyfus case; and I began to see something of the struggle between East and West in the Sino-Japanese war." Du Bois, *The Oxford W. E. B. Du Bois* (New York: Oxford University Press, 2007), 15.

16. On the racial politics of gaslighting, see Angelique M. Davis and Rose Ernst, "Racial Gaslighting," *Politics, Groups, and Identities* (2017): 1–14.

17. "7 Ways We Know Systemic Racism Is Real," Ben & Jerry's website, https://www.benjerry.com/whats-new/2016/systemic-racism-is-real, accessed March 22, 2018.

18. See Eduardo Bonilla-Silva, *Racism Without Racists: Color-Blind Racism and the Persistence of Racial Inequality in America* (2003; Lanham, MD: Rowman & Littlefield, 2017), and Joe R. Feagin, *The White Racial Frame: Centuries of Racial Framing and Counter-Framing* (2008; New York: Routledge, 2013).

19. Matt Bruenig, "The Top 10% of White Families Own Almost Everything," Demos.org, September 5, 2014, http://www.demos.org/blog/9/5/14/top-10-white-families-own-almost-everything.

20. See also David R. Roediger, *The Wages of Whiteness: Race and the Making of the American Working Class* (London: Verso, 2007).

21. Emily Badger, "Whites Have Huge Wealth Edge over Blacks (but Don't Know It)," *New York Times*, September 18, 2017, https://www.nytimes.com/interactive/2017/09/18/upshot/black-white-wealth-gap-perceptions.html.

22. See M. W. Kraus, J. M. Rucker, and J. A. Richeson, "Americans Misperceive Racial Economic Equality," *Proceedings of the National Academy of Sciences of the United States of America* 114, no. 39 (January 1, 2017): 10324–31.

CHAPTER 1: THE IDIOT'S GUIDE TO CRITICAL RACE THEORY

1. Harris, "Whiteness as Property," 1724.

2. Loewen, *Lies My Teacher Told Me*, chapter 3.

3. Phil Rosenthal, "Mike Ditka: 'No Oppression in Last 100 Years,'" *Chicago Tribune*, October 10, 2017, http://www.chicagotribune.com/sports/breaking/ct-ditka-20171010-story.html.

4. John McWhorter, "Racism in America Is Over," *Forbes*, December 30, 2008, https://www.forbes.com/2008/12/30/end-of-racism-oped-cx_jm_1230mcwhorter.html.

5. A number of other scholars have addressed the role of sociology in obscuring racial oppression and reinforcing the racial status quo. For prominent examples, see James B. McKee, *Sociology and the Race Problem: The Failure of a Perspective* (Urbana: University of Illinois Press, 1993); Noel A. Cazenave, *Conceptualizing Racism: Breaking the Chains of Racially Accommodative Language* (Lanham, MD: Rowman & Littlefield, 2015); and

Aldon D. Morris, *The Scholar Denied: W. E. B. Du Bois and the Birth of Modern Sociology* (Oakland, University of California Press, 2015).

6. See Eduardo Bonilla-Silva and Gianpaulo Baiocchi, "Anything but Racism: How Sociologists Limit the Significance of Racism," in *Handbook of the Sociology of Racial and Ethnic Relations*, Handbooks of Sociology and Social Research, ed. Hernan Vera and J. R. Feagin (Boston: Springer, 2008).

7. William Julius Wilson, *The Declining Significance of Race: Blacks and Changing American Institutions* (Chicago: University of Chicago Press, 1978). Note that Wilson's argument about the declining explanatory power of race focused on African Americans' gains in the labor market. On this point, see Aldon D. Morris, "What's Race Got to Do with It?," *Contemporary Sociology* 25 (1996): 309–13. Although Wilson conceptually minimizes structural racism and generally avoids acknowledging white supremacy in contemporary society, his work highlights class divisions among African Americans as well as the plight of poor and working-class blacks. See William Julius Wilson, *The Truly Disadvantaged: The Inner City, the Underclass, and Public Policy* (Chicago: University of Chicago Press, 1987).

8. For a review of the key texts that established the field of critical race theory, see Richard Delgado and Jean Stefancic, *Critical Race Theory: An Introduction* (New York: New York University Press, 2001); Richard Delgado and Jean Stefancic, *Critical Race Theory: An Annotated Bibliography* (Charlottesville, VA: Virginia Law Review Association, 1993); and Kimberlé Crenshaw, Neil Gotanda, Gary Peller, and Kendall Thomas, *Critical Race Theory: The Key Writings That Formed the Movement* (New York: New Press, 1996).

9. Ira Katznelson, *When Affirmative Action Was White: An Untold History of Racial Inequality in Twentieth-Century America* (New York: W. W. Norton, 2006).

10. See Leslie Picca and Joe Feagin, *Two-Faced Racism: Whites in the Backstage and Frontstage* (London: Routledge, 2007): "In the North American case, from the 1600s to the 1960s, whites benefited greatly from 'affirmative action' programs provided by federal, state, and local governments more or less for whites only. These included the nineteenth-century and early twentieth-century provision by the federal government of hundreds of millions of acres of land for viable farm homesteads in many states. From that agricultural land many white families built up wealth that they passed to several later generations of whites, who often translated it into such things as good education, white-collar jobs, and good housing. Tens of millions of whites today are affluent because of a few large scale federal programs of land allocation. Yet this land, for the most part, was not made available to black Americans and other Americans of color who were present in those states during the same decades—because of widespread, sometimes violent, white opposition and discrimination." (29–30)

11. Sally Kohn, "Affirmative Action Has Helped White Women More Than Anyone," *Time*, June 27, 2013, http://ideas.time.com/2013/06/17/affirmative-action-has-helped-white-women-more-than-anyone.

12. "To Keep Its Stock Pure: A History of Eugenics at Harvard," WBUR, March 8, 2016, http://www.wbur.org/radioboston/2016/03/08/eugenics-at-harvard.

13. Jamiles Lartey, "Racism at Harvard: Months After Protests Began, Students Demand Concrete Change," *Guardian*, April 13, 2016, https://www.theguardian.com/education/2016/apr/13/racism-harvard-law-school-slaveholder-seal.

14. Mills, *The Racial Contract*, 18.

15. On forms of white racial ignorance, see also Jennifer Mueller, "Producing Colorblindness: Everyday Mechanisms of White Ignorance," *Social Problems* 64, no. 2 (2017): 219–38.

16. Karen E. Fields and Barbara J. Fields, *Racecraft: The Soul of Inequality in American Life* (London: Verso, 2012).

17. Audrey Smedley and Brian D. Smedley, *Race in North America: Origin and Evolution of a Worldview*, 4th ed. (Boulder, CO: Westview Press, 2012).

18. See Gillian White, "In DC, White Families Are on Average 81 Times Richer Than Black Ones," *Atlantic*, November 26, 2016, https://www.theatlantic.com/business/archive/2016/11/racial-wealth-gap-dc/508631/.

19. Stokely Carmichael and Charles V. Hamilton, *Black Power: The Politics of Liberation in America* (New York: Random House, 1967), 4.

20. Ibid.

21. Ibid.

22. Crystal Marie Fleming, "To Be Clear, White Supremacy Is the Foundation of Our Country. We Won't Destroy It by Toppling Statues," *The Root*, August 19, 2017, http://www.theroot.com/to-be-clear-white-supremacy-is-the-foundation-of-our-c-1797990783.

23. CNN Transcript: *State of the Union*, August 20, 2017, http://transcripts.cnn.com/TRANSCRIPTS/1708/20/sotu.01.html.

24. On color-blind racism within the United States, see Bonilla-Silva, *Racism Without Racists*.

CHAPTER 2: LISTEN TO BLACK WOMEN

1. Cherrie Moraga and Gloria Anzalduá, *This Bridge Called My Back: Writings by Radical Women of Color* (New York: Kitchen Table/Women of Color Press, 1981), 94.

2. If you haven't heard of the Nardal sisters, let me be the one to suggest that you check out their work. Jeanne and Paulette Nardal were French Caribbean women who were involved in raising racial consciousness during the Negritude movement in France. See Tracey D. Sharpley-Whiting, *Negritude Women* (Minneapolis: University of Minnesota Press, 2002), and Jennifer

Anne Boittin, "In Black and White: Gender, Race Relations, and the Nardal Sisters in Interwar Paris," *French Colonial History* 6 (2005): 119–35.

3. Salma Hayek, "Harvey Weinstein Is My Monster Too," *New York Times*, December 13, 2017, https://www.nytimes.com/interactive/2017/12/13/opinion/contributors/salma-hayek-harvey-weinstein.html.

4. Amy Kaufman, "Celebration of Women Filmmakers Triggers Heated Debate Among Salma Hayek, Jessica Williams and Shirley MacLaine," *Los Angeles Times*, January 28, 2017, http://beta.latimes.com/entertainment/movies/la-et-mn-female-filmmakers-lunch-race-debate-20170128-story.html.

5. Audre Lorde, *Sister Outsider: Essays and Speeches* (1984; Berkeley, CA: Crossing Press, 2007), 127.

6. See Felice Léon, "The Real Woman Behind 'Me Too,'" *The Root*, October 20, 2017, https://www.theroot.com/watch-the-real-woman-behind-me-too-1819716901.

7. Women of Color Network, *Women of Color Network Facts & Stats: Domestic Violence in Communities of Color*, National Resource of Domestic Violence (Harrisburg, PA: Women of Color Network, June 2006), 2, http://www.doj.state.or.us/wp-content/uploads/2017/08/women_of_color_network_facts_domestic_violence_2006.pdf.

8. Vickie M. Mays, "Black Women, Work, Stress, and Perceived Discrimination: The Focused Support Group Model as an Intervention for Stress Reduction," *Cultural Diversity and Mental Health* 1, no. 1 (1995): 53–65, https://www.ncbi.nlm.nih.gov/pmc/articles/PMC3650252/.

9. Adrienne Davis, "Slavery and the Roots of Sexual Harassment," in *Directions in Sexual Harassment Law*, ed. C. MacKinnon and R. Siegel (New Haven, CT: Yale University Press, 2003), 457–78; Angela Davis, "Reflections on the Black Woman's Role in the Community of Slaves," *Massachusetts Review* 13, nos. 1/2 (1972): 81–100.

10. Dorothy Roberts, *Killing the Black Body: Race, Reproduction, and the Meaning of Liberty* (New York: Vintage Books, 2017), 21.

11. Linda Goler Blount, "Maternal Health and Black Women," in *Our Bodies, Our Lives, Our Voices: The State of Black Women & Reproductive Justice Policy* (Washington, DC: National Black Women's Reproductive Justice Agenda, 2017), 51, http://blackrj.org/wp-content/uploads/2017/06/FINAL-InOurVoices_Report_final.pdf.

12. Roberts, *Killing the Black Body*, 285.

13. Andrea J. Ritchie, *Invisible No More: Police Violence Against Black Women and Women of Color* (Boston: Beacon Press, 2017), 104.

14. Kimberlé Crenshaw et al., *Say Her Name: Resisting Police Brutality Against Black Women* (New York: African American Policy Forum, 2015), 4, http://www.aapf.org/s/merged_document_2-1.pdf. As an example of the reflexive centering of black men even in contexts of identical targeting, see this article, wherein the author asserts that in addition to being racist, stop-and-frisk is also "a sexist policy, as men are the ones who suffer the

public humiliation." Tony Miguel, "Stop and Frisk: Racist and Ineffective," MSNBC.com, December 14, 2012, http://www.msnbc.com/the-cycle/stop-and-frisk-racist-and-ineffective.

15. See Crenshaw et al., *Say Her Name*. See also Ritchie, *Invisible No More*, and Kate Abbey-Lambertz, "These 15 Black Women Were Killed During Police Encounters. Their Lives Matter, Too," *Huffington Post, Black Voices*, February 13, 2015, https://www.huffingtonpost.com/2015/02/13/black-womens-lives-matter-police-shootings_n_6644276.html.

16. "'I Use My Love to Guide Me': Surviving and Thriving in the Face of Impossible Situations," conversation at the New School, New York, with CeCe McDonald, Reina Gossett, and Dean Spade, Barnard College, April 21, 2014, http://bcrw.barnard.edu/event/i-use-my-love-to-guide-me-cece-mcdonald-reina-gossett-dean-spade.

17. Jamie Malanowski, "The Underappreciated and Forgotten Sites of the Civil War," *Smithsonian Magazine*, April 2015, https://www.smithsonianmag.com/history/underappreciated-forgotten-sites-civil-war-180954579.

18. Keeanga-Yamahtta Taylor, ed., *How We Get Free: Black Feminism and the Combahee River Collective* (Chicago: Haymarket Books, 2016), 30–31.

19. "A Black Feminist Statement: The Combahee River Collective," as reprinted in ibid., 18; *All the Women Are White, All the Blacks Are Men, but Some of Us Are Brave*, ed. Akasha (Gloria T.) Hull, Patricia Bell-Scott, and Barbara Smith (1982; New York: Feminist Press, 2015), 15. Note that the Combahee River Collective statement was originally published in 1977.

20. "Sojourner Truth," Women's Rights, National Historical Park, New York, https://www.nps.gov/wori/learn/historyculture/sojourner-truth.htm, accessed February 21, 2018.

21. Michele Wallace, "A Black Feminist's Search for Sisterhood," in Hull, Bell-Scott, and Smith, *All the Women Are White, All the Blacks Are Men, but Some of Us Are Brave*, 9.

22. Kimberlé Crenshaw, "Demarginalizing the Intersection of Race and Sex: A Black Feminist Critique of Antidiscrimination Doctrine, Feminist Theory and Antiracist Politics," *University of Chicago Legal Forum* 140 (1989): 149. For a good overview of intersectionality, see Patrick R. Grzanka, *Intersectionality: A Foundations and Frontiers Reader* (Boulder, CO: Westview Press, 2014).

23. Moya Bailey, "More on the Origin of Misogynoir," Tumblr, April 27, 2014, http://moyazb.tumblr.com/post/84048113369/more-on-the-origin-of-misogynoir.

24. "A Black Feminist Statement," in Hull, Bell-Scott, and Smith, *All the Women Are White, All the Blacks Are Men, but Some of Us Are Brave*, 16.

25. Ibid., 21.

26. Phoebe Lett, "White Women Voted Trump. Now What?," *New York Times*, November 10, 2016, https://www.nytimes.com/2016/11/10/opinion/white-women-voted-trump-now-what.html.

27. Crenshaw et al., *Say Her Name*. See also Ritchie, *Invisible No More*.

28. Cathy Newman, "The Vile Sex Abuse by UN Peacekeepers Is Leaving the United Nations in Tatters," *Telegraph*, April 14, 2016, http://www.telegraph.co.uk/women/politics/the-vile-sex-abuse-by-un-peacekeepers-is-leaving-the-united-nati.

29. Guilaine Kinouani, "Since I Gave You a Phone It's Not Rape," *Open Democracy*, November 25, 2016, https://www.opendemocracy.net/5050/guilaine/since-i-gave-you-phone-it-s-not-rape.

30. "Herstory," Black Lives Matter website, https://blacklivesmatter.com/about/herstory, accessed February 21, 2018.

31. National LGBTQ Task Force, "Black Feminism and the Movement for Black Lives: Barbara Smith, Reina Gossett, Charlene Caruthers," YouTube video, January 23, 2016, https://www.youtube.com/watch?v=eV3nnFheQRo, accessed February 21, 2018.

32. bell hooks, *Sisters of the Yam: Black Women and Self-Recovery* (1994; New York: Routledge, 2015), 41.

CHAPTER 3: ON RACIAL STUPIDITY IN THE OBAMA ERA

1. Xuan Thai and Ted Barrett, "Biden's Description of Obama Draws Scrutiny," CNN.com, February 9, 2007, http://www.cnn.com/2007/POLITICS/01/31/biden.obama/.

2. Barack Obama, transcript, "World AIDS Day Speech—2006 Global Summit on AIDS," December 1, 2006, http://obamaspeeches.com/095-Race-Against-Time-World-AIDS-Day-Speech-Obama-Speech.htm.

3. For full video of the Boston event, see C-SPAN, "Obama Campaign Event," February 4, 2008, https://www.c-span.org/video/?203903-1/obama-campaign-event.

4. Democrats Abroad, "Who We Are," http://www.democratsabroad.org/, accessed February 21, 2018.

5. Note that Republicans Abroad dissolved and was replaced with Republicans Overseas in 2013. For a brief history of Democrats Abroad and Republicans Abroad, see Jay Sexton and Patrick Andelick, "Will Americans Abroad Tip the Balance in November?," *Newsweek*, March 28, 2018, http://www.newsweek.com/will-americans-abroad-tip-balance-november-440818.

6. France 24, "Obama J'ai Fait Un Reve," YouTube video, April 4, 2008, https://www.youtube.com/watch?v=Yr07jxqyrQY.

7. Democrats Abroad, "Where on Earth Will YOU Vote?," YouTube video, July 24, 2008, https://www.youtube.com/watch?v=amukRM9SSoo.

8. Not exactly the same thing as Charlamagne Tha God's book *Black Privilege: Opportunity Comes to Those Who Create It* (New York: Touchstone, 2017).

9. Spoiler alert! In Jordan Peele's 2017 film *Get Out*, the "sunken place" refers to a scene in which a white hypnotist exerts mind control over the black

protagonist. I use the term to simply indicate the dynamics of internalized oppression, or even false consciousness, to borrow Marx's formulation.

10. Jessica Purkiss and Jack Serle, "Obama's Covert Drone War in Numbers: Ten Times More Strikes Than Bush," Bureau of Investigative Reporting, January 17, 2017, https://www.thebureauinvestigates.com/stories/2017-01-17/obamas-covert-drone-war-in-numbers-ten-times-more-strikes-than-bush. See also Medea Benjamin, *Drone Warfare: Killing by Remote Control* (London: Verso, 2013), and Crystal Marie Fleming, "War Crimes We Can Believe In," Aware of Awareness, October 8, 2017, https://awareofawareness.com/2017/10/08/war-crimes-we-can-believe-in.

11. For a systematic review of Obama's drone policy, see Benjamin, *Drone Warfare.*

12. Glenn Greenwald, "Obama Killed a 16-Year-Old American in Yemen. Trump Just Killed His 8-Year-Old Sister," *Intercept*, January 30, 2017, https://theintercept.com/2017/01/30/obama-killed-a-16-year-old-american-in-yemen-trump-just-killed-his-8-year-old-sister.

13. For analysis of Obama's historic role in deporting undocumented people, see Tanya Marie Golash-Boza, *Deported: Immigrant Policing, Disposable Labor, and Global Capitalism* (New York: New York University Press, 2015). As Golash-Boza points out, during "the first five and a half years of his presidency, Obama deported more than two million people—more than the sum total of all people deported before 1997" (5).

14. I am thinking here of Obama's silence on the crimes of Daniel Holtzclaw, the Oklahoma police officer who stood trial for sexually assaulting black women and girls.

15. For an accessible description of neoliberalism, see George Monbiot, "Neoliberalism: The Ideology at the Root of All Our Problems," *Guardian*, April 15, 2016, https://www.theguardian.com/books/2016/apr/15/neoliberalism-ideology-problem-george-monbiot.

16. Kirk Noden, "Why Do White Working-Class People Vote Against Their Interests? They Don't," *Nation*, November 17, 2016, https://www.thenation.com/article/why-do-white-working-class-people-vote-against-their-interests-they-dont.

17. Adolph Reed Jr., "Nothing Left: The Long, Slow Surrender of American Liberals," *Harper's*, March 2014, http://harpers.org/archive/2014/03/nothing-left-2/.

18. Jonah Birch and Paul Heideman, "The Trouble with Antiracism," *Jacobin*, October 11, 2016, https://www.jacobinmag.com/2016/10/adolph-reed-blm-racism-capitalism-labor/.

19. David Leonhardt, "Barack Obama: A Free-Market-Loving, Big-Spending, Fiscally Conservative Wealth Redistributionist," *New York Times Magazine*, August 20, 2008, http://www.nytimes.com/2008/08/24/magazine/24Obamanomics-t.html.

20. Barack Obama, "Toward a 21st-Century Regulatory System," *Wall Street Journal*, January 18, 2011, https://www.wsj.com/articles/SB10001424052748703396604576088272112103698.

21. Mark Hensch, "Obama to Net $400K for Wall Street Speech: Report," *Hill*, April 24, 2017, http://thehill.com/homenews/news/330337-obama-to-net-400k-for-wall-street-speech-report.

22. Tressie McMillan Cottom, "The Problem with Obama's Faith in White America," *Atlantic*, December 13, 2016, https://www.theatlantic.com/politics/archive/2016/12/obamas-faith-in-white-america/510503.

23. On Obama's twelve years at the University of Chicago School of Law, see Jodi Kantor, "Teaching Law, Testing Ideas, Obama Stood Slightly Apart," *New York Times*, July 30, 2008, http://www.nytimes.com/2008/07/30/us/politics/30law.html. Obama's course syllabi are available via the *New York Times*, http://www.nytimes.com/packages/pdf/politics/2008OBAMA_LAW/Obama_CoursePk.pdf, accessed February 21, 2018.

24. Ta-Nehisi Coates, "My President Was Black," *Atlantic*, January/February 2017, https://www.theatlantic.com/magazine/archive/2017/01/my-president-was-black/508793/.

25. Transcript: Barack Obama's Speech on Race, NPR, March 18, 2008, http://www.npr.org/templates/story/story.php?storyId=88478467.

26. Ibram X. Kendi, *Stamped from the Beginning: The Definitive History of Racist Ideas in America* (New York: Nation Books, 2016), 493.

27. William Darity Jr., "How Obama Failed Black Americans," *Atlantic*, December 22, 2016, https://www.theatlantic.com/politics/archive/2016/12/how-barack-obama-failed-black-americans/511358.

CHAPTER 4: TRUMP COUNTRY

1. Adam Serwer, "The Nationalist's Delusion," *Atlantic*, November 20, 2017, https://www.theatlantic.com/politics/archive/2017/11/the-nationalists-delusion/546356/.

2. Team Coco, "Dan Rather on the Age of Trump: This Is Not Normal," Conan on TBS, December 4, 2017, available on YouTube, https://www.youtube.com/watch?v=_LyevPdfbeo.

3. Cleve R. Wootson Jr., "Trump Rages About Leakers. Obama Quietly Prosecuted Them," *Washington Post*, June 8, 2017, https://www.washingtonpost.com/news/the-fix/wp/2017/06/08/trump-rages-about-leakers-obama-quietly-prosecuted-them/?utm_term=.0933e2f61c5e.

4. James Risen, "My Life as a New York Times Reporter in the Shadow of the War on Terror," *Intercept*, January 3, 2018, https://theintercept.com/2018/01/03/my-life-as-a-new-york-times-reporter-in-the-shadow-of-the-war-on-terror.

5. James C. Goodale, "Only Nixon Harmed a Free Press More," *New York Times*, July 31, 2013, https://www.nytimes.com/roomfordebate/2013/05

/21/obama-the-media-and-national-security/only-nixon-harmed-a-free-press-more.

6. Risen, "My Life as a New York Times Reporter in the Shadow of the War on Terror."

7. Michael Kranish and Robert O'Harrow Jr., "Inside the Government's Racial Bias Case Against Donald Trump's Company, and How He Fought It," *Washington Post*, January 23, 2016, https://www.washingtonpost.com/politics/inside-the-governments-racial-bias-case-against-donald-trumps-company-and-how-he-fought-it/2016/01/23/fb90163e-bfbe-11e5-bcda-62a36b394160_story.html?utm_term=.b3b3be075fb6.

8. Yuself Salaam, "I'm One of the Central Park Five. Donald Trump Won't Leave Me Alone," *Chicago Tribune*, October 12, 2016, http://www.chicagotribune.com/news/opinion/commentary/ct-donald-trump-central-park-five-guilty-20161012-story.html.

9. Maureen Dowd, "When Hillary and Donald Were Friends," *New York Times*, November 2, 2016, https://www.nytimes.com/2016/11/06/magazine/when-hillary-and-donald-were-friends.html?mtrref=www.google.com&gwh=B9AAD01D0FD49862A5C61D6C7943DA14&gwt.

10. David Leonhardt, Twitter, January 15, 2018, https://twitter.com/DLeonhardt/status/952893671342559232.

11. John Haltiwanger, "Trump Isn't Alone. Five Racist Quotes from Modern Presidents," *Newsweek*, January 12, 2018, http://www.newsweek.com/trump-racist-quotes-modern-us-presidents-780168.

12. See, for example, David Leonhardt and Ian Prasad Philbrick, "Donald Trump's Racism: The Definitive List," *New York Times*, January 15, 2018, https://www.nytimes.com/interactive/2018/01/15/opinion/leonhardt-trump-racist.html; and Christianna Silva, "Trump's Full List of 'Racist' Comments About Immigrants, Muslims and Others," *Newsweek*, January 11, 2018, http://www.newsweek.com/trumps-full-list-racist-comments-about-immigrants-muslims-and-others-779061.

13. Brandon Carter, "Rep. Wilson: Trump White House Is 'Full of White Supremacists,'" *Hill*, October 20, 2017, http://thehill.com/homenews/house/356459-rep-wilson-trump-white-house-is-full-of-white-supremacists.

14. See Keegan Hankes, "Breitbart Under Bannon: How Breitbart Became a Favorite News Source for Neo-Nazis and White Nationalists," Southern Poverty Law Center, March 1, 2017, https://www.splcenter.org/hatewatch/2017/03/01/breitbart-under-bannon-how-breitbart-became-favorite-news-source-neo-nazis-and-white.

15. Christianna Silva, "Trump Administration Doesn't Care About Nazis: The US Voted Against UN Resolution Condemning Nazism," *Newsweek*, November 22, 2017, http://www.newsweek.com/trump-administration-doesnt-care-about-nazis-us-voted-against-un-resolution-720489.

16. On the US government's covert collaboration with Nazi scientists under the classified project known as "Operation Paperclip," see Linda Hunt, *Secret Agenda: The United States Government, Nazi Scientists, and Project Paperclip, 1945 to 1990* (New York: St. Martin's Press, 1991); Annie Jacobsen, *Operation Paperclip: The Secret Intelligence Program That Brought Nazi Scientists to America* (New York: Back Bay Books, 2015); and Eric Lichtblau, *The Nazis Next Door: How America Became a Safe Haven for Hitler's Men* (Boston: Houghton-Mifflin, 2014). A book review of Jacobsen's *Operation Paperclip* published by the CIA itself admits that the United States recruited numerous "prominent Nazis," including Werner von Braun, Hubertus Strughold, and General Reinhard Gehlen, for scientific, military, and intelligence projects. See Jay Watkins, "Intelligence in Public Literature: *Operation Paperclip: The Secret Intelligence Program to Bring Nazi Scientists to America*," *Studies in Intelligence* 58, no. 3 (October 6, 2014), https://www.cia.gov/library/center-for-the-study-of-intelligence/csi-publications/csi-studies/studies/vol-58-no-3/operation-paperclip-the-secret-intelligence-program-to-bring-nazi-scientists-to-america.html.

17. Alexis C. Madrigal, "Remembering the Nazi Scientist Who Built the Rockets for Apollo," *Atlantic*, March 23, 2012, https://www.theatlantic.com/technology/archive/2012/03/remembering-the-nazi-scientist-who-built-the-rockets-for-apollo/254987.

18. Daniel A. Gross, "The US Government Turned Away Thousands of Jewish Refugees, Fearing That They Were Nazi Spies," *Smithsonian Magazine*, November 18, 2015, https://www.smithsonianmag.com/history/us-government-turned-away-thousands-jewish-refugees-fearing-they-were-nazi-spies-180957324/.

19. US Holocaust Museum, "Voyage of the St. Louis," https://www.ushmm.org/wlc/en/article.php?ModuleId=10005267, accessed February 21, 2018.

20. On the significance of referring to Japanese "internment" camps as concentration camps, see Roger Daniels, "Words Do Matter: A Note on Inappropriate Terminology and the Incarceration of the Japanese Americans," In *Nikkei in the Pacific Northwest: Japanese Americans and Japanese Canadians in the Twentieth Century*, ed. Louis Fiset and Gail Nomura (Seattle: University of Washington Press, 2005), 190–214.

21. A 1982 congressional report published by the Commission on Wartime Relocation and Internment of Civilians acknowledges the role of anti-Japanese racism and ignorance on the part of white Americans in implementing and rationalizing the incarceration policy. Commission on Wartime Relocation and Internment of Civilians, "Summary," *Personal Justice Denied* (Washington, DC: Commission on Wartime Relocation and Internment of Civilians, 1982), https://www.archives.gov/files/research/japanese-americans/justice-denied/summary.pdf, accessed February 21, 2018. Of particular interest is this passage from the report: "The promulgation of Executive

Order 9066 was not justified by military necessity, and the decisions which followed from it—detention, ending detention and ending exclusion—were not driven by analysis of military conditions. The broad historical causes which shaped these decisions were race prejudice, war hysteria and a failure of political leadership. Widespread ignorance of Japanese Americans contributed to a policy conceived in haste and executed in an atmosphere of fear and anger at Japan. A grave injustice was done to American citizens and resident aliens of Japanese ancestry who, without individual review or any probative evidence against them, were excluded, removed and detained by the United States during World War II." (18)

22. See Roger Daniels, "Incarceration of the Japanese Americans: A Sixty-Year Perspective," *History Teacher* 35, no. 3 (2002): 303.

23. A 2014 article published in *Tablet*, a Jewish magazine, draws connections between FDR's anti-Japanese racism and his failure to help Jewish refugees fleeing the Holocaust. See Rafael Medoff, "Why Didn't FDR Help European Jews? Hints in His Decision to Intern Japanese Americans," *Tablet*, February 14, 2014, http://www.tabletmag.com/jewish-news-and-politics/162780/roosevelt-japanese-internment. Though FDR is known to have made public statements in support of Jewish people, he nonetheless refused to intervene and help Jewish refugees attempting to escape the death camps of Nazi Germany.

24. Gregory H. Robinson, *By Order of the President: FDR and the Internment of Japanese Americans* (Cambridge, MA: Harvard University Press, 2001), 38.

25. Albert Marrin, *Uprooted: The Japanese American Experience During World War II* (New York: Alfred A. Knopf, 2016), 85.

26. African American Policy Forum, "Trail of Tears," http://www.aapf.org/trail-of-tears, accessed February 21, 2018. On Jackson's role in facilitating ethnic cleansing, see Howard Zinn, *A People's History of the United States* (New York: Harper Collins, 2015), chapter 7, particularly pp. 125–30.

27. Thomas Jefferson and Nicholas E. Magnis, "Thomas Jefferson and Slavery: An Analysis of His Racist Thinking as Revealed by His Writings and Political Behavior," *Journal of Black Studies* 29, no. 4 (1999): 491–509.

28. Haltiwanger, "Trump Isn't Alone. Five Racist Quotes from Modern Presidents."

29. For recent analysis of the intersections between immigration, neoliberalism, and racism, see Leah Perry, *The Cultural Politics of U.S. Immigration: Gender, Race, and Media* (New York: New York University Press, 2016).

30. Kai Wright, "The United States of Anxiety, Episode 4: The Media That Created Trump," *Nation*, October 13, 2016, https://www.thenation.com/article/the-media-that-created-trump.

31. Arun Venogupal, "Long Island Woman Feels a Trump Presidency Will Rescue America from Its Elites," NPR, October 15, 2016, https://www.npr.org/2016/10/15/498056601/long-island-woman-feels-a-trump-presidency-will-rescue-america-from-its-elites.

32. Tessa Berenson, "White House on 'Shithole' Comment: President Trump Isn't a 'Scripted Robot,'" *Time*, January 16, 2016, http://time.com/5105238/white-house-on-shithole-comment-president-trump-isnt-a-scripted-robot.

33. Melissa Mahtini, "Jay-Z Slams Trump's 'Shithole' Comment as 'Hurtful,'" CNN.com, January 28, 2018, https://www.cnn.com/2018/01/27/us/jay-z-van-jones-on-trump-cnntv/index.html.

34. Feagin, *The White Racial Frame*, 3. For Feagin, the white racial frame is one of three pillars of systemic racism, the other two being discriminatory practices favoring whites and the institutionalization of the racial hierarchy.

35. Ibid., 10.

36. Unfortunately, some nonwhite minorities also join in the great American pastime of joking about violence against people of color, as shown by the case of Jason Lai, a former San Francisco cop, who was caught, along with several other cops, exchanging racist and homophobic text messages referring to black people as "nigs," "barbarians," and "wild animals." Not satisfied with merely insulting African Americans, Lai also sent texts reading "Indian ppl are disgusting" and "I hate that beaner." Lai himself is Chinese American. Internally oppressed minorities notwithstanding, white supremacist joking seems to be an especially prevalent practice among white men. See Scott Glover and Dan Simon, "'Wild Animals': Racist Texts Sent by San Francisco Police Officer, Documents Show," CNN.com, April 26, 2016, https://www.cnn.com/2016/04/26/us/racist-texts-san-francisco-police-officer/index.html. Of course, Lai is not alone. Jeff Adachi, a public defender, argued that the racist texts, which were sent by numerous officers in San Francisco, point to a "deep culture of racial hatred and animus against blacks, Latinos, gays and even South Asians." Other police departments across the country have also been wracked by scandals involving racist texting. See Thomas Fuller, "San Francisco Police Chief Releases Officers' Racist Texts," *New York Times*, April 29, 2016, https://www.nytimes.com/2016/04/30/us/san-francisco-police-orders-officers-to-complete-anti-harassment-class.html.

37. This student journal entry was cited in Picca and Feagin, *Two-Faced Racism*, 5–6, as well as in Feagin's *The White Racial Frame*, 11–12.

38. On the prevalence of racist joking among young whites, see N. L. Cabrera, "'But We're Not Laughing': White Male College Students' Racial Joking and What This Says About 'Post-Racial' Discourse," *Journal of College Student Development* 55, no. 1 (2014): 1–16; and Bonilla-Silva, *Racism Without Racists*. On Donald Trump's racist "jokes" about Native Americans, among others, see Lauren Gambino, "Trump Makes 'Pocahontas' Joke at Ceremony Honoring Navajo Veterans," *Guardian*, November 28, 2017, https://www.theguardian.com/us-news/2017/nov/27/trump-makes-pocahontas-joke-at-ceremony-honoring-navajo-veterans.

39. Bonilla-Silva, *Racism Without Racists*, 80.

40. Ibid., 222.

41. Adam Serwer, "The Nationalist's Delusion," *Atlantic*, November 20, 2017, https://www.theatlantic.com/politics/archive/2017/11/the-nationalists-delusion/546356/.

42. Taryn Finley, "Omarosa Says Donald Trump Is 'Racial' But 'Not a Racist,'" *Huffington Post*, December 15, 2017, https://www.huffingtonpost.com/entry/omarosa-donald-trump-racial-not-racist_us_5a33e557e4b040881be9f178.

43. "Sen. Hatch on Trump: 'I Don't Think There's a Racist Bone in His Body,'" video, *Washington Post*, August 17, 2017, https://www.washingtonpost.com/video/politics/sen-hatch-on-trump-i-dont-think-theres-a-racist-bone-in-his-body/2017/08/17/c14d7168-834b-11e7-9e7a-20fa8d7a0db6_video.html.

44. Kai Wright, "United States of Anxiety, Episode 2: Who Owns the Deed to the American Dream?," podcast, *Nation*, September 29, 2016, https://www.thenation.com/article/the-united-states-of-anxiety-episode-2-segregation-and-the-trump-phenomenon/. Note that Mrs. Johnson is Patty's mother. In particular, listen to timestamp 21:20, where Johnson describes her perception of Trump's racial attitudes.

45. Michael Tesler, "The Return of Old-Fashioned Racism to White Americans' Partisan Preferences in the Early Obama Era," *Journal of Politics* 75, no. 1 (2013): 110–23. Tesler defines "old-fashioned racism" as characterized by three features: "(1) desire for social distance between the races, (2) beliefs in the biological inferiority of blacks, and (3) support public policies insuring racial segregation and formalized discrimination" (114).

46. Tesler presents whites with low educational attainment as duped or misinformed about the racial politics of the two parties, suggesting that college-educated whites were better informed about the progressive racial policies of the Democratic Party and that it took the election of a black Democratic president for working-class whites to catch on. In making his case, Tesler points to the Democrats' implementation of civil rights legislation—and the virulently racist opposition of Republicans such as Barry Goldwater—as indicators that the two parties take a radically different approach to racial politics.

47. See Tesler, "The Return of Old-Fashioned Racism to White Americans' Partisan Preferences in the Early Obama Era," 121. Though Tesler was prescient about the reemergence of white supremacist politics, I question his description of white working-class voters as misinformed dupes who somehow missed the memo about the Democrats' racial inclusivity. Isn't it possible that working-class whites actually had a more accurate understanding of the two parties' racial positioning prior to Obama's election, given that both Republicans and Democrats are deeply implicated in maintaining the racial status quo? Though it is certainly true that conservative

politicians like Reagan engaged in dog-whistle racism, stigmatizing African Americans and other people of color as "welfare queens" and violent criminals, Democrats have demonstrated that they are more than willing to play that game too. Michelle Alexander, author of *The New Jim Crow: Mass Incarceration in the Age of Colorblindness* (New York: New Press, 2012), has strongly criticized Democratic politicians' use of racist imagery and messaging to attract the support of white voters, notably in their efforts to pass the crime bill and welfare reform. Alexander notes that Bill Clinton mastered the fine art of blaming conservatives for racism in his presidential campaign speeches but "capitulated entirely to the right-wing backlash against the civil-rights movement and embraced Reagan's agenda on race crime welfare and taxes—ultimately doing more harm to black communities than Reagan ever did." See Michelle Alexander, "Why Hillary Clinton Doesn't Deserve the Black Vote," *Nation*, February 10, 2016, https://www.thenation.com/article/hillary-clinton-does-not-deserve-black-peoples-votes.

48. Ta-Nehisi Coates, "The First White President," *Atlantic*, October 2017, https://www.theatlantic.com/magazine/archive/2017/10/the-first-white-president-ta-nehisi-coates/537909/.

49. Christian Parenti, "Listening to Trump," *Jacobin*, November 22, 2017, https://www.jacobinmag.com/2016/11/trump-speeches-populism-war-economics-election/. On the data discrediting the "class not race" argument, see Mehdi Hassan. "Top Democrats Are Wrong: Trump Supporters Were More Motivated by Racism Than Economic Issues," *Intercept*, April 6, 2017, https://theintercept.com/2017/04/06/top-democrats-are-wrong-trump-supporters-were-more-motivated-by-racism-than-economic-issues/; and Michael Tesler, "Views About Race Mattered More in Electing Trump Than in Electing Obama," *Washington Post*, November 22, 2016, https://www.washingtonpost.com/news/monkey-cage/wp/2016/11/22/peoples-views-about-race-mattered-more-in-electing-trump-than-in-electing-obama.

50. Vincent L. Hutchings, "Change or More of the Same? Evaluating Racial Attitudes in the Obama Era," *Public Opinion Quarterly* 73, no. 5 (2009): 917–42. Hutchings makes a strong case that racial attitudes among white liberals did not change drastically or become significantly more progressive or egalitarian in the decades preceding Obama's election. Younger whites also share many of the racial worldviews of prior generations. On this point, see p. 929 in particular: "In short, on matters of public policy dealing explicitly with race, there is little evidence that the racial divide is declining among younger cohorts."

51. By comparison, 42 percent of white Republicans describe blacks as "lazier" and 26 percent of Republicans think blacks are less intelligent. See Aaron Blake, "Republicans' Views of Blacks' Intelligence, Work Ethic Lag Behind Democrats at Record Clip," *Washington Post*, March 31, 2017, https://www.washingtonpost.com/news/the-fix/wp/2017/03/31/the-gap-between-republicans-and-democrats-views-of-african-americans-just

-hit-a-new-high. Original GSS data is accessible via the National Opinion Research Center. See GSS Data Explorer, https://gssdataexplorer.norc.org/variables/vfilter, accessed February 21, 2018.

52. Hutchings, "Change or More of the Same?," 926. The statistic refers to white voters who supported Obama in 2008.

53. The anecdote of the racist Obama supporters, mentioned by Jamelle Bouie, was originally reported on the blog *FiveThirtyEight*. See Sean Quinn, "On the Road: Western Pennsylvania," *FiveThirtyEight*, October 18, 2008, https://fivethirtyeight.com/features/on-road-western-pennsylvania.

54. See also Michael Tesler, "Obama Won Lots of Votes from Racially Prejudiced Whites (and Some of Them Supported Trump)," *Washington Post*, December 7, 2016, https://www.washingtonpost.com/news/monkey-cage/wp/2016/12/07/obama-won-lots-of-votes-from-racially-prejudiced-whites-and-some-of-them-supported-trump/?utm_term=.9c0c8ac36fd2.

55. On Obama's conciliatory racial politics and exceptionalism, see Hutchings, "Change or More of the Same?"

56. Daniel A. Effron et al., "Endorsing Obama Licenses Favoring Whites," *Journal of Experimental Social Psychology* 45, no. 3 (2009): 590–93.

57. W. E. B. Du Bois, *Darkwater: Voices from Within the Veil* (1920; Mineola, NY: Dover Publications, 1999), 27.

58. W. E. B. Du Bois, *Black Reconstruction in America: An Essay Toward a History of the Part Which Black Folk Played in the Attempt to Reconstruct Democracy in America, 1860–1880* (1935; Oxford, UK: Oxford University Press, 2007). See also Ella Meyers, "Beyond the Wages of Whiteness: Du Bois on the Irrationality of Antiblack Racism," *Insights from the Social Sciences* (Social Science Research Council) (March 21, 2017), http://items.ssrc.org/beyond-the-wages-of-whiteness-du-bois-on-the-irrationality-of-antiblack-racism/.

59. Harris, "Whiteness as Property," 1759.

60. Bonilla-Silva quoted in John Blake, "The New Threat: 'Racism Without Racists,'" CNN.com, November 27, 2014, https://www.cnn.com/2014/11/26/us/ferguson-racism-or-racial-bias/index.html.

CHAPTER 5: FAKE RACIAL NEWS

1. Ida B. Wells, *A Red Record: Tabulated Statistics and Alleged Causes of Lynching in the United States*, 1895, Project Gutenberg, https://www.gutenberg.org/files/14977/14977-h/14977-h.htm, accessed February 21, 2018.

2. Rachaell Davis, "Soledad O'Brien Blasts Mainstream Media for Normalizing White Supremacy," *Essence*, September 8, 2016, https://www.essence.com/2016/09/08/soledad-obrien-media-normalizing-white-supremacy.

3. On the pervasiveness of white supremacist views among members of the majority population, see Feagin, *The White Racial Frame*; Bonilla-Silva, *Racism Without Racists*.

4. Stuart Hall, "The Whites of Their Eyes," in *Gender, Race, and Class in Media: A Critical Reader*, ed. Gail Dines and Jean M. Humez (Thousand Oaks, CA: SAGE Publications, 1995), 20. Thanks to Leah Perry for pointing me to this citation.

5. Ben Child, "Why Is Hollywood Still Using 'Yellowface' in 2016?," *Guardian*, October 5, 2016, https://www.theguardian.com/film/2016/oct/05/yellowface-hollywood-asian-stereotypes-birth-of-a-dragon.

6. Evelyn Diaz, "Ridley Scott Still Won't Apologize for Racist Exodus Casting," BET.com, September 16, 2015, https://www.bet.com/news/celebrities/2015/09/16/ridley-scott-still-won-t-apologize-for-racist-exodus-casting.html.

7. Rebecca Sun and Rebecca Ford, "Where Are the Asian-American Movie Stars?," *Hollywood Reporter*, May 9, 2016, https://www.hollywoodreporter.com/features/are-asian-american-movie-stars-890755.

8. "Whitewashing," *Last Week Tonight with John Oliver*, HBO, February 23, 2016, available on YouTube, https://www.youtube.com/watch?v=XebG4TO_xss.

9. Elizabeth Monk-Turner et al., "The Portrayal of Racial Minorities on Prime Time Television: A Replication of the Mastro and Greenberg Study a Decade Later," *Studies in Popular Culture* 32, no. 2 (2010): 101–14. On stereotyped images of Latinos and Latinas, see also Clara E. Rodriguez, *Latin Looks: Images of Latinas and Latinos in the US Media* (New York: Westview Press, 2008).

10. Anna Swartz, "How Stanford Sex Offender Brock Turner's Mugshot Exposes a Double Standard in the Media," *Mic*, June 7, 2016, https://mic.com/articles/145488/how-stanford-rapist-brock-turner-s-mugshot-exposes-a-double-standard-in-the-media#.iCZZG7GtR.

11. Aaron Rupar, "Before Denouncing Bannon, the New York Times and Washington Post Partnered with Him," *Think Progress*, November 28, 2016, https://thinkprogress.org/steve-bannon-new-york-times-washington-post-clinton-cash-d59d6492546/. See also Dylan Byers, "New York Times, Washington Post, Fox News Strike Deals for Anti-Clinton Research," *Politico*, April 20, 2015, https://www.politico.com/blogs/media/2015/04/new-york-times-washington-post-fox-news-strike-deals-for-anti-clinton-research-205791.

12. Hadas Gold, "The Huffington Post Ending Editor's Note That Called Donald Trump 'Racist,'" *Politico*, November 9, 2016, https://www.politico.com/blogs/on-media/2016/11/the-huffington-post-ending-its-editors-note-about-donald-trump-231044.

13. Jesse Leavenworth and Kevin Canfield, "Courant Complicity in an Old Wrong," *Hartford Courant*, July 4, 2000, http://articles.courant.com/2000-07-04/news/0007040049_1_slave-trade-courant-andriena-baldwin. The original headline was "A Courant Complicity, an Old Wrong."

14. Feagin, *The White Racial Frame*, 74.

15. Thank you to Leah Perry for reminding me to underscore this point.

16. Ibid., 70.

17. Ibid., 79: "West Coast newspapers generated campaigns against the white-termed 'yellow peril'—that is, Japanese and other Asian Americans."

18. Historian Erika Lee also examines the transnational dimension of anti-Asian racism throughout the Americas. On this point, see Erika Lee, "The 'Yellow Peril' and Asian Exclusion in the Americas," *Pacific Historical Review* 76, no. 4 (2007): 537–62.

19. Ida B. Wells, *Southern Horrors: Lynch Law in All Its Phases*, 1892, Project Gutenberg, http://www.gutenberg.org/files/14975/14975-h/14975-h.htm, accessed February 21, 2018.

20. Paula Giddings, *Ida: A Sword Among Lions: Ida B. Wells and the Campaign Against Lynching* (New York: Amistad, 2009).

21. For additional insights into African American responses to lynching, see Koritha Mitchell, *Living with Lynching: African American Lynching Plays, Performance, and Citizenship, 1890–1930* (Urbana: University of Illinois Press, 2012), and Crystal Nicole Feimster, *Southern Horrors: Women and the Politics of Rape and Lynching* (Cambridge, MA: Harvard University Press, 2011).

22. Giddings, *Ida*, 208.

23. Wells, *A Red Record.*

24. Giddings, *Ida*, chapter 3.

25. Wells, *A Red Record.*

26. Wells, *Southern Horrors.*

27. Using statistics compiled by the *Chicago Tribute*, a white newspaper, *A Red Record* also revealed that the vast majority of lynching victims were not accused of rape in the first place.

28. Wells, *Southern Horrors.*

29. See Michael Corcoran, "Democracy in Peril: Twenty Years of Media Consolidation Under the Telecommunications Act," *Truthout*, February 11, 2016, http://www.truth-out.org/news/item/34789-democracy-in-peril-twenty-years-of-media-consolidation-under-the-telecommunications-act; and Ashley Lutz, "These 6 Corporations Control 90% of the Media in America," *Business Insider*, June 4, 2012, http://www.businessinsider.com/these-6-corporations-control-90-of-the-media-in-america-2012-6.

30. See above note for sourcing. Another 2016 list compiled by *Business Insider* identified Alphabet (Google), the Walt Disney Company, Comcast, 21st Century Fox, and Facebook as the world's leading media companies, all of which were led by white male CEOs. See Lara O'Reilly, "The 30 Biggest Media Companies in the World," *Business Insider*, May 31, 2016.

31. Austen Hufford, "Who Is Dr. Patrick Soon-Shiong, the New Owner of the LA Times?," *Wall Street Journal*, February 7, 2018, https://www.wsj.com/articles/who-is-dr-patrick-soon-shiong-the-new-owner-of-the-la-times-1518024711.

32. American Society of News Editors, ASNE Newsroom Diversity Survey, October 10, 2017. Overall findings and detailed tables available at

http://asne.org/diversity-survey-2017 and at http://asne.org//Files/census/2017%20ASNE%20diversity%20survey%20tables.pdf. See also "How Diverse are US Newsrooms?," with data visualized by Google, https://googletrends.github.io/asne/. Note that the percentage of minority representation is somewhat better for newspapers with daily circulations of five hundred thousand or more where racial minorities constitute 23.4 percent of the workforce.

33. Martin Gilens, "Race and Poverty in America: Public Misperceptions and the American News Media," *Public Opinion Quarterly* 60, no. 4 (1997): 515.

34. From ibid. (emphasis added): "In fact, blacks do compose a large proportion of the American underclass; just how large a proportion depends on how the underclass is defined. *But even those definitions that result in the highest percentages of African Americans do not approach the magazine portrait of the underclass as 100 percent black.* One such definition counts as members of the underclass only poor residents of census tracts with unusually high proportions of (1) welfare recipients, (2) female-headed households, (3) high school dropouts, and (4) unemployed working-age males. . . . By this definition, 59 percent of the underclass is African American. However defined, it is clear that the American underclass contains substantial numbers of nonblacks, in contrast to the magazine underclass composed exclusively of African Americans." (526)

35. Note that though the poverty *rate* is lower for whites than for most other ethnoracial groups, whites still make up the majority of the poor. On the relationship between racialized perceptions of poverty and opposition to welfare, see Gilens, "Race and Poverty in America": "The public's exaggerated association of race and poverty not only reflects and perpetuates negative racial stereotypes but it also increases white Americans' opposition to welfare. Whites who think the poor are mostly black are more likely to blame welfare recipients for their situation and less likely to support welfare than are those with more accurate perceptions of poverty. In one national survey, 46 percent of the white respondents who thought African Americans make up more than half of the poor wanted to cut welfare spending. In contrast, only 26 percent of those who thought blacks compose less than one-quarter of the poor wanted welfare spending cut (*Los Angeles Times*, 1985)." (517) What this means, concretely, is that white Americans' opposition to poverty programs that they themselves would benefit from is largely driven by their overinflated perception of poverty among people of color (and especially blacks).

36. See Color of Change, *Not to Be Trusted: Dangerous Levels of Inaccuracy in TV Crime Reporting in NYC; the Color of Change News Accuracy Report Card* (Oakland, CA: Color of Change, March 2015), https://s3.amazonaws.com/s3.colorofchange.org/images/ColorOfChangeNewsAccuracyReportCardNYC.pdf.

37. Ibid., 8.
38. Ibid., 9.
39. Ibid., 4.
40. Ibid., 11.

41. Lisa Wade, "Racial Bias and Media Coverage of Violent Crime," *Sociological Images*, April 9, 2015, https://thesocietypages.org/socimages/2015/04/09/racial-bias-and-media-coverage-of-violent-crime/.

42. In their analysis of racial bias in the media, Robert Entman and Kimberly Gross conclude that "prejudicial pretrial publicity and troubling coverage associating minorities with crime and violence will continue to be the norm rather than the exception, ultimately causing more harm for nonwhite than white defendants." (131–32) See Robert M. Entman and Kimberly A. Gross, "Race to Judgment: Stereotyping Media and Criminal Defendants," *Law and Contemporary Problems* 71 (Fall 2008): 93–133.

43. Robert Smith et al., "Implicit White Favoritism in the Criminal Justice System," *Alabama Law Review* 66 (2015): 871–913. On page 898, the authors analyze the results of a 2004 study conducted by Jennifer L. Eberhardt and colleagues: "Specifically, Eberhardt and her colleagues found that, when primed with white faces, participants were not only slower to identify weapons compared to when participants were primed with black faces, but also that they were slower to identify weapons compared to participants who were not primed at all. Although the participants were entirely unaware of whether or not they had even been primed, simply seeing a white face for mere milliseconds made it significantly harder for them to perceive a weapon than when they saw no face at all." For the original study, see Jennifer L. Eberhardt et al., "Interpersonal Relations and Group Processes—Seeing Black: Race, Crime, and Visual Processing," *Journal of Personality and Social Psychology* 87, no. 6 (2004): 876–93.

44. Peggy McIntosh, "White Privilege: Unpacking the Invisible Knapsack," *Peace and Freedom Magazine*, July/August 1989, 10–12.

45. Peggy McIntosh, "White Privilege, Color and Crime: A Personal Account," in *Images of Color, Images of Crime: Readings*, 3rd ed., ed. Coramae Richey-Mann and Marjorie S. Zatz (Los Angeles: Roxbury Publishing Company, 2006), 52–60.

46. For reaction to the *Times* shutting down Tanzina Vega's race beat, see Margaret Sullivan, "In a Time of Racial Turmoil, Why Change Course on Covering Race?," *New York Times*, January 29, 2015, https://publiceditor.blogs.nytimes.com/2015/01/29/in-a-time-of-racial-turmoil-why-change-course-on-covering-race/; Chris Ip, "What Will Happen to the *New York Times'* Race Beat?," *Columbia Journalism Review*, January 28, 2015, http://archives.cjr.org/behind_the_news/what_will_happen_to_the_new_yo.php; and "Amid National Racial Turmoil, New York Times Drops Its Race Beat," *Here and Now*, WBUR, January 30, 2015, http://www.wbur.org/hereandnow/2015/01/30/new-york-times-race-ethnicity.

47. Zaid Jilani, "The New York Times Promises Truth and Diversity, Then Hires Climate-Denying Anti-Arab White Guy," *Intercept*, April 14, 2017, https://theintercept.com/2017/04/14/new-york-times-promises-truth-and-diversity-then-hires-climate-denying-anti-arab-white-guy.

48. See Kimberly Ricci, "Almost Everyone, Even the NYT Writer Who Profiled a 'Heartland' Nazi, Thought the Piece Was a Bad Idea," *Uproxx*, November 26, 2017, http://uproxx.com/news/nyt-profile-nazi-normalize-reactions.

49. Sady Dole, Twitter, November 25, 2017, https://twitter.com/sadydoyle/status/934558246861406208.

50. Sean McElwee, Twitter, November 25, 2017, https://twitter.com/SeanMcElwee/status/934483205004103680. As of this writing, the tweet had received nearly 48,000 retweets and 70,000 likes. For the original articles, see John Eligon, "Michael Brown Spent Last Weeks Grappling with Problems and Promise," *New York Times*, August 24, 2014, https://www.nytimes.com/2014/08/25/us/michael-brown-spent-last-weeks-grappling-with-lifes-mysteries.html; and Richard Faussett, "A Voice of Hate in America's Heartland," *New York Times*, November 25, 2017, https://www.nytimes.com/2017/11/25/us/ohio-hovater-white-nationalist.html.

51. Eric Alterman, "The Media Must Stop Normalizing Nazis," *Nation*, December 13, 2017, https://www.thenation.com/article/the-media-must-stop-normalizing-nazis.

CHAPTER 6: INTERRACIAL LOVE 101

1. Williams, "Common Says Black People Showing Love to White People Is the Cure to Racism."

2. Mesfin Fekadu, "Q&A: John Legend on Race, Common, Sam Smith and 'Blurred Lines,'" *San Diego Union Tribune*, March 21, 2015, http://www.sandiegouniontribune.com/sdut-john-legend-blurred-lines-verdict-may-set-scary-2015mar21-story.html.

3. M. Scott Peck, *The Road Less Travelled: A New Psychology of Love, Traditional Values and Spiritual Growth* (New York: Simon & Schuster, 1978).

4. Note that black men were also historically victims of sexual abuse at the hands of white enslavers. On this, see Thomas A. Foster, "The Sexual Abuse of Black Men Under American Slavery," *Journal of the History of Sexuality* 20, no. 3 (2011): 445–64.

5. Christina Sharpe, *Monstrous Intimacies: Making Post-Slavery Subjects* (Durham, NC: Duke University Press, 2010).

6. Sylviane Diouf, "Remembering the Women of Slavery," *New York Public Library Blog*, March 27 2015, https://www.nypl.org/blog/2015/03/27/remembering-women-slavery.

7. Angela Davis, "Reflections on the Black Woman's Role in the Community of Slaves," *Black Scholar* 3, no. 4 (1971): 12.

8. Davis, "Slavery and the Roots of Sexual Harassment," 472.

9. On the history of racial mixture and the establishment of a racial hierarchy in the US, see Treitler, *The Ethnic Project*. Chapter 6 in particular examines the historical experiences of African Americans and anti-blackness within the history of race mixing and anti-miscegenation laws and punishment.

10. "Commentary: Jill Scott Talks Interracial Dating," *Essence*, March 26, 2010, https://www.essence.com/2010/03/26/commentary-jill-scott-talks-interracial.

11. See Chinyere Osuji, *Boundaries of Love: Interracial Marriage from the United States to Brazil* (New York: New York University Press, forthcoming). Note that while race mixture is traditionally celebrated in Brazil, Osuji's research shows that white family members still disapprove of intermarriage with blacks.

12. On the relationship between white supremacy and inegalitarian sex, see Gloria Wekker, *White Innocence: Paradoxes of Colonialism and Race* (Durham, NC: Duke University Press, 2016).

13. Picca and Feagin, *Two-Faced Racism*, 95.

14. Ibid., 95–96.

15. "Fired Fort Lauderdale Cop Holds Up Black Girlfriend to Prove He's Not Racist," *CBS News*, June 15, 2015, https://www.cbsnews.com/news/fired-fort-lauderdale-cop-jason-holding-black-girlfriend-hearing.

16. On color and phenotypic variations within families, see Lori L. Tharps, *Same Family, Different Colors: Confronting Colorism in America's Diverse Families* (Boston: Beacon Press, 2017).

17. Elizabeth Hordge-Freeman, *The Color of Love: Racial Features, Stigma, and Socialization in Black Brazilian Families* (Austin: University of Texas Press, 2015).

18. Edward Telles, *Race in Another America: The Significance of Skin Color in Brazil* (Princeton, NJ: Princeton University Press, 2006).

19. Zeba Blay, "Black Woman Says Ex-Boyfriend Became More Racist During Trump Campaign," *Huffington Post*, November 30, 2016, https://www.huffingtonpost.com/entry/black-woman-says-ex-boyfriend-became-more-racist-during-trump-campaign_us_583ef012e4b0ae0e7cdb088d.

20. TaLynn Kel, "My Husband's Unconscious Racism Nearly Destroyed Our Marriage," *The Establishment*, May 26, 2016, https://theestablishment.co/my-husbands-unconscious-racism-nearly-destroyed-our-marriage-6eaeec301161.

21. Christopher Ingraham, "Three-Quarters of Whites Don't Have Any Non-White Friends," *Washington Post*, August 25, 2014, https://www.washingtonpost.com/news/wonk/wp/2014/08/25/three-quarters-of-whites-dont-have-any-non-white-friends/?utm_term=.3d2f3b8a856f.

22. Picca and Feagin, *Two-Faced Racism*.

23. Brittney Cooper, "The Politics of Being Friends with White People," *Salon*, August 13, 2013, https://www.salon.com/2013/08/13/the_politics_of_being_friends_with_white_people.

CHAPTER 7: BECOMING RACIALLY LITERATE

1. Max Fisher, "This Map Shows Where the World's 30 Million Slaves Live. There Are 60,000 in the U.S.," *Washington Post*, October 17, 2013, https://www.washingtonpost.com/news/worldviews/wp/2013/10/17/this-map-shows-where-the-worlds-30-million-slaves-live-there-are-60000-in-the-u-s/?utm_term=.260c2dc188ce. On the present day legality of slavery in the United States, see Ava DuVernay's film *13th*, as well as Randal John Meyer, "Slavery Is Still Legal in the United States," *Newsweek*, August 25, 2015, http://www.newsweek.com/slavery-still-legal-united-states-365547.

2. Meredith L. Biedrzycki et al., "Root Exudates Mediate Kin Recognition in Plants," *Communicative & Integrative Biology* 3, no. 1 (2010): 28–35.

3. W. E. B. Du Bois, "I Won't Vote," *Nation*, October 20, 1956, https://www.thenation.com/article/i-wont-vote/.

4. Martin Luther King Jr., "Beyond Vietnam: A Time to Break Silence," April 4, 1967, King Encyclopedia, http://kingencyclopedia.stanford.edu/encyclopedia/encyclopedia/enc_beyond_vietnam_4_april_1967, accessed February 21, 2018.

5. Ibid.

6. For insight into King's internationalism and interest in African empowerment and his reflections on Ghanian independence, see his sermon "The Birth of a New Nation," delivered April 7, 1957, available online at https://kinginstitute.stanford.edu/king-papers/documents/birth-new-nation-sermon-delivered-dexter-avenue-baptist-church.

7. Dana Goldstein, "Sterilization's Cruel Inheritance," *New Republic*, March 4, 2016, https://newrepublic.com/article/130796/sterilizations-cruel-inheritance.

8. Devah Pager and Hana Shepherd, "The Sociology of Discrimination: Racial Discrimination in Employment, Housing, Credit, and Consumer Markets," *Annual Review of Sociology* 34 (2008): 181–209; Dalton Conley, *Being Black, Living in the Red: Race, Wealth, and Social Policy in America* (Berkeley: University of California Press, 1999).

9. Tia Cross, Freada Klein, Barbara Smith, and Beverly Smith, "Face-to-Face, Day-to-Day—Racism CR," in Hull, Bell-Scott, and Smith, *All the Women Are White, All the Blacks Are Men, but Some of Us Are Brave*, 52–56.

10. Note that this methodology was used in the "two-faced racism" study by Picca and Feagin, wherein students kept journals about racial incidents over a period of several weeks.

11. See "About Us," Project Implicit, https://implicit.harvard.edu/implicit/aboutus.html, accessed April 19, 2018.

12. Ann Gibbons, "How Europeans Evolved White Skin," *Science*, April 2, 2015, http://www.sciencemag.org/news/2015/04/how-europeans-evolved-white-skin. See also Marissa Fessenden, "Europeans Haven't Been White for Very Long," *Smithsonian Magazine*, April 3, 2015, https://www.smithsonianmag.com/smart-news/heres-how-europeans-quickly-evolved-lighter-skin-180954874.

13. Hannah Devlin, "First Modern Britons Had 'Dark to Black' Skin, Cheddar Man DNA Analysis Reveals," *Guardian*, February 7, 2018, https://www.theguardian.com/science/2018/feb/07/first-modern-britons-dark-black-skin-cheddar-man-dna-analysis-reveals?CMP=share_btn_tw.

14. Christianna Silva, "Why Are So Many Native Americans Killed By Police?," *Newsweek*, November 11, 2017, http://www.newsweek.com/more-native-americans-are-being-killed-police-including-14-year-old-who-might-708728.

15. David B. Oppenheimer, "Color-Blindness, Racism-Blindness, and Racism-Awareness: Revisiting Judge Henderson's Proposition 209 Decision," *Berkeley Journal of African-American Law & Policy* 13, no. 229 (2011): 254.

16. Pew Research Center, "How Blacks and Whites View the State of Race in America," June 14, 2016, http://www.pewsocialtrends.org/interactives/state-of-race-in-america.

17. Howard C. Stevenson, *Promoting Racial Literacy in Schools: Differences That Make a Difference* (New York: Teachers College Press, 2014).

18. "Brown v. Board at Fifty: 'With an Even Hand,'" Library of Congress website, https://www.loc.gov/exhibits/brown/brown-brown.html, accessed March 22, 2018.

19. David J. Kelly et al., "Three-Month-Olds, but Not Newborns, Prefer Own-Race Faces," *Developmental Science* 8, no. 6 (2005): F31–F36.

20. On best practices for addressing race and racism with children, see Stevenson, *Promoting Racial Literacy in Schools*; Jennifer Harvey, *Raising White Kids: Bringing Up Children in a Racially Unjust America* (Nashville: Abingdon Press, 2017); Melinda Wenner Moyer, "Teaching Tolerance: How White Parents Should Talk to Their Young Kids About Race," *Slate*, March 30, 2014, http://www.slate.com/articles/double_x/the_kids/2014/03/teaching_tolerance_how_white_parents_should_talk_to_their_kids_about_race.html; Erin Winkler, "Here's How to Raise Race-Conscious Children," *BuzzFeed*, June 11, 2017, https://www.buzzfeed.com/erinwinkler/tips-for-talking-to-children-about-race-and-racism?utm_term=.htLdmJ9ow#.ia439mlV5; and Stephanie Pappas, "How to Talk About Race to Kids: Experts Advice for Parents," *Live Science*, July 25, 2016, https://www.livescience.com/55524-how-to-talk-to-kids-about-race-experts-advice.html. For a dissenting view that argues against burdening children with racial anxieties, see Steele, *Whistling Vivaldi*.

21. For a brilliant critique of color blindness and its false equivalencies, see Osagie K. Obasogie, *Blinded by Sight: Seeing Race Through the Eyes of the Blind* (Redwood City, CA: Stanford University Press, 2014). In particular, Obasogie's analysis of the film *Guess Who's Coming to Dinner* (and its modern remake, starring Ashton Kutcher) illustrates how postracialism and color-blind ideology in the post–civil rights era attempt to render racial context and questions of power irrelevant.

22. James Baldwin, *No Name in the Street* (New York: Dial, 1972), 93–94.

23. For an excellent documentary about Jane Elliott's work and her "brown eyed/blue eyed" social experiment, see *A Class Divided*, *Frontline*, 1985, available online at the PBS website, https://www.pbs.org/wgbh/frontline/film/class-divided/.

24. *An Unfinished Crusade: An Interview with Jane Elliott*, PBS *Frontline*, January 1, 2003, available online at https://www.pbs.org/wgbh/frontline/article/an-unfinished-crusade-an-interview-with-jane-elliott/.

25. On abolitionism, see Dan Berger et al., "What Abolitionists Do," *Jacobin*, August 24, 2017, https://www.jacobinmag.com/2017/08/prison-abolition-reform-mass-incarceration; The Next System, "Towards the Horizon of Abolition: A Conversation with Mariame Kaba," November 9, 2017, https://thenextsystem.org/learn/stories/towards-horizon-abolition-conversation-mariame-kaba.

26. W. K. Kellogg Foundation, "Racial Equity Resource Guide," database, http://www.racialequityresourceguide.org/organizations/organizations/sectionFilter/Racial%20Healing, accessed February 21, 2018.

27. Heather Long, "There's a Serious Proposal to Give Babies Born in the United States $20,000 (or More)," *Washington Post*, January 8, 2018.

28. Octavia Butler, "NPR Essay—UN Racism Conference," https://www.npr.org/programs/specials/racism/010830.octaviabutleressay.html, accessed February 21, 2018.